Angels in Vietnam: Women Who Served

Angels in Vietnam: Women Who Served

Stories and poems by and about the women who served in Vietnam

Jan Hornung

Writers Club Press
San Jose   New York   Lincoln   Shanghai

Angels in Vietnam: Women Who Served

All Rights Reserved © 2002 by Janine Hay Hornung

No part of this book may be reproduced or transmitted in any form or by any means, graphic, electronic, or mechanical, including photocopying, recording, taping, or by any information storage retrieval system, without the permission in writing from the publisher.

Writers Club Press
an imprint of iUniverse, Inc.

For information address:
iUniverse, Inc.
5220 S. 16th St., Suite 200
Lincoln, NE 68512
www.iuniverse.com

ISBN: 0-595-24090-9

Printed in the United States of America

To all veterans of all wars:

*Welcome Home
and
Thank You*

"Never bend your head. Always hold it high.
Look the world straight in the eye."

           Helen Keller, 1880–1968

Contents

List of Illustrations and Pictures xv
Foreword xvii
Preface xix
List of Abbreviations xxv
List of Contributors xxix
Introduction xxxiii

CHAPTER 1: *Women Who Served* 1
    The Woman Veteran/Women Who Served 2
    Better Than Medicine 4
    Women in War 5
    Sisters 7
    The Angels of Vietnam 10
    Gung Ho 11
    Colonel Maggie 12

CHAPTER 2: *Wives and Mothers and Daughters* 18
    The Night Before 18
    The Suitcase and The Duffle Bag 20
    Veteran of the Vietnam War 22
    You 23
    A Dogfaced Soldier 24
    Becky Died 26
    A Daughter's Love 27
    I Am Off To War, My Gentle Carol 28
    Carol—Has It Been A Hundred Years? 29

CHAPTER 3: *The Nurses* 31
    Blended Like A Fine-Tuned Instrument 31

Doing Their Best *32*
The Caring Was From The Heart *32*
I See You Walking *32*
I Can Still See Her Face *34*
Thank You, Ma'am *35*
I Wish I Knew Her Name *36*
I Stand and Salute *37*
Duet With Death *38*
They Are Angels *41*
I Am Sadness *42*
To The Nurses *43*
Lend Me *45*

CHAPTER 4: *Judy's Story* *47*
The Injured *50*

CHAPTER 5: *Chrissy* *52*
Farewell *52*
Pilot in Triage *53*
The Colors of Christmas *53*
Bits and Pieces *55*
A Measure of Success *55*

CHAPTER 6: *Nam Nurses* *60*
Veteran's Day *60*
Dear Little Boy of Mine *63*
You're In The Army Now *65*
Beautiful Vietnam *66*
Quang Tri *68*
Army Nurse Corps *70*

CHAPTER 7: *Gary's Angel* *73*
Warrior and The Nurse *74*
Angel of Mercy *78*
I Felt I'd Died *81*
Finding Judy *83*

The Art of Medicine	83
War No More	86
CHAPTER 8: *From New Zealand*	88
Sister	88
Australia and New Zealand in Vietnam	90
Body Bags	91
The Last Step	93
CHAPTER 9: *Australian and New Zealand Nurses in Nam*	94
RAANC, Royal Australian Army Nursing Corps in Vietnam	94
The New Zealand Involvement in Vietnam	97
The Car	98
CHAPTER 10: *Donut Dollies*	100
They Brought Smiles	100
The American Red Cross in Vietnam	100
Donut Dolly Blue	101
Carrying On The Tradition	103
Proud To Be A Donut Dolly	105
When Did It Begin?	123
CHAPTER 11: *Once Upon A Time*	124
We Smiled Anyway	124
A Brief History of Red Cross Clubmobiles in W.W. II	130
CHAPTER 12: *To Say Goodbye*	132
CHAPTER 13: *Christmas in Vietnam*	140
The Day It Snowed In Vietnam	140
Project Concern International	148
Christmas in Vietnam, 1966	149
A Christmas Visit Remembered	153
CHAPTER 14: *Christmas in Vietnam*	156
In My Heart Forever	156
Boosting Morale	157
A Year To Kill	157

CHAPTER 15: *Post Traumatic Stress Disorder* *160*
   Ambushed *160*
   Flashbacks *161*
   A Soldier's Prayer *161*
   Memories Penetrating the Shroud of Death: PTSD
      The Shroud of Lost Innocence and Life *163*
   Julie *165*
   The Dam Burst *168*
   Midnight Movie *169*
   PTSD *171*
CHAPTER 16: *A Woman Looks Back At War* *173*
CHAPTER 17: *Veterans Resource Network Association* *178*
   Are you a Vet? *178*
   Why? *181*
CHAPTER 18: *The Healing Continues* *183*
   Souvenirs *183*
   Psyched *184*
   Seasons of Siege *187*
   Parts is Parts *190*
   Do You Know *193*
   Nightmare of a Soldier *194*
CHAPTER 19: *My Name is Karen* *196*
   And The War Goes On *197*
   Soldier's Medal *201*
CHAPTER 20: *Seeking God* *203*
   God, a Soldier, and a Red Cross Worker *203*
   God, I'd Really Like To Know *206*
   Parade of Fear *207*
   I Only See Blue Pajamas *210*
CHAPTER 21: *Nightingale Mom* *212*
   The War Comes Home *212*

CHAPTER 22: *FYI* *217*
   For Your Information *217*
   Operation Babylift *218*
   Where is Vietnam? *219*
   What They Said *219*
   Who Was Ho Chi Minh? *221*
   Why Vietnam? *222*
CHAPTER 23: *Love Stories and Poems* *225*
   A Moment *225*
   Deanna's Love Story *226*
   Love's Good Vibrations *228*
   Love and War *233*
   An Affair To Remember *236*
   My Visits With Jack *239*
   ANZAC Day *248*
CHAPTER 24: *Vietnam Light* *249*
CHAPTER 25: *Return to Vietnam* *257*
   My Thirty Year Anniversary Trip *257*
   Civilian Women in Vietnam: Army Special Services *267*
CHAPTER 26: *The Vietnam Veterans' Memorial* *270*
   The Wall *270*
   The Vietnam Veterans' Memorial *272*
   My Brother *273*
   Images of Freedom *275*
   Honoring our Heroes *276*
CHAPTER 27: *In Memory* *277*
   Folded Flag *277*
   Roll Call *278*
   Thanksgiving Day *288*
CHAPTER 28: *Welcome Home* *289*
   Gathered In *289*
   Aftermath *291*

    Soldier's Farewell *293*
    What Is A Vietnam Veteran? *294*
    If Only *298*
CHAPTER 29: *God Bless America* *299*
    bird of a single flight *300*
    A Stronger America *301*
    The Cab Driver *302*
    My Fellow Americans *304*
    God Bless America *305*

About the Author 307
Appendix 309
Glossary 317
Index 321

# List of Illustrations and Pictures

Cover photo courtesy of Judith Baker Williams and Alice Nolen-Walston. On the cover, 1st Lt. Judith Baker, left, and 2nd Lt. Alice Nolen, prepare the Receiving Ward at the 67th Evacuation Hospital in Qui Nhon, in November 1968.

Dog Tags, a drawing by Melody Hay 1
Penni Evans 9
Colonel Maggie 17
The Morning After 40
Lt. Mary Hyland 41
Watching for Dustoff, a drawing by Sarah Hay 45
Welcome 57
Chrissy and Children 58
Farewell 59
Chateau Quang Tri 68
Incoming 69
On the Road to Hue 70
Vung Tau 116
Bob Hope, 1967 117
Donut Dolly 118
The Old Lady 119
The Soldiers and The Children 120
Children are Wonderful 121
Dauntless 122

Once Upon A Time 129
Lt. Sebek 138
Jim, a painting by Julie Parker 159
Certificate of Achievement 202
Jack and Kathy 255
Roy and the President 256

FOREWORD

by David "Hack" Hackworth
(U.S. Army, colonel, retired)

As a war veteran, including Vietnam, I know firsthand the unspeakable horrors and pain that many of our country's fighting men have endured over the centuries. From the American Revolution to Desert Storm, men have bravely gone into battles that many did not survive. With the exception of the Vietnam era, the majority of Americans have always supported their men during wartime. The United States attempted to correct this injustice with the dedication of the Vietnam Veterans' Memorial, "The Wall," in 1982.

It is the thousands of women, however, who served their country during the Vietnam War, who were overlooked for decades. The value of women in supportive roles during Vietnam is not well known. The fact is that for over a decade, approximately 11,000 American women served one-year tours in Vietnam. The majority of those women were in the military serving as nurses, administration workers, air traffic controllers, and more. The others, civilians, volunteered to go with organizations such as the American Red Cross. Eight of the military women lost their lives in Vietnam; their names are on "The Wall." Fifty of the civilian women died. Although these women were not in combat directly, there was no safe place in Vietnam.

In 1993, with the dedication of the Vietnam Women's Memorial, America finally said, "Thanks, Welcome Home," to these women.

Jan Hornung has gathered some of these women's stories, poems, and pictures in this book. Several men Vietnam veterans also contributed their stories and poems honoring the women who aided them in country. Although Jan was too young for Vietnam, she realized the importance of serving her country and did so in the Army in the 1980s. Her desire is to make sure that people know about the brave women who served in Vietnam, and that is why this book is so important to her and to thousands of others who were involved in or affected by our involvement in Vietnam—a war we should never forget, a kind of war we should never repeat.

David "Hack" Hackworth (U.S. Army, colonel, retired)

Colonel (retired) David "Hack" Hackworth spent 26 years in the United States Army. He retired in 1971, but continues to stay active in military issues with his writing and guest appearances on national radio and television talk shows. From 1990 to 1996, he was *Newsweek's* contributing editor for defense. In addition to Hackworth's international bestseller, *About Face*, he has written several books including *Hazardous Duty, The Price of Honor,* and *Steel My Soldiers' Hearts.* His column, *Defending America,* appears weekly in newspapers across America and on his Web site. Find out more about this passionate watchdog of America's military at www.hackworth.com.

PREFACE

A journey of a thousand miles begins with a single step, and the road to wartime healing begins with one shared memory at a time. The unspoken memories often do not go away. They may go deep inside the soul where they lie dormant like a volcano that finally blows after years, decades, of saving up the pain.

Not all the memories of wartime are painful. Some people remember the happy moments, the moments of respite from a madness called war—moments of sharing, of giving, of laughter, even moments of love.

Many of the images of war portrayed in the poems and stories in this book are disturbing. Some may bring a tear to the reader's eyes, others may bring a smile to the heart. Whatever the reader's response, keep in mind that the images are real. The poets and storytellers are real. The Vietnam experience was real for over a quarter of a million American men and women and for thousands more from New Zealand, Australia, Thailand, Korea, the Philippines, and Vietnam.

I have been thinking of writing this book for over 15 years. I did not serve in Vietnam, but I flew helicopters in the Army with many wonderful Vietnam veteran crew chiefs and pilots. In addition to the men, I kept thinking about the courage as well as the suffering of the women who also served our country during this time. As a writer, it occurred to me that I could do something to tell their stories. Then it dawned on me—who better to tell their stories than the women veterans and the men who knew them? So began my search for those who wanted to share their stories. I set up a Web site, http://www.geocities.com/vietnamfront, to find those who wanted to be a part of this project. The response was wonderful.

Many Vietnam veterans wrote to encourage me in my endeavor. Some women veterans wrote to say they could not share a poem or story, but that they were grateful for my wanting to do this. Some shared their stories but wish to remain anonymous. Some women wrote a note to tell me why they went to Vietnam. One woman's simple yet poignant statement expresses many others' comments to me, "I was young, and I felt I could do something for our men in Vietnam and for my country."

Many of the men and women who served their country in Vietnam know they have to let their war memories out for themselves as well for those who can no longer speak for themselves—those whose hands they held during death, whose faces they saw once and never again, those whose cries they shushed. Over 58,000 American men, nearly five dozen military and civilian American women, approximately 500 Australians, and 39 New Zealanders did not come home alive from Vietnam. For those that survived, the journey continues, the healing goes on.

Thank you to all of you who contributed to this book with stories, poems, pictures, and words of support, encouragement, and friendship. Thank you to all of you whose names may not appear in this book but still contributed through your e-mails with words of support.

To all Vietnam veterans, "Welcome Home and Thank You."

Jan Hornung

ACKNOWLEDGEMENTS

A Special Thanks

This book was a work of the heart for me. Each and every person that e-mailed, called, wrote, or I met in person was just as excited about this book as I am. Each one of you that contributed poems, stories, pictures, information, contacts, and support is forever in my gratitude. Thanks to the marvels of e-mail, I was able to keep in communication with everyone who contributed from around the world—from across the United States, including Alaska, to New Zealand and Australia.

A special thanks to the artists who have brought some of the poems and stories to life with their wonderful talents: Sarah Hay, Melody Hay, and Julie Parker.

A special thanks to Ruth Hay for her tireless editing abilities. A special thanks to Hal Hay for downloading and uploading hundreds of e-mail correspondences between me and Ruth Hay.

A special thanks to my new friends Patty Bright Fortenberry, Vietnam Donut Dolly, and her husband, Steve Fortenberry, a Vietnam veteran. I had the good fortune and honor to meet them in May of 2001.

A special thanks to Mike Subritzky in New Zealand, The Kiwi Kipling, and author of *The Vietnam Scrapbook—The Second ANZAC Adventure*. He went above and beyond the call of duty helping me make contacts and finding information during my research for this book. His beautiful and heartfelt poetry contributes significantly to *Angels in Vietnam*.

A special thanks to Christina Sharik, Army Mom, for her wonderful contributions. Christina reminds us all that everyone is affected by war, especially the moms who send their sons and daughters.

A special thanks to Diana Sebek, Dancing Spirit, for her moving stories, *To Say Goodbye* and *My Visits With Jack*. Diana kept me grounded throughout the writing of this book with her sharing, humor, and friendship.

A special thanks to Deanna Hopkins and her husband, James M. Hopkins. Deanna took on the task of writing the Introduction, and she provided contacts and support that kept me going when I thought, "How am I ever going to do this project?"

A special thanks to Linda Beall, the editor of *The Better Half*, for introducing me to her relatives Phyllis Nelson and Nancy Landauer, who both shared wonderful stories for this book.

A special thanks to Ann Caddell Crawford, founder of *Military Living Publications* and author of *Vietnam Light* for sharing her story.

A special thanks to Chris Schneider for her support and wonderful poetry, story, and picture contributions for this book. And a special thanks to her daughter, Karli Schneider, for sharing her poem about her mother.

A special thanks to Janis Nark, for sharing her words of inspiration and hope.

A special thanks to all of the women who bared their souls by contributing heartfelt stories, poems, or pictures—Mary "Chris" Banigan, Dr. Narelle Biedermann, Sharon Vander Ven Cummings, Mary Hyland Daines, Sandie Elgin, Diane Evans, Penni Evans, Elma Ernst Fay, Pat Hewatt, Sharon Huffman, Ann Kelsey, Judy Blackman Kigin, Marsha Klein, Nancy Quirk Lilja, Jackie Norris, Karen Offutt, Mary Standard, Maria Sutherland, Pam Miley-Terry, Kimmie Thomas-Bowles, Diana Waite, Lindsey Weilbacher, Judy Williams, and Eileen P. Wolfe.

A special thanks to Frank Zamora for his inspiring words and support.

A special thanks to Gary Jacobson, Vice President of The International War Veterans' Poetry Archives, for sharing his poetry and story in tribute to a Vietnam physical therapist. His friendship and support lifted me up many times during this project.

A special thanks to Colonel (retired) David "Hack" Hackworth, author of *About Face, Hazardous Duty, The Price of Honor,* and *Steel My Soldiers' Hearts,* for taking an interest in this project and providing the forward.

A special thanks to the men, the Vietnam veterans who thought enough of the women who served in Vietnam to share a poem or a story in tribute to them: Vinny Alestra, Paul "Doc" Baviello, Dane Brown, Joe F. Casal, Dan with the 9th Infantry Division, James Dempsey, J.B.F., Sonny Gratzer, Larry Harty, Doc Hollywood, Johnny Hutcherson, Pat Kenny, Rick Lewis, Arthur E. Long Jr., Jim McColloch, Bill McDonald, John A. Moller, Dan Mouer, Anthony W. Pahl, Jim Schueckler, and David Lloyd Smith.

A special thanks to each of you who contributed stories and poems and, for personal reasons, wish to remain anonymous.

Thanks to everyone who contributed favorite quotes for the beginning of each chapter.

I have great admiration for each and every one of you.

>To each of you, I extend a hearty
>*Welcome Home and Thank You!*
>Jan Hornung

LIST OF ABBREVIATIONS

ACAV—Armored cavalry assault vehicle
Air Cav—1st Cavalry Division (airmobile), activated July 1, 1965
ALSG—Australian Logistic Support Group
ANZAC—Australian and New Zealand Army Corps
APC—Armored Personnel Carrier
ARC—American Red Cross
ARVN—Army of the Republic of Vietnam, the military of the Republic of Vietnam (South Vietnamese government) until its collapse in 1975.

Bde—Brigade
Bn—Battalion
BOQ—Bachelor Officer's Quarters

C-130—A large transport aircraft for moving troops and equipment
Cammo—Camouflage
CO—Commanding Officer
Col. —colonel
CORDS—Civil Operations and Revolutionary Development Support

DIV—Division, usually consists of 3 brigades in the military
DMZ—Demilitarized zone

ER—Emergency Room

GI—A soldier; literally means Government Issue.

HHC—Headquarters, Headquarters Company

ICU—Intensive Care Unit
IV—Intravenous
IWVPA—International War Veterans' Poetry Archives

LRRP or LRP—Long Range Reconnaissance Patrol
Lt. —lieutenant
Lt. Col. —lieutenant colonel
LZ—Landing Zone

MACV—Military Assistance Command, Vietnam
MARS—Military Affiliate Radio System
MIA—Missing in Action
MOS—Military Occupational Specialty
MP—Military Police

NVA—North Vietnamese Army
NVC—North Vietnamese Communists
NZ—New Zealand

OR—Operating Room

PFC—private first class
POW—Prisoner of War
PSYOP—Psychological Operations
PT—Physical Therapist
PTSD—Post Traumatic Stress Disorder
PX—Post Exchange

R&E—Receiving & Evaluation, Emergency Room/Triage
R&R—Rest and Recreation

RAANC—Royal Australian Army Nursing Corps
Rec—Recreation
Recon—Reconnaissance
RN—Registered Nurse
RNZIR—Royal New Zealand Infantry Regiment
ROK—Republic of Korea
RPG—Rocket-propelled grenade
RVN—Republic of Vietnam, Southern Vietnam

SEA—Southeast Asia
SF—Special Forces
SMH—Service to Military Hospitals, ARC
SMI—Service to Military Installations, ARC
Spc.—Specialist, military rank
SRAO—Supplemental Recreational Activities Overseas, ARC

TDY—Temporary Duty
TOD—Tour of Duty

USAF—United States Air Force
USARV—United States Army, Vietnam
USMC—United States Marine Corps
USO—United Service Organizations

VA—Veterans Administration
VC—Viet Cong; from Viet Nam Cong San (Vietnamese communists). This is what others called the Vietnamese communists. They referred to themselves as the National Front for the Liberation of South Vietnam or the National Liberation Front, inaugurated 1960.

VRNA—Veterans Resource Network Association
VVHP—Vietnam Veterans Home Page
VWMP—Vietnam Women's Memorial Project

WAC—Women's Army Corps
W.W.II—World War II

List of Contributors

Vinny Alestra
Mary "Chris" Banigan
Paul Baviello
Dr. Narelle Biedermann
Dane Brown
Joe F. Casal
Ann Caddell Crawford
Sharon Vander Ven Cummings
Mary Hyland Daines
James P. Dempsey
Sandra K. Elgin
Diane Evans
Penni Evans
Elma Ernst Fay
Kathleen Fennell
Patty Bright Fortenberry
Steve Fortenberry
Sonny Gratzer
David Hackworth
Larry Harty
Melody Hay
Sarah Hay
Pat Hewatt
Doc Hollywood
Deanna Gail Shlee Hopkins
James M. Hopkins

Sharon Long Huffman
Johnny Hutcherson
Gary Jacobson
J.B.F.
Ann Kelsey
Pat Kenny
Judy Blackman Kigin
Marsha Klein
Rev. Nancy Landauer
Rick Lewis
Nancy Quirk Lilja
Arthur E. Long Jr.
Jim McColloch
Bill McDonald
Pam Miley-Terry
John Moller
Daniel Mouer
Janis Nark
Phyllis Nelson
Alice Nolen-Walston
Jackie Lively Norris
Karen Offutt
Anthony W. Pahl
Julie Parker
Patricia Powell
Chris Schneider
Karli Schneider
Jim Schueckler
Diana Sebek
Christina Sharik
David Lloyd Smith
Mary Standard

Mike Subritzky
Maria Sutherland
Diana Waite
Lindsey Stringfellow Weilbacher
Judith Baker Williams
Eileen Wolfe
Frank Zamora

INTRODUCTION

*Real joy comes not from ease or riches
or from the praise of others,
but from doing something worthwhile.*
           Wilfred Grenfell, 1865–1940

When Jan asked me to write something for her book, I wondered if I was qualified enough and up to the task. I am married to a Vietnam Veteran and have been volunteering and contributing to a Vietnam Veterans' Web site (Vietnam Veterans Home Page, VVHP, http://vets.appliedphysics.swri.edu/) since the early '90s. I've been working with Veterans, worldwide, mostly via e-mail and sometimes in person, for this long, also. My brother served in the Air Force in the 1960s, and my daughter served in the Army in the 1980s. But what do I really know about how they feel deep inside? Maybe writing this all down will help me understand, too.

When I started working on the Internet, I was surprised first by the guilt that many Veterans feel and would e-mail me about—guilt because they didn't get to finish the job they'd been sent to do; guilt because they survived the war and came home when many, including friends, died; guilt because their name is not on "The Wall" in D.C.; guilt because they didn't do more so some of those names on "The Wall" wouldn't be there; guilt because their job in country wasn't as "dangerous" as others; guilt because they served Stateside or in another country and weren't sent to Southeast Asia to "actual" combat in this war.

xxxiii

I try to counsel that each had a job to do, no matter what and no matter where, in the "chain of support;" and they have nothing to be guilty about. They did their duty as best they could, and we're so very glad they are alive and with us!

I and others grope for the magic bullet, the words that will take the pain away. We try to understand, we love, we support, we care. We do not make judgements, and we listen. But, it's never enough; and we get frustrated and even angry—angry at the hurt we can't get our hands on and take away.

Then came the one sentence that I heard from a Vietnam Veteran that has stayed with me more than any other and brought this war home to me: "I need to forgive myself."

Decades later, the emotions, for some, are finally coming to the surface after being stuffed for so long; and the PTSD (Post Traumatic Stress Disorder) has to be dealt with. The full extent of how ingrained the trauma and horror has been for so long wasn't fully apparent until I married my husband, "Mike," (James M. Hopkins) who served in country during this war. He is a gentle man who was asked to fight an "enemy" in a land I didn't even know how to pronounce nor spell nor find on a map. I also learned that he has "normal" reactions to very "abnormal" experiences.

I was surprised, also, by the number of women who served in Southeast Asia during this war who had the same PTSD as the men; and some were as suicidal. I don't think I had thought of the women in this way, about what they had seen and endured, too. I've heard many male Vietnam Veterans state that they thought the nurses, at least, had it worse than anyone—they saw the injured bodies and held the dying every day—far more and far longer than most.

I have always thought of war as two "fronts"—the foreign front and the home front. I've also heard Vietnam Veterans state, on more than one occasion, that they thought their spouses, if married, and other family members had it worse back home. At least the Veterans knew where they were and that they were alive. They state that the strain on their families of "not knowing" would be something they could not endure, that they would rather be in Southeast Asia fighting.

I do believe the "Winds of Change," as I have called it for so long, are here; and the Internet and its technology are integral parts to this "Change." Veterans of the Vietnam War, both men and women, and their families and friends are now connected around the globe. They have a "Community" and a "voice" to tell of their experiences—a "Safe Harbor" where there is caring, understanding, acceptance, and support.

This "Change" is being brought on also by another generation or two, now—the youth of our country. I hear from them almost daily, and they are searching for the truth; they want to know what really happened and from a firsthand source—the Vietnam Veterans themselves. I think that their tributes and respect, for those who laid it all on the line for all of us and our freedom, have helped to fan these "Winds of Change."

And, the positive responses that a simple "Thank You" brings from our Veterans never ceases to amaze me. Some Vietnam Veterans tell me it's the first they've heard. It never ceases to amaze me, also, when I see and hear the graciousness and enduring spirit from them every day. There is a Brotherhood and Sisterhood that is sacred between Veterans, a bond forged by "fire." They are there for one another and their countries. They are "still serving."

There is something that this nation and other countries must come to know and hold sacred—when we ask our men and women to serve and send them in harm's way, *our* duty to them does not end when they come back to our shores or take the uniform off. It never ends. We owe them unending respect and support and unending care for their health—mental and physical—if they require it. This needs to be part of the equation and understood when we make the decision to become involved in others' problems.

Thank you all for your service to our country; and to our allies, thank you for your support and for serving your country, too. Thank you all for thinking that our way of life and freedom were worth fighting for. And thank you for your sacrifices so that those I love can sleep safe within our shores at night.

WELCOME HOME!
Deanna Gail Shlee Hopkins

CHAPTER 1

Women Who Served

*You gain strength, courage and confidence by every experience
in which you really stop to look fear in the face.
You must do the thing you cannot do.*
　　　　　　　　　Eleanor Roosevelt, 1884–1962

Dog Tags
by Melody Hay

The Woman Veteran/ Women Who Served

She is a Veteran.
She is a Woman,
a daughter, a wife...
sometimes she typed,
sometimes she pressed
her hand against a wound
and saved a life.
She might have been
an entertainer,
who shared a song, a wink,
a smile—
she might have been a Dolly
or a transportation clerk—
whatever she did, was her work,
and made her feel worthwhile...
Sometimes she stood in oozing mud—
or in a pool of someone's blood.
She is a Veteran.
She's a mother, a daughter,
and a wife—
Some people,
also known as Vets—
owe her their very sacred life.
Accolades for her sacrifices
have oft times been too slow—
Whether she served in a
place that was far, or near—

> the front lines, or the rear
> One thing, above all,
> is abundantly clear…
> she was a Volunteer.
> She never HAD to go.

by Christina Sharik

Christina Sharik is the ex-wife of a Vietnam veteran, the daughter of a World War II Army captain who served in China, and the mother of an Army staff sergeant who has served in Somalia, Bosnia, Germany, and Korea. Christina is a legal secretary living in Florida with her husband, Scott, a dog, a cat, a bird, and a fish. On December 13, 2001, Christina became a grandmother to Tristan Michael Ream. "Talk about proud!" she says.

Read more of Christina Sharik's poetry at her Web site, Army Mom's Safe Haven, www.the-revetment.com/armymom, and in her upcoming book, *Healing the Heartache: Poetry for the Vietnam Generation.*

"I've been writing poetry about Vietnam and its effect on me, pen pals, friends, and my ex since the mid '60s, and I am still writing," says Christina.

Christina Sharik is a Trustee and a member of the Bronze Helmet Award Committee for The International War Veterans' Poetry Archives found at www.iwvpa.net. More of her poetry is also at Vietnam Veterans Home Page at www.vietvet.org.

See Christina's poetry, *The Night Before,* chapter 2; *The Suitcase and The Duffle Bag,* chapter 2; *I Am Sadness,* chapter 3; *Aftermath,* chapter 28; *If Only,* chapter 28; and *The Cab Driver,* chapter 29.

Better Than Medicine

In 1968, Elder Gordon B. Hinckley, who today is the current prophet and President of the Church of Jesus Christ of Latter-day Saints, visited the wounded at the 106th General Hospital in Japan. A few weeks later, Elder Hinckley gave the baccalaureate address at the Dixie College commencement in St. George, Utah. The following excerpt is taken from his address, published in *The Church News*, June 15, 1968:

> Four or five weeks ago my wife and I walked through the wards of a great American Army hospital in Yokohama, Japan. Row on row, floor on floor, stood the beds of Vietnam war casualties.
>
> Our escort was a captain, a physiotherapist, a lovely girl from Maryland, with dark hair and dark eyes, she was beautiful in her white nurse's uniform. Every man lifted his eyes as she passed. There was always a smile for her, but never a leer. I talked with one of the men about her.
>
> "She's different," he said. "She has class. There's something about her that's almost spiritual. She does something for this drab place. She's better than medicine."

The Army captain mentioned in the article above expressed her thoughts over 30 years later: "The patient's statement really could apply to any of the women who served in the military hospitals, not just to me. In addition to what we actually did in our jobs, what's suggested here is that because of the spiritual and other attributes that women possess, we were able to bring comfort to the wounded men—perhaps as much as their medications and treatments did.

"I remember trying to always be friendly, trying to appear happy even when I wasn't, cheering them up, wiping their tears, being a sister to some and a mother to others, caring so much that it sometimes hurt so badly, writing letters home for guys who couldn't use their hands or couldn't see, playing my guitar and singing with the patients on the wards, getting off base with those who could leave, and praying with those who asked me to do so."

Women in War

They talk about a woman's sphere,
As though it had a limit.
There's not a place in earth or heaven.
There's not a task to mankind given...
Without a woman in it.

Kate Field, 1838–96

Throughout wartime history, women have participated in their countries' conflicts in a variety of roles. From nurses to pilots and journalists to spies, women have served when their countries called.

Whether women worked and raised their families while the men fought overseas, tended wounded soldiers, brought entertainment to soldiers far from home, served as non-combat military personnel, or fought alongside their brothers, women have played significant and noteworthy roles throughout wartime history.

During the United States Civil War, nearly 250 women, disguised as men, fought alongside the men of the Confederate Army. Women also have risked their lives as spies in all wars, gathering valuable information for their countries. The Army Nurse Corps and the Navy Nurse Corps sent women overseas in World War I, World War II, the Korean War, and the Vietnam War. In World War II, over 1,000 American women flew every airplane in America's Army Air Corps as the Women's Airforce Service Pilots, WASP.

America sent 40,000 women to Desert Shield and Desert Storm in 1990 and 1991, the largest deployment of women in United States' history; sixteen of these women did not return home alive. Americans knew about and supported the 100-hour war of Desert Storm and the women who served in combat-support positions. During the Vietnam War, however, many had the attitude that "nice girls did not go to war," said Lt. Col. (retired) Janis Nark, a Vietnam Army nurse (chapter 16).

From 1965 to 1973, of the nearly 2,600,000 U.S. military personnel who served in Vietnam, approximately 7,000 of those were "nice girls" who were in the Army, Navy, Marine Corps, and Air Force. They were the nurses (80% of the military women in Vietnam were nurses), physical therapists, occupational therapists, air traffic controllers, aerial reconnaissance photographers, intelligence and language specialists, legal officers, and in security and administrative positions.

Civilian women also served in Vietnam in the American Red Cross, the USO, the Central Intelligence Agency, the U.S. Agency for International Development, and other government agencies. Other women went to Vietnam as journalists, flight attendants, and for various churches and other humanitarian organizations. Women also went to Vietnam with the Special Services, which had several divisions related to morale and recreation. They operated and provided service clubs, libraries, arts and crafts, entertainment, sports, movies, and administered the Rest and Recreation program. There are no official records of how many civilian women served in Vietnam. Some estimate the civilian numbers at approximately three thousand over the span of the war.

Most of the women experienced many of the same dangers and hardships as the men. They were often in the line of fire from rockets and mortars, and they saw firsthand the horrors of death and bloody mutilation. The courageous efforts of these women who saved lives, comforted injured and dying men, and boosted morale has not gone unforgotten by their country or the men veterans who remember them.

Sisters

You are not of my blood
Yet you are my sisters
Uniforms of colours mixed
Green, tan, white, blue
Fatigues or skirts
Civvies of shorts and dresses
Plain to bangles
Sisters All

Some used scissors and IVs
Some used typewriters and telephones
Some used books and crafts
Some used tools of war
Some gave just a smile
Some used cameras and pens
Some used Kool-Aid and flashcards
Some used prayer and taught
Sisters All

Time was relative
You came for a tour—365 days
You came for an assignment
You flew Freedom Birds in-out
You served elsewhere in the world
You stayed in the villages

You lived on a compound
You lived in a hooch or a villa
You lived on the go
Sisters All

You saw smiles, you saw tears
You saw death, you saw courage
You heard laughter, you heard screams
You heard sirens, you heard shells
You felt happy, you felt angry
You felt grief, you felt pain
Maybe you felt nothing at all
Sisters All

Some gave laughter and music
Some gave life in a world of death
Some lent a hand—mother, wife, lover
As a soul left a shattered body behind
Some gave their blood and health
And the health of their children
Some came home to silence
Some came home in flag-draped silver boxes
Some never returned, left behind, unacknowledged
Sisters All

You came back to the World
You spoke briefly, then not at all
About your time in Nam, in service
That was then, this is now you thought
In '82 some came together at the Wall
Now it is 1993 and we dedicated a Memorial
"All Gave Some—Some Gave All"

Gently sisters reaching out to sisters
To lead them out of darkness
Into a world of recognition
Out of the closet and into the world
As Vietnam Veterans
Sisters All

by Penni Evans

Penni Evans
Quang Tri 1970/71
Photo by Robert Sandford
Courtesy of Penni Evans

Penni Evans served in Vietnam as an American Red Cross Donut Dolly from March 1970–August 1970 at Cam Ranh Air Base; August 1970–October 1970, II Field Force at Long Binh; October 1970–November 1970, Cu Chi; and December 1970–March 1971, Quang Tri. Read her poetry, *Ambushed*, chapter 15; *Souvenirs*, chapter 18; *My Brother*, chapter 26; and *Folded Flag*, chapter 27. More of her poetry is at the American Red Cross Vietnam Donut Dollies Web site, www.donutdolly.com, and in her book, *Behind the Heart*.

The Angels of Vietnam

They were angels of mercy dressed in white,
or frequently fatigue green,
They were happy to lend a helping hand
and work behind the scenes.

Whether as an air traffic controller,
a photographer, therapist or nurse,
They were there in Vietnam,
a battleground that was cursed.

They may not have been allowed to fly
or fight while carrying a gun,
But they each did their part,
they went the distance, and then some.

They bled and died, and they suffered
right along with the men,
And for their country, if needed,
they would gladly do it again.

They weren't recognized as heroes,
hardly acknowledged at all,
But where would America be
had they not also answered the call?

They willingly did the mundane jobs
while freeing men to fight,
They held the hands of dying friends,
throughout the long, dark night.

Vietnam was not a popular war
and much patriotism seems to be gone,
But don't think it was never there—
far too many didn't come home.

So when you see a woman in uniform,
or a civilian volunteer,
Think of what they gave in Vietnam
and give them a hearty cheer.

For all the brave women who went and
served their country so well,
They've earned their angel wings already
while in that Vietnam hell.

by Diana Waite

Gung Ho

    Shortly after high school, I enlisted in the U.S. Marine Corps in April 1962 and went through boot camp at Parris Island, South Carolina. I loved it! From there I went to Camp Pendleton, California; and was that ever an experience for a small-town, Southern girl who grew up in the Smoky Mountains.

For me, the old saying "Once a Marine—Always a Marine" is true. I'm still as "Gung Ho" now as I was then. The military has always had my support, especially our disabled veterans who have given so much for their country. I didn't go to Vietnam, but that doesn't mean my feelings didn't go.

I have enjoyed writing poetry since I was a teen-ager. My subjects are widely varied but usually come about due to something that affects me personally or something I feel strongly about. There is nothing I feel more strongly about than our veterans who gave so much for us. This is especially true for our Vietnam veterans who were treated so badly when they came home. They only did what their country asked of them, and their country let them down.

When I retire I will probably return to the South where all of my family lives. Then I hope to devote more time to writing.
Diana Waite

Read Diana Waite's poem *Images of Freedom*, chapter 26.

Colonel Maggie

Nurse, Entertainer, and Honorary Green Beret

Almost everyone knows about all of Bob Hope's trips to Vietnam. He would do his annual Christmas Shows for TV, which were recorded live at some of the safest bases in Vietnam, while surrounded by TV cameras, reporters, and lots of tanks and protective armed troops. I was at his Christmas Day show back in 1966, just north of Saigon. I enjoyed it very much. It was one of a few good memories that I have of my Tour of Duty. But, meeting Martha Raye—better known to the troops, as Colonial Maggie—was the highlight event of the year for me.

I met her in Phu Loi, South Vietnam, in the early part of 1967. She came to our small airfield base camp, without any fanfare at all. She just arrived and began casually talking to us guys there. We, of course, knew of her from all her old movies. I made mention to her that I wanted a photo to show my mother, who was her biggest fan, and she turned that into a five-minute comedy routine about how only the real old folks remembered her. She teased me about that and then put her arms around me. She made fun of everything, including referring to herself as The Big Mouth! The guys in my unit, the 128th Assault Helicopter Company, were really impressed that she had come all the way out to see us. We never had any big-named entertainers ever come through our camp, so her visit was something very special to all of us.

Later that day, I got my chance to get up on stage (the top of a flatbed truck) and get my photo taken with her. I found her to be a very real person, and she gave you the feeling that she really cared about you. There were neither reporters nor TV cameras on her visit. She was there because we were there.

At that time, her reputation was rapidly growing among veterans. We heard many stories about her from the Special Forces units out in the boondocks. When we would fly into almost any small SF camp, the guys would speak most highly of her. She was their hero for sure. She had been traveling to Vietnam (I am told that she paid her own way) and spending weeks and sometimes up to six months at a time in country. She kept this pace up for over nine years during the Vietnam War. She was not there just to entertain the troops, but she also engaged in nursing work wherever it was needed. She spent most of her time out in the field or in the hospitals. She went to some of the most dangerous and remote locations in Nam.

She was not looking for any publicity or photo opportunities; she went where she knew the need was the greatest. She visited base camps that no other entertainers dared to go to. She walked through the mud and rain, and she took the heat and mosquitoes all in stride. No one ever remembers her complaining about the food, the weather, transportation, or life in general. She spent time at places that did not have hot showers, let alone places for women to use a restroom. She had to endure the same hardships that the GIs did. Her job was to keep up our spirits and make us feel loved and appreciated. She didn't come to Nam for a visit—she came to work. That, for her, meant sometimes using her nursing skills and helping with patients.

There were many stories going around about all the battles she had been in while in country. She did not try to shelter herself from harm's way, and she refused over and over again to allow anyone to risk his life to protect or evacuate her to a safer place if she happened to be subjected to any kind of enemy attack. There is one story that made the rounds with the Special Forces units that we ran into, but it somehow never made it into the newspapers or on the evening news shows at that time, that I can recall. I have some of the facts but not all of them. But this story reveals the real character of this wonderful woman warrior.

The story relates how Colonial Maggie, who was also a trained RN, went to entertain and visit a very small Special Forces camp. (It could have been at Soc Trang, around the early part of 1967.) I was told that she and some clarinet player had gone to the camp to entertain, but while they were there the NVA attacked the camp. Mortar rounds and small arms fire were incoming. It appeared that there was a full-scale assault on the base camp. It was uncertain if the camp would be able to hold off the assault.. The camp medic was hit, and so with her being a nurse, she took over and began to assist with the treatment of the wounded who kept pouring into the aid station.

The camp was in great danger for several hours of being overrun. The higher-ups in the military were trying to dispatch helicopters to the camp, but a combination of very bad weather and heavy fighting made that task a very dangerous mission for any crews that would be trying to come in to get the wounded or to pull her out to a safer place. All this time, she was subjecting herself to the dangers of flying shrapnel and incoming automatic rifle rounds. She tended to the task that she was trained for—treating the wounded. She was said to have remained calm and fully active in doing her work—even with all the action taking pace just outside the aid station. She kept focused on treating the wounded and did not seek shelter or safety for herself.

She kept refusing any and all rescue missions. She spent hours putting her skills as a nurse to use treating patients and even assisting with surgery. She was in the operating room for 13 hours; she then went through the aid station talking with the wounded and making sure that they were okay. It was said that she worked without sleep or rest until all the wounded were either treated or evacuated out on a Huey (helicopter). She did not leave that camp until she was satisfied that all wounded were taken care of.

This is just one of the many untold stories about Martha Raye—but ask enough Vietnam veterans about her and you will find even more tales of Colonial Maggie. She finally received some long overdue honors before she died. They ranged from the Jean Hersholt Humanitarian Academy Award in 1968 for entertaining troops in Vietnam to the 1993 Presidential Medal of Freedom for her lifetime of dedication to America. "Colonel Maggie," Martha Raye, also was an honorary member of the Special Forces. She received her prized Green Beret and the title of Lieutenant Colonel from President Lyndon B. Johnson himself.

Known as "Colonel Maggie of the Boondocks" by her many military friends, Martha Raye (born Margaret Teresa Yvonne Reed on August 27, 1916) died October 19, 1994. Raye is buried in the military cemetery at Fort Bragg, North Carolina, an exception to policy she requested in 1992.

by Bill McDonald
128th Assault Helicopter Company
Phu Loi, South Vietnam

Bill McDonald served in Vietnam from November 1966 through November 1967 as a crew chief/door gunner on a Huey UH-1D with the 128th Assault Helicopter Company, at Phu Loi Army Airfield.

"I was wounded, shot up, and shot down. I received several awards including the Distinguished Flying Cross, Bronze Star, Purple Heart, and 14 Air Medals.

"I got out of the Army and married my high school sweetheart, Carol. In January 2002, we celebrated 32 years of marriage. We have two grown children (a son and daughter) and one very wonderful grandson born in 2000. My wife and I are still best friends. We both grew up in Sunnyvale, California, and we share the same friends who go all the way back to the first and second grade.

"I retired from the United States Postal Service, where I was a safety specialist. I now try to help veterans and their families deal with the aftermath of the Vietnam War through my Support Network on my Web site, The Vietnam Experience at www.vietnamexp.com, a Web site that shares the emotional and spiritual experiences of the Vietnam War through poetry, stories, and photos by combat veterans. The Web site has had over half a million visitors as of July 2002.

"I am now involved in the making of a documentary film called *In The Shadow of The Blade* about the effects of the Huey helicopter in Vietnam. The film should be released in late 2003.

"I went back to Vietnam in the spring of 2002 and visited where I was shot down and wounded—was a very healing and emotional trip."
Bill McDonald
The Vietnam Experience, www.vietnamexp.com

Read Bill McDonald's poems *I Am Off To War, My Gentle Carol* and *Carol—Has It Been A Hundred Years?* in chapter 2.

Colonel Maggie
Photo courtesy of Bill McDonald

Colonel Maggie, center, as the troops called nurse and entertainer Martha Raye, often talked with and amused the soldiers during her lengthy trips to Vietnam. Bill McDonald is the soldier standing.

CHAPTER 2

Wives and Mothers and Daughters

There never was a good war or a bad peace.
Benjamin Franklin, 1706–1790

For over a decade, thousands of women sent their hearts and souls to Vietnam along with their loved ones. Day one of the separation was often a lonely, tearful beginning for many young wives of a year or more of praying for and worrying about their husbands going off to war. Approximately 17,500 married American men did not return alive from Vietnam.

The Night Before

(for Rod)

We lay in bed that night
listening to Rod McKuen's records
The Sand, The Sea, the Sky—
he finally fell asleep
and that's when I began to cry—
All kinds of strange imaginings
passed before my eye

as I listened to the ticking
of the minutes on
the alarm clock going by—
After making love and talking,
he finally slept—
I knew the words he said
would be the ones I always kept
inside my head.
We had a son, a baby
9 months old—
and he slept, too, in his
little baby bed...
Innocent of War.
I knew
that when his father returned,
he wouldn't remember him anymore...
I played "The Sea" on "low"
over and over, and then
suddenly, it was morning,
once again—
No matter how I tried to stop it,
the sun rose anyway...
and now it was the "dreaded day"...
Up early, getting dressed
a smile upon my face—
so much to say to each other
and neither was able to speak—
I wanted to scream "Don't go"
but that would never do—
He played with the baby,
Hide and Seek.
You'll be hiding, all right, I thought,

too far away to be found—
I thought of all these things to say
and couldn't utter a sound.
Off to the airport and checked the bags;
regular passengers unknowing
All by himself with a wife
and parents, none of whose fears
were showing...
And then...he was gone...
I broke down in the kitchen
and I said to my mom:
"What if he doesn't come home, Mom?
What if he doesn't come home?"
It'll be ok, she said—
you have us, and you have your son—
it'll be ok...she said again, and again.
It was noon, and he'd been gone
since ten...

by Christina Sharik

The Suitcase and The Duffle Bag

Once, some long lost age ago,
my husband left for war—
It was only called a "conflict"
So I wondered just what for...
At some point, or another
he must have packed his gear—
I don't remember helping him,
just watching him, with fear...
Off he went, with one small wave

and I waited for a year.
Michael began to walk and talk
and I wished his dad were here…
At some point in the fairy tale
my husband did come home
He had a duffle bag this time
and came back home, alone.
But, in the middle of the story
I flew off pretty far—
from PA to Hawaii,
for his two week R&R
My suitcase never emptied then
It was filled with memories…
I emptied it when I got home,
could smell the tropic breeze…
I have pictures of me, somewhere,
in a 2 piece bathing suit
flashing him the "V" sign
and giving a salute—
and every day in Paradise
we loved and laughed and talked—
(he was already different,
even in the way he walked…)
When I got home, I put my case
high upon the bedroom shelf—
until he got home from Vietnam,
where he had lost himself.
Of course, I didn't know that yet.
We were transferred to a base;
By then he was so very strange
that I felt out of place…
I had that suitcase many years—

got rid of it one day,
but not all of the memories—
those times I packed away;
Long after the sad tale ended,
(as all fairy tales must do)
My ex gave Mike his duffle bag
and now he's used it, too…

by Christina Sharik

Read about Christina Sharik, chapter 1, and see her poetry, *The Woman Veteran/Women Who Served*, chapter 1; *I Am Sadness*, chapter 3; *Aftermath*, chapter 28; *If Only*, chapter 28; and *The Cab Driver*, chapter 29.

Veteran of the Vietnam War

She wears, with great honour, the scars of my battles
She's cared for my mind since my body came home.
She's held my hand gently when I've become rattled
She's succoured my heart more times than I've known.
She's helped me fight demons and the ghosts of my war
She's been alongside me through all the terror I've seen
She's convinced me to live when life I wanted no more
She has experienced a hell to which I've never been.
She's tended my wounds with the firmness of true love
She's provided me solace throughout all of my pain
She's fought every conflict with strength from above
And she has done all this
for love,
not for gain.

by Anthony W. Pahl

Anthony W. Pahl, an Australian Vietnam veteran, served with the Royal Australian Air Force, No. 9 Squadron, Vung Tau/Nui Dat, 1969–1970, as a helicopter gunner and leading aircraftsman. From 1962–1973, Australia sent 46,852 personnel to Vietnam. Of those, 494 died serving their country.

Pahl wrote this poem, *Veteran of the Vietnam War*, about and for his wife, Maria. The poem also is a tribute to the many women who loved their soldiers and helped them heal physically and emotionally upon their return.

"My wife and I met when I was 15, and we married in February 1968, five days after I turned 18. Our daughter, Sonia, was born in February 1969 and was 5 months old when I left for Vietnam in June 1969. Our second daughter, Monica, was born in April 1972," Pahl said.

For more stories, poems, and pictures from Anthony W. Pahl, visit his Web site, Bushranger's Revetment at www.the-revetment.net. More of Pahl's poetry also is included in the International War Veterans' Poetry Archives located on the Web at www.iwvpa.net. Anthony Pahl, "Bushranger," is the senior vice president and Web master of the IWVPA.

You

When I watch you
standing in front of my
peers, describing the life
I never saw you live
And
When I watch you
captivate each soul
by describing the dismembered
body of your 18-year-old patient

I say,
When I watch you
you courageous and heroic woman
who used to be called lieutenant
used to be called Chrissy
I stand up
by God, mom,
I stand up.

by Karli Schneider

Karli Schneider is the daughter of Chris Schneider, an Army nurse in Vietnam. Karli wrote this poem when she was 18 years old for her senior high school creative writing class in 2001. It is written in the style of *Miss Rosie* by Lucille Clifton, 1936–present. See Chris Schneider's poetry and story, chapter 5, *Chrissy*.

A Dogfaced Soldier

The Daughter

I was in the Army from 1973 to 1975, but never in Nam. My Dad was there twice. My Dad was in Nam while I was in the 6th grade at Immanuel Lutheran School in Junction City, Kansas. For a school project that year at Christmas time, we all wrote notes in Christmas cards and sent them to Nam.

As you know there were thousands of soldiers and also thousands of cards and letters such as mine being sent. Dad said one morning for mail call the clerk asked who wanted a card addressed to "A Dogfaced Soldier in Vietnam." He volunteered and lo and behold, it was from his own daughter! What a pleasant surprise! I don't have any idea now why I used the term "Dogfaced Soldier," but I'm sure glad I did because it got to him as a result.

by Sharon Long Huffman

The Dad

In July 1965, Arthur E. Long Jr., C Company, 1st Battalion, 26th Infantry, took a train to Fort Lewis, Washington; from there, he went by boat to Vung Tou, Vietnam. He then flew to Bien Hoa and on to Phuoc Vinh, an old French fort and rifle range. He and the other men dug into the rifle range bank and set up tents for sleeping.

Stateside: In October 1965, Bell Telephone and a radio station in Philadelphia started a "Mail-Call Viet Nam." They asked people to send cards and letters to the soldiers in Vietnam, and they would box them up and forward them.

Vietnam: I was a novice stamp collector. We had postage-free service in Vietnam, so I was also collecting those that had return addresses. (I would write roughly twelve letters at night while I was on radio watch.) We started getting letters addressed to "Dogfaced Soldiers," "Fellow Soldiers," "Service Men in Viet Nam," etc. We estimated that our unit was getting approximately 3,000–5,000 cards and letters per day. When multiplied by all the units in Vietnam, that makes roughly 300,000 to 400,000 a day. I would do daily, or when possible, pickup for the mail for my platoon. I would look for stamps and cards with return addresses. At that time, I already corresponded with a 16-year-old in Gary, Indiana, a 19-year-old student in West Chester, Pennsylvania, a 42-year-old in Miami, someone in New York, and numerous others from the Western states. I still have several letters and drawings sent to us. The chances of ever getting a card or letter from someone you knew was around one in a billion. The chances of getting one from Kansas was even less likely, much less Junction City, Kansas, where my family was living at that time.

In early to mid December 1965, I went to pick up mail for my platoon; the mail clerk would sort out the mail and put aside those with return addresses for me. On one of those days he said, "Sgt. Long, would you be interested in this card ?" It was addressed to "Dogfaced Soldier," with the return address, Junction City, Kansas. When I opened it up, I saw a nice religious, handmade card with a Bible verse and a short note. It was signed: Sharon Long—age 11 years. *I attend Immanuel Lutheran Church School…*

I wasted no time comparing the signature with the letters I received from my family back in Junction City, Kansas. I learned later that many of the children attending the church school were military dependants whose fathers were in Vietnam, and they were given the project of making a card with their favorite Bible verse included to send to the troops in combat. They weren't assigned a particular soldier, just any "fellow dogface" in Vietnam.

by Arthur E. Long Jr.

Becky Died

No "Dear John," just a letter from mom saying Becky had died.
We were together just last week in dreams so sweet, and now
just a letter from mom saying Becky had died.

She was crossing the street one dark, rainy night
when a drunk driver took her life,
said the letter from mom saying Becky had died.

Everyone was saying, we would one day marry;
even we thought so;
then Becky died.

by Rick Lewis
Semper Fi

Rick Lewis was a Marine sergeant attached to Golf Company, 2nd Battalion, 7th Marines, 1st Marine Division, Vietnam, 1969–1970. He was engaged to Becky, a freshman at Drake University in Des Moines, Iowa.

Rick and his wife, Mary, reside in Des Moines, Iowa, and in 2001, they celebrated their 30th wedding anniversary. They have two children: Kyle, a college wrestling coach in Sioux City, Iowa, and Kari, a Claims Supervisor for Mercy Medicare and a dance instructor. Rick and his wife are the proud grandparents of triplets, born December 28, 2000, to Kyle and his wife, Shelly.

Rick Lewis is the Revenue Protection Officer with the Postal Service. He is also part of the pastoral staff at a local Bible Church in Des Moines. In addition, Rick is in his twentieth year as a high school wrestling coach.

See Rick Lewis' poem, *God, I'd Really Like To Know*, chapter 20.

A Daughter's Love

Dad, I miss you so,
No words can say.

You are on my mind,
From day to day,

I love you Dad,
And I always will.

This love inside,
No man can kill!

We'll be together.
Again someday.

Either here on earth,
Or God's place,
Far away.

by Sandra K. Elgin

Sandie Elgin wrote this poem in honor of Technical Sergeant James Richard Thomas. He became Missing in Action November 25, 1971, while on a rescue mission with an Air Force pararescue squadron out of Da Nang, Vietnam. For more about Thomas, visit Pararescue, Gone But Not Forgotten at http://members.aol.com/Berly100, a Web site created by Thomas' daughter, Kimmie Thomas-Bowles. Although Sandie Elgin is not a veteran, she writes poems such as *A Daughter's Love* about the Vietnam War and the veterans.

I Am Off To War, My Gentle Carol

October, 1966
San Francisco, California

Gentle Carol.
Your soft voice
still murmurs within my memories.
Your image

hangs onto the very corners
of this young warrior's heart.
I can feel traces of my heart
leaving wet rivers
down my manly cheeks.
Gentle Carol,
must I go?
Must I be taken away
like a fallen leaf
in the cold fall wind?
How far
is a long time?
How many moments
must pass?
Will tomorrow still
be waiting for us?
Gentle Carol,
How many leaves must fall?
How many cold winds
will chill the air?
Will you still be there
and
will I still be
your young warrior poet?

by Bill McDonald

Carol—Has It Been A Hundred Years?

July 1967
Base Camp, South Vietnam

My tired
War torn heart
And body
Wants to stop
The reality of this dream.
I want to wake myself up
And roll over
And find you there.
Memories,
Of your flashing,
sunshine smile,
And soft laughter,
Brings me a moment
Of sanity
In this insane place
Filled with dying
And
Lonesome young poets.

by Bill McDonald
128th Assault Helicopter Company
Phu Loi, South Vietnam
November 1966–1967

Bill and Carol married in 1970. Read about Bill McDonald and his story, *Colonel Maggie,* chapter 1.

CHAPTER 3

The Nurses

*Be not afraid of greatness:
some are born great, some achieve greatness,
and some have greatness thrust upon them.*
William Shakespeare, 1564–1616

Blended Like A Fine-Tuned Instrument

I was wounded April 17, 1968, during Tet. I remember how great the nurses were at Phu Bai. I wasn't there long, and everything is still kind of dazed in my mind, but I do remember the nurses' kindness and compassion and professionalism all blended together like a fine-tuned instrument.

Semper Fi, Dane Brown
1st Battalion, 27th Marines
It's Just A Nam Thing, http://www.itsjustanamthing.com

Doing Their Best

I was fortunate enough to never need the services of the nurses, although I will say that the grunts greatly appreciated the fact that the nurses were there and would do their best for us. The nurses—they saw more death than most grunts.

Dan (anonymous)
9th Infantry Division, Mekong Delta, 1969

The Caring Was From The Heart

I was hospitalized in Nam at a field hospital in Saigon; it wasn't combat related. In my short stay of one week, I shared a room with six men that did have combat-related injuries. During that period of time, I watched the nurses comfort them as time would allow them to. You could tell the caring was from the heart, not part of a dictated protocol. They learned the names of girlfriends and wives, also children if any. I can't pick out any certain one to say who was best; they all were wonderful.

J.B.F.
54th Signal Company, Forward Support and Maintenance, First Logistics, 1965–1966

I See You Walking

I see you walking in 1969,
we all stopped to stare;
one hand holding your jungle hat
on the back of your head.
There, heading for the infirmary,
American girl in olive green,

feminine walk, lush figure,
auburn pigtails below the hatbrim.
Moving away, you never saw us,
and I never bled on your stretcher;
never held your hand, nor saw your face.
But I see you walking...still.
I watched you with wonder and lust,
an American nurse...in Vietnam...
Good God!...but I was only 23,
and now I'm more than twice that.
I didn't know in '69 what I know now,
about me, and maybe about you.
Didn't know the price we'd pay
all this time...all these years.

I saw you then with college eyes,
pink carnations, imagined perfume.
I didn't know the blood you'd see,
I forgot the weapons that I carried.
I still see you walking, that dusty road,
that hair so red...from time to time.
I know you did great good, your tour...
lust and amazement became respect.
I never knew your name, GI Nurse,
but I wish you well, and I hope
that you sleep in peace...
I close my eyes sometimes
and I see you walking.

by James M. Hopkins

With his draft notice in early 1969, James M. Hopkins went from being a graduate student at East Texas State University to being a soldier. By July of that year, he was assigned to the 1st Infantry Division, RVN. He was reassigned to the 9th Infantry Division in 1970. Hopkins got out of the Army in July 1970, and in 1972 he earned a Master of Science in Chemistry. Today, he is happily married to Deanna Gail Shlee Hopkins. Between them, they have five children and eleven grandchildren.

For more of Hopkins' poetry, visit The Sound of Whirling Blades—Poems and Reflections at The Vietnam Veterans Home Page at http://vets.appliedphysics.swri.edu/blades.htm
http://www.vietvet.org/blades.htm (mirror site)

I Can Still See Her Face

There was a nurse at the 85th Evacuation Hospital in Qui Nhon. I was there drawing supplies. I must have looked like the death that surrounded them. I had not showered or shaved for a couple of weeks, and my fatigues were torn and tattered. I was covered with dirt.

This nurse approached and asked if my rifle was loaded and what I wanted. The question seemed foolish, but I answered. After explaining that loaded weapons weren't needed, she escorted me out and promised to secure the medical supplies I needed. She walked me over to her quarters and showed me where the shower was. She promised to return.

I fell asleep on her bed for almost twelve hours. When I awoke she was lying next to me, and I felt safe. It wasn't lust as some stories might end, just safe. When we got up, she got me coffee, and we talked about being a medic in the front. She gave me my supplies, kissed my cheek, and waved goodbye as I walked to the waiting helicopter. I can still see her face. I am thankful for the encounter.

by James P. Dempsey.

In January of 1966, Dempsey was 20 years old. He was assigned to HHC 2/5 and attached to B Company from May 1966–June 1967. He then transferred to HHC First Cavalry Division and was assigned to the DIV LRRP (E Company, 52nd Infantry), then the 75th Ranger Battalion. In 1968, he was discharged after three years. Dempsey re-enlisted in 1969, and he returned to Vietnam in January 1970. Wounded in May 1970, he was evacuated to St. Albans Naval Hospital in Queens, New York. He retired in 1981 as a sergeant first class and became a civilian paramedic and firefighter in Texas. He currently is a consultant on emergency management and EMS.

See *In My Heart Forever*, James P. Dempsey, chapter 14.

Thank You, Ma'am

Thank you Ma'am, from the Vietnam Vet
So many of us will not forget
Your gentle touch while you held our hand
comforting us when we could not stand

You saw the carnage, and you heard our pain
But you stood your ground and you would do it again
Changing our dressings and helping us through
An awful time for me and you

The war was over for us, but not for you
for your tour of duty was not through
The Choppers kept coming from dusk to dawn
as you saw many a young man pass to the beyond

For this I thank you, for a job well done
and helping us get back together as one

They speak of Heroes, seldom a word of you
But this old warrior just wants to say God Bless You.

by Larry Harty

Larry Harty was a nineteen-year-old Huey crew chief with the United States Army's 2nd Signal Group, 1st Signal Brigade, in Long Thanh North, from 1970 to 1971. Harty retired from the Army as a master sergeant. Today, Harty continues to serve the U.S. Army as a civilian bus driver.

"I am married to the same lady I was when I was in Vietnam. I did 23 years in Army Aviation, retiring in 1993," Harty said.

I Wish I Knew Her Name

I was 21 on the second day of my basic training. I went to Fort Polk (Louisiana) for infantry training. They called it Tigerland. My MOS (Military Occupational Specialty) was 11-B-10, light weapons infantry.

I was with the Big Red One, the First Infantry Division, and my company was called the Black Panthers. I was in battles, firefights, I was nearly cut in half by fragments from a missile. My medic was shot in the head trying to get to me. On August 8, 1967, of 105 men, really boys, there that night near Phuoc Loc, 26 died. Twenty-six mothers cried. Twenty-six fathers cried. Twenty-six young, brave men died. Nobody cares...

On August 8, 1967, I was sent to four hospitals before they operated on me. They put me in the corner to "cool off" for 11 days, and then they operated for 21 hours. When I awoke, the nurse told me I had been in the corner to cool off. I did not know what it meant, and I was in no shape to ask or understand. I only learned a few years ago that it meant that in triage, they thought I was virtually dead. So they literally put me in the corner to cool off—to die.

The hospital where the gooks (enemy) attacked was Long Binh. I hated that place so much; you cannot understand unless you were there. They shelled the base, hit the ammo dump and it went off for about two hours. I was on a Stryker frame after being paralyzed and almost cut in two. A young, beautiful nurse threw herself on top of me to protect me. It was the bravest action I ever witnessed. Of all the action I saw, that nurse was the bravest. I wish I knew her name now.

by David Lloyd Smith

I Stand and Salute

The nurses who served in Vietnam in the hospitals and on board the hospital ships were some of the most dedicated and caring people I have ever met. A Marine Corpsman I knew said that if I could just keep my guys alive long enough to get them back to the hospitals to the doctors and nurses, my Marines would be all right.

In many ways their job was harder then ours because they had to fight to keep the guys alive, and each patient became like a brother or a friend. They saw the horror of war every single day and unlike us didn't have a way of releasing their frustrations by going into battle and getting a measure of revenge. The compassion these ladies showed makes me so proud that I, in a small way, could be associated with them. They are our sisters, and I consider them more Vietnam vets then some of the guys on ships or who never came closer than hundreds of miles to the country.

I stand and salute each and every one of them.

Semper Fi
Hm3 "Doc" Buzz Baviello
D Co 1st Bn 5th Marines
RVN 1969–70

Paul "Doc" Baviello's book, *Corpsman Up,* was published in 1994. Read his book online at www.corpsman.com/corpsbook.html at the Navy Corpsman Web site, www.corpsman.com.

"Doc" or "Buzz" Baviello explains, "Corpsman Up! is the cry that echoes across the battlefield when a Marine goes down wounded. More than friends, medical corpsmen are the lifesavers of their unit." His book is a "fictionalized account of the real experiences of a Navy hospital corpsman assigned to a Marine grunt unit in Vietnam" and it "is a tribute to courage, friendship and heroism."

Today, Baviello is a teacher and football coach in California.

Duet With Death

It begins with awareness.
I know he is going to die;
He knows he is going to die.

>As he slips away,
>His color changes to ashen.
>His eyes watch me.

His eyes are fearful—
That he will die,
And there's nothing he can do.

>My eyes are fearful—
>That he will die,
>And there's nothing I can do.

His eyes plead with me
To save him.
I frantically try—knowing I can't.

      We look at each other,
      Locked in a staring contest
      With life and death the stakes.

He blinks—he loses.
His eyes still stare,
But he's not in them anymore.

      I beat his chest—
      A dull lifeless thud
      That fails to revive him.

I beat again—with fear.
His death scares me.
I might die, too.

      I beat again—with anger
      That I can't do more—
      At him—for giving up.

I beat again—with sadness
At the killing war
I am powerless to change.

      His eyes remain vacant.
      His pupils dilate.
      I am alone: the duet is done.

by Mary M. Standard

Mary Standard served as a medical surgical nurse, second and first lieutenant, with the 18th Surgical Hospital, Pleiku, from March to October 1967, and with the 12th Evacuation Hospital, Cu Chi, From October 1967 to September 1968.

The Morning After
Photo courtesy of Mary M. Standard

Mary Standard took this picture at the 12th Evacuation Hospital in Cu Chi, Vietnam, in 1968. It was "the morning after a particularly bad night on duty filled with fresh casualties and incoming rounds. We quietly gathered behind the hootches and sat together for a few minutes before trying to get some sleep. I think this picture shows the fatigue we felt (physically and mentally) and our attempt to hold it inside ourselves as shown by body language."
Mary M. Standard

Lt. Mary Hyland
Photo courtesy of Mary M. Standard

Mary M. Standard captures the feeling of the moment at the 12th Evacuation Hospital in Cu Chi, Vietnam, in 1968, on the face of Mary Hyland Daines. Mary Standard took this picture at the same time as *The Morning After* above.

Lt. Mary Hyland, a 21-year-old nurse, served with the 12th Evac, in ICU, from February 1967 to February 1968. She returned to the states a few weeks after the Tet Offensive. Today, Mary Hyland Daines is an oncology nurse clinical specialist, mother of three, grandmother of one, and wife of a retired Army Reserve colonel (CRNA).

They Are Angels

In Vietnam there were no front lines, and the VC/NVA had no problem hitting a hospital. There were no rules. I had to go to a hospital one time in my year and a half there. I was not feeling well, it was no big deal, but after I got there I couldn't wait to get out of there. I saw the other side of war. This was not a firefight any more, but this was a new war. This was saving lives, even the enemies. They did things that were out of feelings for mankind and because it was the job they chose to do. They were givers of life; healers giving hope where there was none in a very special way, and they did it well in my eyes. They are angels.

I needed help in 1998, and out of nowhere there was hope—an Army nurse that I met online still giving of herself. She was there for me just like she was there 30 years before for others in Vietnam. Their war will never end, and they will be there for others no matter what.

I wish in my small way to thank them all, and say, "You will never be forgotten by U.S. troops. God Bless You."

by Vinny Alestra
27th Combat Engineers, A Company, Vietnam, 1968–1969

I Am Sadness
(for the medical personnel)

I am Sadness.
I cannot cry.
I saved a few
I saw some die…
I feel alone.
I may be Here
but I'm not Home.
I am Sadness…
my heart is Sore
I still see them
in dreams of War.
I sometimes smile—
you think I'm fine

but I'll remember
for all of time.

by Christina Sharik

Read about Christina Sharik, chapter 1, and see her poetry, *The Woman Veteran/Women Who Served*, chapter 1; *The Night Before*, chapter 2; *The Suitcase And The Duffle Bag*, chapter 2; *Aftermath*, chapter 28; *If Only*, chapter 28; and *The Cab Driver*, chapter 29.

To The Nurses

I was a Marine Helo pilot, and we deposited a lot of seriously wounded marines and civilians and a few of the other guys into your professional hands. You were and still are very much appreciated. Thanks for being there.

Like many helo drivers of that era, a large percentage of my hops were medevac. The nurses of my memory do not have clear faces. They are shadows dressed in green, running into the chopper's tornado-like winds pushing gurneys while we tried to minimize time on the ground. They were like darts of hope, running out of the medevac facility bunkers. I remember praying and thanking God that they were there. Knowing that the next time in it might be me on the gurney.

We had no females at the Marble Mountain Marine Air Facility near Da Nang. The only other time we came in contact with the nurses was on shuttle runs from Da Nang to the hospital ships like the U.S.S. Sanctuary.

I was always busy flying the aircraft and didn't concentrate on faces. As I try to remember now, it is as if I was afraid to see a face. I made the mistake once of looking at a Korean Marine who had stepped on a land mine and lost a leg. We took him to the hospital ship in Da Nang Bay. As the corpsmen and nurses hustled the stretcher by my side of the helo, I looked at him, saw his face, and saw that he was holding his leg. I never looked at faces again. I think that is why I can only remember shadowy figures, except for my closest pilot and air crew associates that I spent every waking hour with.

I cannot imagine how bad it would have been if the nurses had not been part of all of it. For me, they represented the sterile and clean part of the world that we had left. Without knowing or having met any of them in Vietnam, they were very much a part of me.

Vietnam was the best damned flying I ever did. The closest thing to that sort of flying since then was a short time of crop dusting when I got out. I would do it all over again, but next time I would take more photos and take some time to go meet the nurses and doctors. Memories are strange things.

by Pat Kenny
HMM-364 Purple Foxes
April 1970–April 1971
USMC
Marble Mountain Air Facility
I Corps

Pat Kenny was 24 when he served in Vietnam. Today, he is a General Securities representative and lives in Richland, Washington.

Jan Hornung 45

Watching for Dustoff
by Sarah Hay

Lend Me

Lend me your eyes
so that I may see
the world as you.
Lend me your heart
so that I may feel
the love as you.
Lend me your love
so that I may
comfort and heal as you.
Lend me your shoes
so I may walk
the same path as you.

> Lend me your hand
> so that I may be as
> strong as you.
> Lend me your hand
> so that I may get up
> and lend you mine.
>
> by Joe F. Casal

Joe Casal served in Vietnam from 1966–1967 as a chief of communications with the U.S. Army. "I am still in contact with the nurse that helped me in Vietnam, she also happened to be my nurse on the PTSD (Post Traumatic Stress Disorder) Program here back in the world."

See Joe Casal's Web site, The Dien Cai Dau Express. "It will supply you with Veteran News, jokes, pictures, and links. Dien Cai Dau Express also sends out a daily newsletter." Visit one of the following sites for more information:

- Dien Cai Dau Express Veterans Newsletter at
  http://hometown.aol.com/number1gijoe/DDExpress.html
  "This page is mainly to inform you of veteran benefits available and all new updates in the laws helping veterans of all wars."

- Dien Cai Dau Express…at
  http://members.aol.com/vet66a/page/index.htm
  "This Home Page is mainly to say WELCOME HOME! to my brothers in combat and to share many links to other Vietnam oriented sites that can be of help to my bro's looking for information about Agent Orange, PTSD, locators services to find their buddies that they served with in Nam, and also to help students that might want to get in touch with any of us that served in Nam; includes pictures."

- Dien Cai Dau Express, Helping To Put A Little Laughter In Your Journey at http://www.geocities.com/vet66a

CHAPTER 4

Judy's Story

Too deep for words is the grief you bid me to renew.
   Virgil, from Aeneid, Roman poet, 70–19 B.C.

Time and time again I have read about us, the nurses who served in Vietnam: "They were calm, professional, and caring."

We were all those things, but the outward appearance and the inner feelings were yet another dichotomy of Vietnam. The following is an example of that two-pronged self. These were my thoughts and feelings during one of about 300 twelve-hour shifts I worked. There is no doubt in my mind that I appeared confident, competent, caring, professional, and calm but...

I'm Lieutenant Baker, I'm 23 years old and a member of the Army Nurse Corps. I have been in Vietnam working in the ER of an Evacuation Hospital for eight months now. Nothing I saw, felt, or imagined prepared me for being here, doing this job and trying to survive emotionally.

When I went on duty tonight to work the 7 p.m. to 7 a.m. shift, the nurses and corpsmen from the day shift told me that an 18-year-old GI had come in a couple of hours ago. He had stepped on a land mine and his legs were a real mess. He was screaming and crying and begged the

47

doctors to save his legs. He's in the Operating Room now and no one knows yet if he lost his legs. The people from the day shift are emotional wrecks; it must have been a terrible show.

Great! The supervisor just called saying that ICU (Intensive Care Unit) is really busy and one of us nurses has to go work there tonight. I am outranked by the other nurse, so here I go! Holy **! They really are busy over here and "all" they want me to do is wait for that kid to get out of surgery and care for him as he wakes up.

Damn! They had to remove both his legs below the knee. I don't want to be here. What am I going to do or say when he wakes up and realizes what happened—damn this war! Maybe he'll sleep until the shift is over. Sure! Right! Oh, no, here he comes—ah, look at this, he's just a boy, this is going to break his mother's heart! You have to get yourself together, Baker; you just can't let him see any pity in your eyes, you know that! Now get it together before he wakes up! He's coming to, maybe not—he's opening his eyes! Keep it together Baker, keep it together! I wish the knot in my stomach would go away—he's looking at me, trying to focus—touch him and smile. DO IT! That look in his eyes, he remembers—he's struggling to raise his head so he can look at his legs—push him back down—no, he's earned the right to face the truth—gently hold his shoulder, let him know you're here and understand. Yea, right, I understand! He saw that they're gone and has fallen back down—he's devastated!

Baker! You will not cry, you can not cry, DON'T CRY!!!! It's the last thing he needs! But he's only a kid—DO NOT CRY!!!—He's turning to say something.

GI: "Can you tell me what the ** I'm suppose to do without my ** legs?"

(Lieutenant Baker thinking to herself again) DON'T CRY!! You can do this—You HAVE to do this! Answer him! Put your hands on him—smooth his hair—I can't do this—yes you can! ANSWER HIM!

Lieutenant Baker: "You're going to have to spend a long time working very hard to learn to walk with artificial legs, and if you can't do that you'll be in a wheelchair and learn to get around in that." Boy, that was just a great big comfort! How can I comfort him when I can't even comfort myself anymore—this damn war!

by Judith Baker Williams, Army Nurse

Judith Baker Williams served in the Army Nurse Corps with the 67th Evacuation Hospital in Qui Nhon, from February 1968 to February 1969.

"The Dustoff pilots and crews did a hell of a job getting the wounded to us in Vietnam. Actually, most of us did a hell of a good job—we should have won that damn war.

"We were the youngest and most inexperienced nurses to ever be sent into a war zone, but nothing could have prepared us for what we saw and had to deal with. But we met the challenge; the survival rate for the seriously wounded was 83%, the highest survival rate of any war.

"We accomplished this with the help of the doctors, of course, but also with the help of our corpsmen who worked tirelessly by our sides and the field and evac medics who did an outstanding job of keeping the wounded alive until they could be delivered into our care. We worked 12 hours a day, six days a week.

"Our battlegrounds were the Emergency Room, OR, Post-Op, Intensive Care Unit, and Surgical Wards. We also fought on a battleground which receives little attention—the Medical Ward, where we encountered diseases not seen in the "Real World" and about which we had to learn quickly. Our enemies were bleeding, raging fevers, infections, fear, and death. We served our Country with Courage, Honor, and Pride."
Judith Baker Williams.

See her Web site, Vietnam Nurses Haven at http://vietnamnurses.com
Also see her "closed" discussion/support list that she started for nurses who served in Vietnam at http://groups.yahoo.com/group/VietNamNursesHaven

The Injured

*Yesterday, all my troubles seemed so far away
Now it looks as though they're here to stay
Oh, I believe in yesterday.*

The Beatles
Yesterday

Over 153,000 men required hospitalization for injuries while serving in Vietnam between 1964 and 1973. Another 150,000 plus required no hospitalization for their injuries but still required treatment. Over 75,000 men were left severely disabled. Of these, over 6,000 lost one or more limbs.

The high percentage of disabilities was, in part, due to the weapons used in Vietnam. Designed to mutilate, kill, and prevent soldiers from returning to battle, weapons such as claymore mines inflicted injuries that required much medical attention. The multiple wounds created by a mine, for example, each needed incision, debridement (surgical removal of dead or contaminated tissue and foreign matter), irrigation, and re-irrigation a few days later to prevent the high risk of infection. If the soldier's wounds were so great that he required amputation of one or more limbs, the soldier then required months, sometimes years, of rehabilitation and medical care.

Three hundred percent more soldiers survived amputation or crippling wounds to the lower extremities in the Vietnam War than in

World War II, and 70% more than in the Korean War. In addition to the excellent medical care provided by the nurses, corpsmen, and doctors, getting the wounded to this care was a critical factor in the survival rate. The medical evacuation helicopters, Dustoff, played a major role in speedy evacuation of the injured. Thanks to the helicopters, a larger percentage of injured men survived in Vietnam than in previous wars. Only 2% of the injured who did make it to a hospital died. A greater percentage survived, but a greater percentage of the soldiers also returned home disabled than in other wars. The nurses, as well as the women in other organizations such as the American Red Cross, were there for them all.

CHAPTER 5

Chrissy

*War marks the men and women
who are caught up in it for life.
It visits them in the hour before sleeping;
it comes to them—
bringing grief, pride, shame, and even laughter—
in the casual moments of everyday life.
It never goes away.*

William Broyles Jr.
Brothers in Arms: A Journey From War to Peace

Farewell

One hundred years from today,
I will be gone and who will remember you?
Not even your family will know that
you died in your boots.

I tenderly bag your dog tags
and bloodied prom picture.

I gently zip you into a plastic, green body bag,
my soul buried beside you.

by Chris Schneider

Chris Schneider, known as Chrissy McGinley in Vietnam, was a medical surgical nurse with the Army Nurse Corps. She was assigned to the 95th Evacuation Hospital, Da Nang, Vietnam, from June 1970 to June 1971. She arrived in country as a 21-year-old second lieutenant.

Today, Chris Schneider lives in Okemos, Michigan, with her husband, Tom, her daughter, Karli, and son, Tommy. Chris has a Master of Science degree in Communication Disorders from Western Kentucky University and works as a speech-language pathologist at Sparrow Hospital in Lansing, Michigan.

"My dream," says Chris, "is to return to Vietnam, with my daughter, to see the country and its people at peace."

Through her poetry, Chris continues to find her own peace with her year in Vietnam.

Pilot in Triage

I still smell your burned flesh
and see your charred body
impaled on a fence.
Did I remember to call the priest?

by Chris Schneider

The Colors of Christmas

All colors are drained from the images
except red and green.

Chopper blades whirl as
I stand in triage surrounded by dying soldiers.
Red blood flows from head and chest wounds,
as a strong metallic smell fills the air.
Glassy eyes stare upward,
as blood trickles from the corner of open mouths.
A gurney, with muddied legs, is pushed to the freezer.
A corpsman follows, carrying a single, bloodied thumb.
A soldier's shiny, red intestines roll to the floor,
as he is turned to his side and into a green, plastic body bag.

I suddenly awake and feel my heart
beating, racing, pounding.
I sit up in bed, next to my sleeping husband,
and wipe perspiration from my head.
Red and green,
green and red,
the colors of Christmas.
"What's wrong with you?" I hear my husband ask.
"There were all these guys," I tell him,
"whole guys, parts of guys, young guys, bleeding guys, dead guys."
"It was just a dream," he tells me.
That's all it was.
It was just a bad dream.
I wipe silent ghost tears from my forehead.
Red and green,
green and red,
the colors of Christmas.

by Chris Schneider

Bits and Pieces

It wasn't GIs with missing limbs,
but limbs with missing bodies
that bothered me most.
Bits and pieces of
star spangled heroes.

by Chris Schneider

A Measure of Success

I was born and raised in Pasadena, California. I was one of six children. Both my mom and dad served in the Navy during World War II. My mom was a Navy nurse and my dad, for a brief hospital stay, was her patient. I attended nursing school at the Los Angeles County Medical Center School of Nursing (1966–1969) and, during that time, I remember Army recruiters coming to the county hospital and talking about nurses being needed in Vietnam. On graduating, a part of me wanted to sign up and go right then, but another part of me was afraid to go because I was inexperienced as a nurse. So, I worked at the county hospital for a year and then signed up to go.

I was 21 years old when I went to Vietnam. I volunteered to go because I had the feeling that I wanted to do something significant with my life. Also, I had two brothers who were draft age at the time. My thinking was that if they had to be there, I wanted to be there to help. The Army was the only branch of the service that would guarantee I would immediately be sent to Vietnam. And so, in April of 1970, I joined the Army.

After six weeks of basic training at Fort Sam Houston in San Antonio, Texas, I left for Vietnam. On arrival in country, I was assigned to the 95th Evacuation Hospital in Da Nang. The 95th was made up of Quonset huts with beds for approximately 320 patients. Our compound bordered the South China Sea. We cared for American GIs, Vietnamese soldiers and civilian adults, Republic of Korea (ROK) marines, Vietnamese children, and prisoners of war. Our patients were transported to us via helicopters, Army ambulances, and occasionally arrived on foot or in fish netting. Nurses worked a minimum of 12 hours a day, 6 days a week. My assignment the first two months was on a surgical ward.

One of my earliest patients was an American soldier who introduced me to some of the harsh realities of wartime nursing. I don't remember his name, but I do remember the stench of pseudomonas that infected his open wounds. I remember that his body was covered with holes and his chest burned, and I remember that my ward was filled that night. One hour after having his dressings changed, he grew more restless and I hurried to his bed to see what I could do to make him more comfortable. I turned on his bed light and I remember the horror of finding giant red ants crawling over his face and in and out of the open wounds on his chest, arms, and legs.

After eight to ten weeks on the surgical ward, I transferred to receiving and pre-op, the triage and pre-operative area for casualties from the field. I remained there the entire rest of my tour. One of my fonder memories from receiving and pre-op is how the soldiers all loved to smell our perfume. So I would wear a whole lot more perfume than I needed to. I have vivid memories of wounded, even dying, soldiers looking up at me and saying, "You smell so good. Please don't leave me." What made this assignment difficult is that there was so much death, and the patients were all so young. It was hard to place eighteen-year-old bodies in a bag.

The part of Vietnam that I loved was the feeling that I made a difference in the lives of my patients, the intensity of that experience, and the camaraderie that existed with the people I worked with. But there was another side to Vietnam, too, a side that terrified me. Morale was low, racial tension was escalating, drug usage was widespread, and violent acts by GIs against other GIs were increasing. My own hootch had to be sandbagged, at one point, because it was directly behind our commanding officer's trailer, and GIs, on our own compound, had threatened to blow it up.

If asked would I do it all again, I know what my answer would be. My year in Vietnam will always be one of the most significant times in my life because my experiences there taught me what a big difference one person can make in the lives of others. In the words of Ralph Waldo Emerson, "…to know even one life has breathed easier because you have lived. This is to have succeeded."

by Chris Schneider

Welcome
Photo courtesy of Chris Schneider

Sign outside the compound of the 95th Evacuation Hospital, Da Nang, Vietnam.

Chrissy and Children
Photo courtesy of Chris Schneider

Lt. Chrissy McGinley outside the 95th Evac with two Vietnamese patients.

Farewell
Photo courtesy of Chris Schneider

Chrissy McGinley leaving the 95th Evac for the last time to return stateside. "En route home, I fly from Da Nang to Cam Rahn Bay. After a few days there, I board a freedom bird and head back to the world."
Chris McGinley Schneider.

CHAPTER 6

Nam Nurses

Life is either a daring adventure or nothing.
                              Helen Keller, 1880–1968

Veteran's Day

For thirty years, I have not "felt" Veteran's Day
Even having been a nurse in Vietnam.
I was a nurse doing what nurses do. It was my job.
Seeing the Wall was awesome in its magnitude but
Who did I know there?

I knew my Neighbor's son who died in Vietnam. He was there.
I knew that "One" who died, or that "One" who "surely died"...
who I met in the Emergency Room.
Yes, truly an emergency room of living and dying:
Head wounds, burns, multiple gunshot wounds, land mines,
White phosphorus burns, chest wounds, amputees,
tropical infections foreign to men from a faraway country.

But did I know them? I tried not to.
Don't look long in the face; Never look in the wallet.

Don't see whose mother's son was this or
whose wife became a young widow,
or, whose life was changed forever.

But surely, I do know them!
Like the soldiers who knew those who fought beside them,
who fought in their platoon;
Like the men who met the enemy in the most
intimate of exchanges of Life and Death,
so did we who met our patients, our brothers,
in a continuum of life at its intensity.

As did the soldiers, nurses rotated:
injected into a moment in the length of war,
a moment in the life of "One."
Caring for One was entering into the stream of life
of all those whose energies mingled to make a war.

As the soldier: sharing in the sounds of life and death,
feeling the saltiness of life, tears of a failing energy,
touching the bloody essence of a life moving into a new eternity.

As the soldier: sharing the struggle to live, to overcome
gross insult to God's most unique creation, man.

As the soldier: coping with burdens carried heavy on young shoulders.
Burdens tangible, burdens not visible unless you looked into those eyes
searching for reason in the unreasonable.

As the soldier: seeing the innocence of a generation
yanked, stolen, and beaten into submission to the reality of death.

As the soldier: seeing, hearing, smelling, tasting and feeling
a massacre of the human spirit.
   Seeing bodies of flesh festering with volcanic fumaroles
      from Willful Pandering of man's union with chemistry.
      Flesh ripped and separated by the ingenuity of a war machine.
   Hearing and feeling the thunder of explosion bent on destruction,
      pulsating and tearing fragile eardrum and shattering the confidence of understanding.
   Smelling the package of life seared and carbonized, an amalgam
      of bone and flesh, of dirt, sweat, blood, of useless uniformity.
   Tasting the salt of tears exploding into the dry caverns of fears.
   Feelings...scattered, shattered and unattached,
      held until...still trying to find reason in the unreasonable.
   Feelings...
Yes, Veteran's Day:
My brothers on the Wall whose struggle ended, whose unity is etched in granite,
reach out to me, taking my hand and
the hand of One...this One whom I met for a short intense moment.
We are Veterans.

by Nancy Quirk Lilja

"Fumaroles are holes or vents from which steam and other gases escape; "volcanic fumaroles" is an allusion to that. Willful Pandering (WP) is an allusion to White Phosphorus. Once that chemical got on the skin it could not be washed off with water. It took a special chemical. And as long as it was on the skin it kept burning and these little wisps of smoke escaped from the skin...like the steam venting from the fumaroles in the sulfur lakes in Yellowstone Park."
Nancy Quirk Lilja.

Captain Nancy A. Quirk served in Vietnam with the Army Nurse Corps at the 3rd Surgical Hospital, Binh Thuy/Can Tho, IV Corps, March 1970 to January 1971. From January 1968 to January 1970 she was at the 249th General Hospital (Evacuation) in Japan. After serving 11 months in country, at the age of 25, Nancy was medevaced stateside due to illness that required surgery.

Nancy Quirk Lilja is the recipient of the Meritorious Unit Commendation, National Defense Service Medal, Vietnam Service Medal, and Vietnam Campaign Medal w/60 Device, and Bronze Star Medal.

"I worked till 1975 and quit. I loved nursing. After 30 years, I am told I have chronic PTSD. I wrote a few pieces as part of my therapy in moments of inspiration," Nancy said.

Nancy is married with one son.

Dear Little Boy of Mine

Mama-san…dressed in the black cotton tunic
and pants of the peasant Vietnamese,
her back straight, arms outstretched,
carried her offering into the lull of the ER.

Her regal, resigned countenance moved
quietly on callused brown bare feet.
My eyes lifted from my task to see a determined Mama-san
walk the length of the ER alone.
Time stopped.
Her toddler lay flaccidly in her arms.
Our eyes met, both of us knowing,
looking for hope in each other's eyes,
questioning.
Grief was on hold, waiting to be released.

With great care she passed her child to me.
She made an offering of his life,
of his future, and of her future.
A sacrificial goat on the altar of war.
With stony grief etched in her small brown face,
Mama-san offered us her child,
his head crushed under a deuce and a half,
U.S. made and driven.

Tuan's dear little dark head, scant with hair,
with its mask of humanity in place was flattened –
only inches deep, ear to ear.
How pliable, how incomplete his growth, how malleable.
A beautiful child of God made for loving.

Mama-san's slow walk is a frequent replay in my cerebral
movie theatre but the scene ends too quickly.
Line after line of "Did I's" end the credits.

Today, I would fold her in my arms,
share in her loss in a communion of pain.
Then, I was riveted to my place in history,
ineffectual in sisterhood and motherhood.
Yes, today I would hug her, and share her sorrow.
Today, I would weep with her.
Today, I think of her often.

by Nancy Quirk Lilja

See Nancy Quirk Lilja's poem *Memories Penetrating the Shroud of Death: PTSD*
The Shroud of Lost Innocence and Life, chapter 15.

You're In The Army Now

We, the nurses who went to Vietnam, were mostly young, right out of school. Many of us had no nursing experience beyond what we had acquired in school. When the Army recruiter came around shortly before graduation, he convinced me that I would get excellent experience and training in the service, which I did. He also convinced me that my country needed me, that the young men of my generation needed me—and they did.

That is how I justify that year so long ago, a year of grueling work hours and never-ending casualties—they needed me. At the age of 21, in 1967, when most young women were still in college or newly married, I was on my way to Vietnam as a second lieutenant in the U.S. Army. The recruiter was right—I learned a lot that year. I learned to not flinch at horrible sights and smells, I learned to hold the hand of a dying patient, and I learned to not run away from soldiers as they dealt with their amputations. I learned to wear a flak vest and steel pot during alerts. I learned not to cry and how to pray. Oh did I ever pray. I sometimes prayed for sleep. And when sleep came, I prayed to wake up from the nightmares.

Over 30 years later, I look back at my time in Vietnam, and I know I'd go again. I'd do it all over again, when I was young—because they needed me. I've never in my life since felt that anyone needed me as much as those wounded soldiers did. I hope some of them remember my face; I certainly remember theirs.

by a Lieutenant, (anonymous), Army Nurse Corps, Vietnam.

Beautiful Vietnam

In 1965, as a 22-year-old first lieutenant, just recently out of college, I was on my first active duty assignment as a pediatric nurse at Ft. Carson, Colorado.

After only 8 months there, many of us who joined the Army Nurse Corps at the same time, began receiving orders for overseas assignments. Many went to Germany and France, but I got to go to Vietnam! Being young and single, I welcomed the opportunity for adventure and travel.

After a month's training at Ft. Lewis, Washington, our group boarded a regularly scheduled United Airlines flight from Seattle-Tacoma to San Francisco, in full battle gear—fatigues, boots, and loaded canteen belt. We saw a lot of jaws drop and eyes widen from the civilians aboard the plane as we walked bulkily sideways down the aisle past them to our seats. We thought it was hilarious!

Boarding an old troop ship at Oakland Army base, we left at dusk. Passing under the well-lit Oakland Bay Bridge and Golden Gate Bridge was a beautiful sight. We were about 10 nurses in one small room—bunk beds, and one bathroom—but we survived the month long trip, still talking to each other when the trip was over. Debarking in Cam Ranh Bay, we were ferried by helicopter up to our 523rd Field hospital in Nha Trang. That chopper ride was our first view of Vietnam. Lush green fields, and rice paddies everywhere. Beautiful.

I was assigned to a medical unit (as compared to the surgical unit), where our GIs were treated mainly for malaria, dengue fever, hepatitis, or standard illnesses. Occasionally we had a patient with blackwater fever or snakebite. Fatigues and boots were our duty apparel for security reasons. Our work schedule was basically 8-hour shifts, 6 days a week. During the Tet Offensive, however, it was 12-hour shifts, and 7 days a week.

Nha Trang was a beautiful little town with a gorgeous white sandy beach. Walking through town, one enjoyed many small, open-air shops and the slender women in their ao dais (the traditional dress of

Vietnamese women, consisting of a long tunic that is slit on the sides and worn over loose trousers.) Most people were wearing what looked like pajamas, with loose-fitting, full-length bottoms and tops. There were conical hats, cyclos, bicycles, pleasant aromas from sidewalk food stands, staccato tones and inflections of the Vietnamese language being spoken, white-washed buildings with red tile roofs from the French colonial period, bare feet or thongs, and smiling children.

Remember, this is only late 1965, when things were relatively calm.

My most interesting and memorable experiences were when I had the wonderful opportunity of going out on delivery flights to Special Forces camps. This is where I saw the dense jungle beneath our wings, the isolated, heavily fortified camps with adjoining montagnard villages, elevated longhouses for living quarters, colorful clothing worn by the native women, dusty bare feet with splayed toes, children being children—laughing, giggling, and curious. Hardpan red soil in the dry season, slippery, slimy in the rainy monsoon season. Isolated airstrips surrounded by dense jungle.

This is the Vietnam I remember. Beautiful country, beautiful people.

These are my memories, which I shall always remember and cherish.

by Marsha Klein
Army nurse
523rd Field Hospital, Nha Trang
September 1965 to September 1966

What an experience for a 22 year old and all that served there. I was acquainted with many dust-off pilots, and the 52nd Aviation who made deliveries into the Special Forces camps. It will certainly be a year of my life that I will always remember!
Marsha Klein

Quang Tri

Chateau Quang Tri
Photo courtesy of Mary "Chris" Banigan

My happy home in Quang Tri. It was a real dump but a real fixer-upper! Chateau Quang Tri—my Green Palace. Chateau Quang Tri is my palace in paradise decorated in OD Green, though I suggest Hunter Green to be more sophisticated. The decor complete with 50-gallon drums and sandbags creates the warmth and protection desired by all.
Mary "Chris" Banigan.

Mary "Chris" Banigan served with the 18th Surgical Hospital in Quang Tri, the 27th Surgical Hospital in Chu Lai, and the 91st Evacuation Hospital during her two tours in Vietnam, May 1969–May 1970 and October 1970–October1971. Banigan arrived in country as a first lieutenant and departed a year later as a captain. "I worked R&E (Receiving & Evaluation, Emergency Room/Triage) and the OR (Operating Room), and I volunteered on MedCap (Medical Civic Action Program, a type of civic action program whereby military personnel shared time and resources in the community to provide medical care and services to Vietnamese civilians) at the Leprosarium and Provincial Hospital in Hue during my first tour; on my second tour, I was primarily assigned to the OR.

"We (nurses) were a hardy bunch—we worked hard—we played hard and when it was necessary, we were all up to our ears in whatever needed to be done!"
Mary "Chris" Banigan

See more of Banigan's pictures in Vietnam at *What A Long, Strange Trip, 18th Surg, Quang Tri* at http://www.illyria.com/chris/vnchris7.html.

Incoming
Photo courtesy of Mary "Chris" Banigan

A Dustoff (Huey) helicopter arrives with wounded at the 91st Evacuation Hospital in Chu Lai in 1971.

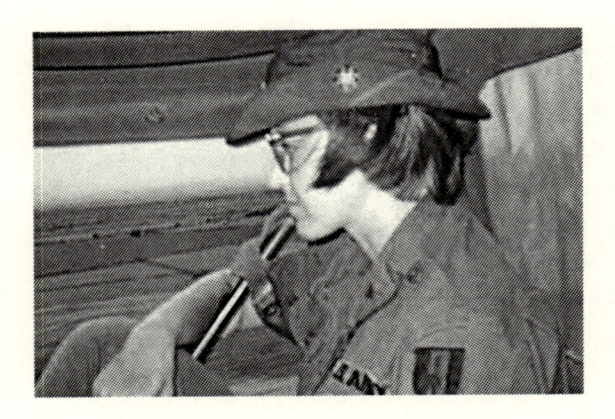

On the Road to Hue
Photo courtesy of Mary "Chris" Banigan

"The picture was taken before or after monsoon season, but I think it might have been in the spring of 1970, because I think it was after moving to Quang Tri. I was on the way to Hue on a MedCap outing. I suspect we visited the Provincial Hospital and then went over to the Leprosarium. Depending on the availability of transportation and the weather, I sometimes traveled by ambulance, deucy, jeep or chopper." Mary "Chris" Banigan

Army Nurse Corps

Women answered the call for nurses in 1775 during the American Revolution (1775-1783). At this time, the second Continental Congress authorized medical support funds to pay female nurses. These civilian women cared for wounded soldiers in General George Washington's Continental Army.

It was less than a hundred years later, in 1861, when America once again called upon female nurses to come to their country's aid. Nurses volunteered for forty cents a day to be a part of the Women Nurses of the Union Army during the Civil War.

In 1887, the Surgeon General established the Army's Hospital Corps, made up of enlisted men. In 1898, however, the military medical personnel were overwhelmed with injured and sick soldiers during the Spanish-American War. Dr. Anita Newcomb McGee, at the request of the Surgeon General, recruited women nurses for the Army. McGee, vice president of the Daughters of the American Revolution, only accepted women with completed nurse's training and a good recommendation. Over 1,500 nurses qualified and served in Cuba, Puerto Rico, the Philippines, Hawaii, China, Japan, and on the hospital ship Relief.

On February 2, 1901, Congress passed a law creating a permanent Army Nurse Corps. It wasn't until 1920, however, that military nurses began wearing rank—second lieutenant, lieutenant, captain, and major. The Navy Nurse Corps was established in 1908.

At the beginning of World War I in 1914, 403 nurses were on duty with the Army Nurse Corps. The Army began training nurses in 1918 with the establishment of The Army Schools of Nursing. By the end of the war in 1918, over 22,000 women had served as nurses in the military. Over the next few years, the numbers continued to drop, and only about 600 women were on active duty as nurses in 1935. Anticipating possible involvement in World War II, the military increased this number to over 4,000 by 1939. From this time until the end of the war in 1945, 56,793 women served in the Army as nurses. In World War II, military nurses took on the new role of flight nurses. Having flight nurses aboard evacuation aircraft greatly increased an injured soldier's chance of survival. After the war, the numbers of military nurses once again dropped to about 2,500 by 1947.

Just a few years later, from 1950–1953, the military once again utilized the nursing corps in the Korean War. This time, 540 nurses served in Korea with MASH (Mobile Air Surgical Hospital) units. Other nurses also served in Japan. Many nurses stayed in Korea after the war, teaching

Republic of Korea Army nurses. In 1958, three nurses of the Army Nurse Corps went to Vietnam to assist the United States Military Advisory Group in Saigon. These women were the first of approximately 8,000 military nurses who served in Southeast Asia during the Vietnam War.

Although Congress has never drafted female nurses into the military, 900 male nurses were drafted for the Army Nurse Corps and Navy Nurse Corps during the Vietnam War.

CHAPTER 7

Gary's Angel

Yes, we're different, world's apart.
Claudine Longet
Until It's Time For You To Go

I was severely wounded, receiving a head wound in Vietnam, while on combat operations with the 1st Air Cavalry '66–'67, as a combat infantryman. I was in a coma for about three weeks at Nha Trang, then shipped to the 106th in Yokohama, Japan.

There I met my Angel of Mercy, Judy Blackman. Her compassion and giving nature pulled me back when many thought I'd surely die. When able, Judy took me places around the city. I called our times dates. She probably thought of it as therapy. Our song: "Yes, we're different, worlds apart, we're not the same. We laughed and played at the start like in a game. You could have stayed outside my heart, but in you came. And here you'll stay until it's time for you to go." I'd like to hear from Judy and thank her.
Gary Jacobson.

Warrior and The Nurse

A combat infantry warrior
Ravaged in body and spirit
From the cruel war come to die
Bit the bloody bullet with his name on it.

Lying on his deathbed rough like the eagle tough
With a nation's blood on his wearied hands
Filling his wounded and repressive heart
Bloodied spent from alien lands.

Just a man wounded by war's inconsolable hate
The boy's innocence beat out of him
Just a boy in violence grown irate
Thrust into the armor of a man.

In far and away Japan waited an angel of mercy
Calling softly to sons of freedom born,
Calling far and away across the China Sea gently,
"Come ye brothers by the cruel war shorn."

"Come from Vietnam's tremulous evil bore
From blistering conflagration
Come to Japan's alien shore.
I will treat boys rent by war's devastation."

"Come ye tired and sorely wounded
By hatred's slings and arrows oppressed.
Gather under my angelic wings unfolded
Here I'll soothe body and soul by battle repressed."

"Embrace again sweet life
Feel my tender touch beleaguered soul restoring
Far from war's maddening strife
Summon inner strength from the depths in healing."

Said the warrior, "Sweet angel with loving touch,
Honor a brother depraved by beastly war's dearth.
Reestablish in my soul humanity's worth
Oh, a perfumed, porcelained hand, means so much."

"Honor a sacred tradition of comfort giving.
Pull a neighbor from death's door
Bring back love and joy of living,
Giving with sunny hope from compassion pour."

"Remind me of my humanity.
Mend my wounded heart so much in need.
Restore misplaced value's sanity.
Restore respect left back in the field to bleed."

Great mercy distills from beings in divine sympathy
As sisters deeply aware of spirit inside suffering
For those wounded in body and spirit, share empathy
In sensitivity the pain relieving
To father, brother, son, bestow tender virtue
Nurtured loving imbue.

A lady officer, and an embattled grunt private
Knowing days together were grimly numbered
Living in a moment snatched from immoral war's fate
By the sands of time encumbered
In but a fleeting island of time before…

Before he must go his way...
And she return to tend teeming thousands more
Depart from budding love games in innocence play
To tend boys receipts from this bloody war.

For he was not a king,
Just a warrior—just a soldier—just a man
She was not a dream,
She was an angel, disguised on earth as woman.

Lost for a fleeting moment from overseers above
They played the game,
Danced the dance of purest love
Though they were not the same...

Too far from carnage to heaven's brightest star
For the boy ripped from war's raging mist
Is a journey exceeding far...
Far too for the master nurse therapist.

The warrior was too soon carried back
Back to "the world"
Back on silvered wings unfurled
Leaving behind his nurse caring
Showing others in gentle passion compassion...
Through tender mercy bearing
Her slice of home far from home sharing.

A seed once planted so long ago
Without nourishing sun and rain did not grow
Souls burnt by the pull of worlds tearing apart

Felt brief love with no beginning…and no end
Fallen silent through ages the beating heart,
The ways of the world cannot in the end bend.

My angel, my nurse, Judy Blackman, told me time and again,
our song was:

"Until It's Time For You To Go"
by Claudine Longet…
With a composite at the end by Neil Diamond, Buffy St John,
Glenn Yarbrough.

You're not a dream, you're not an angel, You're a man.
I'm not a queen, I'm a woman, Take my hand.
We'll make a space in this life that we planned,
And here you'll stay until it's time for you to go.

Yes we're different, worlds apart, we're not the same.
We laughed and played at the start, like in a game.
You could have stayed outside my heart but in you came,
And here you'll stay until it's time for you to go.

Don't ask why, Don't ask how,
Don't ask forever of me.
Love me, love me, now.

This love of mine has no beginning, it has no end,
I was an oak, now I'm a willow, I can bend…
And though I'll never in my life see you again
Still I'll stay until it's time for you to go…

Here I'll stay until it's time for you to go…
Yes I'll stay until it's time for you to go…

by Gary Jacobson

"The imagery in Gary's poems is often a kaleidoscope of thoughts and feelings, ripped directly from his heart; this verse (below) is particularly raw and real emotion."
Mike Subritzky, The Kiwi Kipling

Angel of Mercy

The war ended suddenly for me on that April afternoon in 1967. I was blown unconscious and was put on a dustoff helicopter, never again to see or hear from my brothers in arms for 34 years. I suffered rather a severe head injury that ruined my whole day.

As for the head injury, the pains, the constant ringing in varying tones in both ears—these are just things I have to take in stride. The alternative being unacceptable. Please understand, Vietnam combat vets have a lot of baggage they need to contend with, depending on how much blood they got on their hands and how much of it was their enemies', their buddies', or their own. There needs to be healing, not only of the body but also of the spirit within.

I don't tell too many people about my wounds because I don't want people being sorry for me, or even worse, when I flub up, them saying, "Oh, that's why." I would hate that.

I was on the fifth day on patrol in the boonies that we grunts called "the killing zone," walking at point on the right flank of our operation. A sniper had shot directly at me three different times that particular morning—shooting at anybody, but I happened to be closest to his line of fire, so his bullets whizzed by my ear and pocked the dirt at my feet. Lucky me!

Later down the trail, it was blazing hot and we were all dog-tired. So when our company commander signaled for a break, we immediately began to move into a big circle called a defensive perimeter, all guarding out and watching one another's backs. I had my eye on a shade tree to sit under, scouring the horizon and really looking at the bushes anxiously to see my little friend hiding, waiting to have a fourth shot at me. But I should have looked down a little closer because I tripped a piano trip-wire booby trap. That detonated a grenade, which in turn set off a mortar round. As soon as I was hit, I blacked out. I felt no pain; nothing except the out-of-body experience I describe in my poem *I Felt I'd Died*. I was in a coma for about three weeks.

When I was stabilized, they sent me from the aid station in Nha Trang to Japan. My medical records say I had substantial brain damage. I didn't know much for a couple of months. I had to learn to walk again, to talk and even to write again. It's like when you zero in to make a shot on a target in the practice range—my shot would have been so far off it would have made the sergeants in the control tower run for cover.

I was sprayed with shrapnel from head to foot. My left leg was swollen like a balloon, and they had to give me shots in the stomach (heparin) twice a day for one month to relieve what they thought was a blood clot. I learned to look forward to the midnight shot. For some unclear reason (smile) I couldn't get to sleep knowing it was coming.

I now have a triangular plate in the back of my head measuring three by four inches. Three inches into my brain is a jagged piece of shrapnel about the size of a quarter. No, they didn't take it out, and I'd like them to leave it well enough alone, thank you.

My poor mother. She received a telegram that I had been wounded in the head, neck and leg; then, heard nothing more for over two months—hearing not if I was OK, not what hospital—nothing. She about went out of her head with grief not knowing if I was dead or alive. She told me later she erected a kind of shrine for me with my picture, some flowers, and a candle with "an eternal flame." She prayed to it, and she sent my name to a number of temple prayer circles.

I am a miracle. The doctors that look at me cannot understand, because the path the shrapnel took into my head should have without doubt, and without any chance, either killed me, or made me a human vegetable for life. But I'm not, and they wonder why. And sometimes I wonder why.

Of the four hospital neurological wards I was in, of all the head injury patients, no matter how small a wound, I retained more of myself from before the wound than any of them. I don't know why!

If Nam was hell, then my 14 months in Army hospitals was Hell's Hell. But it did teach me compassion. For during that time I couldn't feel sorry for myself because I couldn't look around without seeing someone very much worse off than I. I saw some real horrors there, both in my neurological ward and next door in the burn ward. I saw big, strapping, good-looking men who were relegated for the rest of their lives slobbering in a wheelchair with vacant, mindless expressions. I saw families come in and tend to their son who was strapped to a bed in an endless coma for the rest of his life. I saw men who literally looked like creatures from the black lagoon—all flesh charred like a bubbling black ash, no ears, no nose, no hair, no features, only a hole for a mouth. I empathize with some who feel the ones who died were the lucky ones. It's like the parable, "I cried because I had no shoes, until I met a man who had no feet."

Judy Blackman, my Angel of Mercy at the 106th hospital in Japan where patients from Vietnam were sent, was a physical therapy nurse, an officer. I was a lowly specialist 4th class. When I came to in Japan, a lot of the patients around me, as they later were to tell me, thought I was surely dead. Judy made me embrace life again. She spent time with me, and when I was able to walk, we went on several "dates" to the seashore, and to several local restaurants, and to the home of a Japanese couple who belonged to my church. I rather think those dates were as much therapy from the master therapist than anything, because we both knew my time was limited before I was shipped to a hospital closer to home. We were attracted to each other, the wounded combat warrior and his angel therapist, and Judy told me "our song" was one sung by Claudine Longet. She kept playing the record for me *Until It's Time For You To Go*.

Here I'll stay until it's time for you to go…Yes I'll stay until it's time for you to go… I still can't read those words without crying; my words now are written through a river of tears.

I am Gary Jacobson. I served with B Company, 2nd of the 7th, First Air Cavalry '66–'67, as a combat infantryman operating out of LZ Betty near beautiful downtown Phan Thiet, fallen in combat due to a booby trap, and now on 100% disability rating. Here is a poem I wrote of my memories of that time when:

I Felt I'd Died

Above a battlefield far away,
My mind in black unconscious lay.
Tethered by a silver thread in heavens sky,
Hovering in God's palm, twixt heaven and earth am I.

Wound in a park swing then let go,
With no more hate to seek my country's foe.
Left behind, heart and breath careening,
No longer man but only being.

An exploding mortar spun to death and fate,
Raised me to the door of heaven's gate.
Spinning on a tenuous strand of life bereft,
I'm blind to "the world" I hadn't yet left.

Hanging dangling on a silver thread,
No longer alive—but neither dead,
Buoyed above the belligerent crowd,
Bobbing like a cork with the sky my shroud.

Floating unfettered without rhyme or reason,
Above the earth in a peaceful season,
Drifting on currents of sweet oblivion beatified,
Heedless of nirvana's nothingness tide.

No longer am I a soldier sustaining oppression,
War weapons wielding powerful fists of suppression.
No more to remember man's "inhumanity to man" war,
That pitiless beast of blood, guts, and gore.

Till a voice groaning below yanked me back,
From purest light to the war wolves pack,
To tired soldier faces with camouflage painted,
To hot sweaty soldiers with Nam's blood tainted.

Who's that groaning below? Who can it be?
Suddenly imposed on my senses I see…It's me!
Suddenly aware it's me down there sighing,
At the base of the silver tether, It's me down there dying.

From the valley of the shadow, to war's glory unfurled,
Platoon medic Bryant talked me back to "the world."
Pulled back from the bright tunnel of light,
Now returned to fight the good fight.

by Gary Jacobson

Finding Judy

Gary Jacobson searched for his "angel of mercy" via various Vietnam Internet sites. In 2001, Judy, who is married with five children, received a letter about Gary from the Vietnam Women's Memorial Project (for more about this project and Sister Search, see chapter 26). She read the poem on his Web site and contacted him.

"Finding her was almost like washing away the years. She is truly a wonderful person, and writing her gave me a deep insight into what feelings she had way back then. We have written several long letters and restored a lot of common ground. She answered many of my questions, and we are now old friends.

"It has been the fulfillment of a dream."
Gary Jacobson

The Art of Medicine

Voltaire (1694–1778) is credited with the following profound statement: "The art of medicine consists of amusing the patient while nature cures the disease." Perhaps that's one of the reasons the U.S. military sent those who had been injured in Vietnam to hospitals, that must have seemed like oases, in Japan, the Philippines, Okinawa, and Hawaii before sending them back to the medical facilities nearest to their homes in the States.

Of course, the main reason was because the rate of physical recovery was faster if a wounded man had a few weeks (to psychologically recover) between the time he was dragged, bloody and frightened, from a foxhole in Vietnam and the time he was safely back in "the world" with family and friends.

Having just been transferred from Walter Reed, I had been in Japan for less than a week when I met Gary. We were walking to church with some friends, heading for our off-base chapel in Yokohama. Gary and I hit it off right from the start, and for the next few weeks, most of my off-duty time was spent with him, meandering along the streets of Yokohama taking in the sights and culture of Japan or hanging out on post when he couldn't get a pass. Gary's comment (that I probably thought of our outings as therapy) might have had more truth to it than either of us knew at the time. To me they really were dates, but Voltaire might have thought of them as "the art of medicine!"

Gary and I were both 23, and, in addition to simply enjoying being together, we had quite a lot in common. He had been to college a couple of years, and he had been on a church mission for two years. By dating, however, we were being a bit daring, not only because I was an officer (a first lieutenant) and he was enlisted (a PFC), but also because I was a physical therapist and he was a physical therapy patient. Being young, I guess we figured that certain established military taboos could simply be disregarded! We sort of threw caution to the wind and just had a lot of fun and good times together until he was shipped back to the States. Gary and I have found it hard to remember many of the details of our times together, but the letters I had written home to my parents have brought to mind some of the lost memories and emotions of those days.

In one letter home I wrote: "There are only 600 patients as of yesterday, and tons are leaving this weekend. One of my patients told me that the hospitals in RVN are full and they're clearing us out now so we can get a fresh load in... The helicopter just landed and is taking away some patients. Should be 2–3 more after this one leaves. Every time I hear one I think of Gary leaving... he's leaving in 2 weeks and I'll never see him again. We'll just have fun until it's time for him to go."

Gary and I wrote on and off over the next couple of years, but we lost touch with each other about a year after he got out of the Army. That was around the time I married Mike Kigin, the finance officer of the nearby 249th General Hospital. Often through the years I would think about Gary and wonder what had happened to him. It's always sad to lose contact with good friends, and I think that point hit home to most of us even more so after the terrorist attacks of last September. Therefore, it was truly amazing to me when, a month after 9/11, I received a letter from a woman working on the Vietnam Women's Memorial Project's Sister Search (chapter 26). She had seen the poem Gary had written, which she said brought tears to her eyes. She suggested that I contact Gary, so after mustering up my courage, I e-mailed him. It's been great fun re-connecting after so long, and we've been enjoying catching up with each other's lives and families.

My husband Mike and I live in Arlington, Virginia, (about five minutes from the Pentagon). I'm still working as a PT, but instead of treating battle-scarred GIs, I now give hugs and hot packs to a bunch of neat elderly folks at Little Sisters of the Poor (a senior citizen residential facility). We have five children, the youngest of whom is a midshipman at the U.S. Naval Academy, the only one of our kids, so far, to follow in our military footsteps. Mike and I have traded our Army uniforms for Boy Scout uniforms, and we have been dedicated Scout leaders/volunteers for more years than I'd like to admit! Our three sons are Eagle Scouts, which is a source of great pride in our family.

I have been awestruck at the beautiful poetry I have read on Gary's Web site. He seems to have a natural gift of being able to put words together in such a way that the reader can really feel the emotion that he's trying to convey, the feelings that he has inside. I am truly touched that Gary would have written such a lovely tribute to me, but I believe that much of what he expresses in *Warrior and the Nurse* could be said about all the women who helped take care of the Vietnam casualties during those most trying of times. Those brave young men were the true heroes of our day, and we as caregivers considered it an honor and a privilege to be able to share a bit of ourselves with them as we helped them to recover both physically and emotionally from their wounds. I think Voltaire was right—amusing the patient is "the art of medicine!"

by Judy Blackman Kigin

War No More

My goal in writing is to educate people who have no idea of the realities of war, the horrors and the trauma. I wish the stories of what happened there to never die. I want them to live on in the telling and retelling until they become a firmly established part of our memory. I was the sports editor of my college daily newspaper (BYU's [Brigham Young University] Daily Universe) when I was drafted, and like so many others, Nam changed the direction of my life indelibly and forever. Nam imbedded my soul with a new set of senses—forever.

Many veterans have written me saying that for the first time in 33 years they read words that expressed exactly what they felt, and that for the first time they were able to sit down in front of the computer with their families and show them what war was like for them. School teachers have written me saying they think my "Tour" (Vietnam Picture Tour, http://pzzzz.tripod.com/namtour.html) should be required viewing for their students.

I wrote this because all the people of the world continually need to understand how important an event war is. War will always be a determining factor of not only who we are, but it will determine our very futures, as well as the futures of our wives and children. I sincerely hope we will not doom our children to fight senseless battles as did we, shackling them to similar fates suffered by their fathers in the latest in a series of "war-to-end-all-wars!" If we do not learn the history of war and its terrible implications, learning there is no glory in war, only death, destruction of values and misery, then we are doomed to repeat it! And the next war will inexorably come! Sometimes war is a necessary evil—sometimes not—sometimes there's Vietnam!

My fervent wish is that we will come to understand the horrors of war, that we can work for peace evermore, making war-no-more!

by Gary Jacobson

Gary Jacobson, "Gazza," is vice president and Awards Committee Coordinator of The International War Veterans' Poetry Archives found at http://www.iwvpa.net.

Gary Jacobson's story, *A Soldier's Story*, and more of his poetry and pictures are at Vietnam Picture Tour at http://pzzzz.tripod.com/nam-tour.html.

"Visit my Vietnam Picture Tour from the lens and poet's pen of a combat infantryman, from one who's walked the walk, and can talk the talk. Take a walk in the park with the 1st Air Cavalry on combat patrol, that in reality will give you the taste of Nam on your tongue, leave the pungent smell of it in your nostrils, and imbed textures of war in your brain as though you were walking beside me. A walk in the park referred to combat patrol out into the boonies, out into the jungle where Charlie lived, out where your chances of living or dying were a roll of the dice."

Gary Jacobson

Read Gary's poems *Love's Good Vibrations*, chapter 23; *An Affair To Remember*, chapter 23; read Gary's comments regarding September 11, 2001, *A Stronger America* and *My Fellow Americans*, chapter 29.

CHAPTER 8

From New Zealand

Who'll come a-waltzing Matilda with me?
Andrew Barton "Banjo" Patterson, 1864–1941

Sister

Young man, you ask me who I am,
and why I wear this faded yellow ribbon…

I am the woman, who held your dying uncle's hand,
and wrote a letter once that broke your grandma's heart.

I am she, who met the 'Dust-Off' at the door,
and carried bloodied, broken bodies through to triage.

Then cut through muddied boots and bloody combat gear,
and washed away the blood and fear and jungle.
I kept the faith when even hope was lost,
and cried within, as young lives ebbed away.

Those hours when death, frosted dying eyes,
mine, was the last smile many young men saw.

I have the voice, that blinded eyes remember,
and the touch of reassurance through the pain.

In darkest night when combat would return,
it was my name that many soldiers called.

I have dressed their wounds, and wiped away their tears,
and often read them letters sent from mom.

I hugged them close, and willed each one my strength,
and smiled and prayed that each boy made it home.

And here today, you ask me who I am...
I am the Nurse, who served in Vietnam.

by Mike Subritzky, The Kiwi Kipling

Born in Kati Kati, New Zealand, Mike Subritzky served in the Royal New Zealand Navy, Royal New Zealand Artillery, Royal New Zealand Air Force, U.S. Navy-Task Force 43 Antarctica, and Polish (Independent) Reserve Brigade. Although he did not go to Vietnam, Mike is no stranger to war with 13 tours of duty to his credit, including the Rhodesian war.

As a writer and war poet, Mike is able to bring war veterans of all nations together in a common unity of healing, courage, and understanding. Mike Subritzky is the author of several books including his most recent, *The Flak Jacket Collection*. His book *The Vietnam Scrapbook—The Second ANZAC Adventure* was nominated for New Zealand Book of the Year Awards 1996 and named Book of the Quarter by Texas State University April–June 1998. Mike was also honored by the New Zealand ex-Vietnam Services Association by having a copy of his book laid at the Vietnam War Memorial Wall in Washington, D.C. during the 1997 pilgrimage. Mike also received the American Vietnam Veterans (honorary) Distinguished Service Medal 1997, "for his contribution to all veterans of the Asian conflict and immortalizing the Vietnam veterans of New Zealand for all time."—United States Congressional Cold War Citation 2000. His numerous poetry awards have certainly earned him the title of The Kiwi Kipling.

See more of Mike Subritzky's poetry at The Flak Jacket Collection, New Zealand war poetry, http://www.geocities.com/mike_subritzky.

Mike Subritzky is the president and co-founder of the International War Veterans' Poetry Archive, http://www.iwvpa.net.

Read Mike Subritzky's poetry, *Midnight Movie,* chapter 15; *Soldier's Farewell,* chapter 28; and *bird of a single flight,* chapter 29.

Australia and New Zealand in Vietnam

The United States wasn't the only country to send their sons and daughters to the aid of South Vietnam. In the mid-1960s, Australia and New Zealand also sent troops to the war. Over 500 Australians, including seven civilians, thirty-eight men of the Royal New Zealand military services and one New Zealand civilian nurse, Sister Lesley Cowper, lost their lives in country.

Australia began sending military advisors in 1962, and in 1965, the 1st Battalion, Royal Australian Regiment, went to fight alongside the U.S. 173rd Airborne Brigade in Vietnam. Approximately 50,000 Australian military personnel served in Vietnam from 1962 until their involvement in the war ended in 1973. An estimated 2,500 to 3,000 Australians were wounded during this time.

Australia sent her women as well—over 200 nurses served in country from 1964 to 1972. Of these, one nurse died, Barbara Black, in 1971, in Vung Tau, due to illness.

The New Zealand government did not keep records of the Royal New Zealand Air Force personnel who served in Vietnam. Historians estimate that approximately 4,500 New Zealanders served in Vietnam.

Body Bags

Body bags slick, shining green,
white nylon zips unable to stem
the knowing of limp slack lines
and men who once were friends.

Floppy hands and heavy carry
to waiting helicopter doors,
and mates who once smiled
now stacked on aluminum floors.

Congealed blood and torn boots
by the bamboo groves
and thumping rotor blades
taking away the stiffened hands.

Stacked, flopped, almost liquid
in the obscene formlessness of plastic,
hiding the end product of insanity
and the awful work of jumping mines.

Taking from your pocket a letter
still unread, but opened by shrapnel,
and here an arm, and there a leg
neatly body-bagged, and bloody well dead.

The ashes of unshown grief choking us
along with the red dust as you go away,
now a mere dot in the vault of the sky
wrapped with your memories in a bag.

by Lt. John A. Moller
RNZIR Whiskey Two, Vietnam

John Moller is a New Zealand Maori (Native New Zealander), who wrote some of the most powerful and moving poetry to come out of the Vietnam conflict. *Body Bags* and his poem *The Last Step* lend themselves to the nursing side of Vietnam and bring home the horror of that conflict.

John Moller joined the New Zealand Army at age 16, and at 21 was selected for officer training. In 1968–1969 he served in Vietnam as an infantry platoon commander with Whiskey 2 Company, Royal New Zealand Infantry Regiment (RNZIR) and was based at Nui Dat in the Phuoc Tuy Province, in South Vietnam. In total, John Moller served 17 years in the New Zealand Army and upon retirement became active in veterans' affairs and Agent Orange issues. He is the current president of the New Zealand Vietnam Association. His war poetry appears in numerous anthologies, and he has also published a personal collection of his war poetry in his book, *The Punji Pit*. (information provided by Mike Subritzky)

The Last Step

Had enough time to cry
"My God"
as the innocent track
leapt up in a moment
of sound and fury—
and the jumping mine
cut him in two
at his pubic hair line.

And in the dark shadows
on the sides of the track
his friends all retched
and gently reached back,
pulling their bayonets
to prod the bloody track.

Fighting down their fear
and wanting to run,
but knowing if they did
they'd be dead, every one;
feeling for the trip-wires
and the shining prongs,
inch by inch all prodding
the leaf mould and the slime.

by Lt. John A. Moller
RNZIR Whiskey Two, Vietnam

Read more of John Moller's poetry at The International War Veterans' Poetry Archives, http://www.iwvpa.net. Read about him and his book, *The Punji Pit, Poems of the New Zealanders in the Vietnam War,* at http://maori2000.com/moller.

CHAPTER 9

Australian and New Zealand Nurses in Nam

Do unto others as you would have them do unto you.
                                           Matthew 7:12

RAANC, Royal Australian Army Nursing Corps in Vietnam

In April 1967, four nursing sisters left Australia bound for an experience that they would never forget. By December 1971, a total of forty-three nursing sisters from the RAANC had served in Vietnam. Their tour of duty was twelve months, and they worked in an environment unlike anything that most had ever worked before. Despite the unveiling of the National Service Nurses Memorial in Anzac Drive, Canberra, in 1999, much of Australian society is unaware that Australian women served in Vietnam. These women touched the lives of hundreds of Australian, New Zealander, American, Korean and Vietnamese soldiers and officers, as well as the lives of Vietnamese civilians. And yet their work has often gone unrecognized. The following article is taken from the work that has been conducted by Dr. Narelle Biedermann, and is not the opinion of the Department of Defence.

Many of the nursing sisters that went to Vietnam were considerably inexperienced nurses, particularly in trauma and intensive care nursing. Most had completed their general nursing training and midwifery training within three years of being posted to Vietnam, and few believed that they were prepared for the experience of nursing in a war zone. Unlike the Australian soldiers, the nursing sisters were not given any training to prepare them for their twelve months in Vietnam, and many had no idea of what to expect. For some, their first "taste" of Vietnam was getting off the plane to see dozens of body bags being loaded on to a plane bound for America or Australia. Others remembered their first nursing experience was shrouded with terror, when a dust-off chopper arrived and unloaded wounded casualties at their feet. One nurse reported that on her first day in Vietnam, she was asked to remove the soldier's boot, and when she did, the entire foot came off with it. Others had several days in which they could explore their surroundings before they were needed.

The nurses worked in all facets of the 8th Field Ambulance (until April 1968) and the 1st Australian Field Hospital (until December 1971): triage, intensive care, surgical ward, medical ward, operating theatres, and Regimental Aid Post. Some found that they were working in the surgical or medical ward, which functioned just like it did in a civilian hospital, except the patients were all young, fit Australian "boys" who had become sick or wounded in a war zone. Others found themselves working in environments for which they had no experience, training or knowledge.

"You were just expected to get on with it. That was it," one nurse reported. Everything that happened in the war affected the hospital, and ultimately, the nurses. For every battle or operation, injured soldiers were brought into the hospital that required treatment: the Tet Offensive, Battle for Fire Support Base Coral and Balmoral, Battle of

Long Kahn, and the myriad operations that were conducted in the Phouc Tuy Province. Every time a soldier was wounded, their job began, and sometimes they didn't stop for thirty-six hours. One nurse remembered: "the dust-off chopper came in and we got to work on the casualties. Some time later, someone asked, 'What day is it?' We had been going non-stop for thirty hours, and we didn't know if it was night or day. The casualties just kept coming."

Most will tell you that it wasn't all hard work in Vietnam. There were barbecues, parties, visits to Nui Dat, parties, swimming at the beach, parties—anything to relax and unwind from the sights and smells of the hospital. They were always consciously aware that they were the only females among thousands of men; a "round eye." Despite the harsh climate, they wore their traditional grey dress uniforms, with stockings and starched veil, "because the boys would feel secure on seeing us in our uniforms. If they reached us alive, they knew that they were going to make it home, and we did everything to ensure that they made it."

Nursing in Vietnam was unique in some ways. It required immense dedication and commitment to care for wounded soldiers who could be lying on a stretcher in triage within twenty minutes of being wounded. Clinically, the nurses took part in practices that would change the management of casualty resuscitation and wound surgery. Despite the trauma and horror of nursing in a war zone, the majority found the experience to be extremely rewarding and the most positive thing they had ever done, as one nurse indicated: "I am so glad that I went. If the phone rang right now to go overseas, I would be packed and out of the door before I had a chance to say goodbye to anyone."

by Dr. Narelle Biedermann
Royal Australian Army Nursing Corps (RAANC) in Vietnam
Reprinted with permission. This article also appears on the Mildura Vietnam Veterans' Web site, The Australian Involvement in Vietnam,

http://users.mildura.net.au/users/marshall, *RAANC in Vietnam*, http://users.mildura.net.au/users/marshall/medic/nurses2.html.

For further details about RAANC in Vietnam, please contact Dr. Narelle Biedermann (narelle.biedermann@jcu.edu.au), School of Nursing Sciences, James Cook University, Townsville QLD 4811 Australia.

"I am the daughter of an Australian Vietnam Veteran who grew up in a home that suffered the effects of the war. After high school I joined the Reserves as a medic. Whilst a medic, I began my nursing training and upon graduation, transferred in the Australian Regular Army as a Nursing Officer. I am married to an Infantry Officer and we have one daughter, Mikaelie. I am now on the inactive Reserve list, and am a lecturer at the School of Nursing Sciences at James Cook University, Queensland, Australia."
Dr. Narelle Biedermann

The New Zealand Involvement in Vietnam

Nine New Zealand military nurses and one Red Cross worker served in The Republic of South Vietnam from 1967 to 1971. The nine nurses were members of the Royal New Zealand Army Nursing Corps, attached to the 1st Australian Logistic Support Group (ALSG), 1st Australian Field Hospital, Vung Tau. Nurses with the rank of lieutenant are called Sister, and captains are called Charge Sisters. Sisters worked as the ward nurses and the Charge Sisters were in charge of the wards or the department in which they worked.

"Sister Margaret Torry was the first of us to go in 1967. Next were Charge Sister Maureen Alexander and Sister Jill Murphy, followed by me (Charge Sister Pam Miley-Terry) and Sister Margaret Whineray.

Charge Sister Claire Jacobson took my place when my TOD (tour of duty) was finished. Sister Karen Clark (deceased in 2000) served with Claire Jacobson. Sister Daphene Shaw and Charge Sister Anne Griffen were the last to go in 1971.

"There was one member of The NZ (New Zealand) Red Cross, Isabel Beaumont, (not a nurse) who went up to SVN (South Vietnam) in 1970 and was posted to the Australian Red Cross unit at 1st Australian Field Hospital, Vung Tau. She was a welcome addition to the number of those excellent ladies."

Charge Sister Pam Miley-Terry

The Car

"We have a car and would like the NZ sisters to have it," I was told by Victor company officers when I was visiting Nui Dat. What a morale booster that would be for us I thought. "It needs a bit of fixing up but does go," he said.

My thoughts were that it would have to be an ANZAC sisters car—speaking to our CO (commanding officer) at the hospital (1st Australian Field Hospital), 1 ALSG, Vung Tau—permission was given with much positive prompting from me.

Did I explain that the car was commandeered? (Under wartime conditions of course). The truth of the matter was the car was found in the jungle in the Courtney Rubber by 1 Platoon Victor, 3 Victor Company (4 R.A.R.N.Z) 27 November 1969. It had belonged to a French Rubber Planter but used by the Viet Cong (No. Plate NVA 001). A 1948 Citroen, black.

The car was choppered back to Nui Dat and then the arguments as to who should have it began and ended with the decision to give it to the Kiwi sisters. One of the soldiers had worked with a Citroen company and was able to get the car in running order. The car was duly delivered to NZ Workshops and among other things was painted a beautiful mauve pink.

The day came for the delivery—photos—Major Q. Rhodda handed it over to us. No speedometer/no key start/only a push button. A beautiful mauve pink car complete with bullet holes.

Petrol was supplied by various depots about 1 ALSG. We could drive the car in the confines of the camp only at 15 kilometers per hour and driving on the right. The Provosts (Military Police), had a trial with us, as it was quite difficult to maintain at 15 km per hour when there was no speedometer let alone drive on the right hand side.

All would go well until one had to change roads. The car proved a real morale booster for us. The medical orderlies thought they could use it but were firmly informed that it was for the sisters only.

Whenever any of the nurses went on R&R they were impelled to bring decorations back. Thus we had stick-on flowers, feet, and one of the girls brought back an old fashioned horn—bulb and trumpet type.

Yes, the car had many uses. Even provided a place to sit with someone when some privacy was wanted.

This is the true story of the car; a New Zealand-acquired innovation. Thanks to the big hearts of the men of 1 Platoon, Victor 3 Company, of the Royal New Zealand Infantry.

Thanks guys!

by Pamela Miley-Terry
Charge Sister ex RNZNC, February, 1969–February, 1970, Vietnam. Reprinted with permission: *The Vietnam Scrapbook—The Second ANZAC Adventure,* by Mike Subritzky.

CHAPTER 10

Donut Dollies

Second (star) to the right and straight on till morning.
James M. Barrie, 1860–1937
Peter Pan

They Brought Smiles

The grunts will always feel close to the Donut Dollies; they brought smiles and a few minutes of laughter without judging us. This was during a time when many of our peers judged us quite harshly for doing what we were ordered to do. I suspect that the Donut Dollies also felt that judgment, both in Vietnam and when they returned home.

I don't know how many actually served, but how often do you hear of a woman mentioning having been a Donut Dolly?

Dan (anonymous), 9th Infantry Division, Mekong Delta, 1969

The American Red Cross in Vietnam

From 1962 to 1974, the United States sent paid volunteers from the American Red Cross to assist the military personnel in Vietnam. The young women of the American Red Cross served in the hospitals, arranged emergency leave for soldiers, passed on information to the soldiers from home, and provided recreational activities. The American Red Cross in Vietnam was divided into three groups: The SMH (Service to Military Hospitals), the SMI (Service to Military Installations), and the SRAO (Supplemental Recreational Activities Overseas).

The SMH of the American Red Cross provided social work and recreational therapy for the injured and rehabilitating patients in the hospitals. The SMI passed on communications from the soldiers' families back home in regards to emergencies, births, and deaths. They also arranged compassionate emergency leaves for the soldiers who were returning stateside due to a death or serious illness of a family member.

The SRAO, or Donut Dollies, brought games and conversation to the soldiers in the field. They also ran recreation centers for the enlisted men. They offered a smile, games, and a break from the war for the military personnel. The Donut Dollies traveled by jeep and helicopter to reach the soldiers wherever they could. Thousands of men, far from home and loved ones, participated in American Red Cross recreational activities at military command posts as well as remote field sites during the Vietnam War.

Information courtesy of Sharon Vander Ven Cummings, American Red Cross SRAO "Donut Dolly," April 1966–April 1967. See her story, *Once Upon A Time*, chapter 11.

Donut Dolly Blue

Memorial Days pass and too little thought given
To the memory of Donut Dollies in Blue who were striven.
Over one hundred years of unashamed tears fell from the eyes
Of Red Cross Ladies whose exploits should be recognized.

Their own battle—and they fought the good fight—
Largely unrewarded, demands a lost soul to show their light.
Some had it good, dancing in The Nam in the night on moonlit beach,
While others lived in bunkers when rockets left the breech.

Of the three millions of Viet Nam vets, most Dollies made it home,
But left large pieces of their life when they lived in someone's Rome.
They shared the loss of life, someone else's and their own,
And today will share their grief at the foot of a friend's headstone.

Visits on mountain tops and riding choppers high above,
Trying hard to keep the pasted smile and a look of love
For grunts who dreamed of hamburgers and shakes
Who forged hard ahead to stop the thought of seeing their own wakes.

Dollies made men dream of girls back home, of girls with rounded eyes,
Seeing only the slanted kind, and remembering bad goodbyes.
Would they make it home, these unwashed grunts,
Who spent long, long hours counting days and months?

If they didn't, probably their last beautiful memory
Was of seeing Donut Dollies, erasing thoughts of enemy.
Thank you, Dollies, all of you, who volunteered to the last woman.
You were all that made Viet Nam fun for many Infantrymen.

What G.I. could ever forget, one beautiful American girl
Driving an ACAV, laughing and giving it a whirl?
And at night in the dark, his memories would last
Even though so many years have passed.

Thank you the for the games you played, Ladies in Blue,
And for saying the names of men you really never knew.

And even though their dreams are stuck amid bamboo,
To a man, count on the fact that they remember you.

by Sonny Gratzer

George M. "Sonny" Gratzer served in Vietnam from 1967–68 as a captain commanding Company B, 2nd Battalion, 2nd Infantry, 1st Infantry Division. He is the recipient of the Silver Star with Oak Leaf Cluster, the Soldiers Medal, the Bronze Star with Valor (1st Oak Leaf Cluster), the Purple Heart (2nd Oak Leaf Cluster), the ARCOM (Army Commendation, 2nd Oak Leaf Cluster), the Combat Infantryman's Badge, the Vietnamese Cross of Gallantry (with Silver & Gold Stars), and other awards. Gratzer is the author of *General Issue Blues: Vietnam to Here, A Warrior's Tour;* and *Mountain Meadow Amore.* See his Web site, General Issue Blues, at http://www.sonnygratzer.com.

Carrying On The Tradition

My mother was an American Red Cross Donut Dolly in World War II, and that's how she met my pilot father. Of course, I grew up hearing all about her adventures and thought it sounded like the greatest job imaginable!

Lo and behold, one day when I was a senior in college at the University of Denver, she called me on the phone and told me she had just seen an article in the paper about the Red Cross. They were looking to recruit young women for the very same program in Vietnam. I hustled right down to my local Red Cross and talked with one of their staff about the program. They gave me all the info they could, and tried to be realistic with me about how tough the job could be. Nothing they said dimmed my enthusiasm for such an adventure, and I applied. Several months later they sent me to San Francisco for an interview (of course my mother went with me), and I was accepted into the program, due to leave in July 1967, one month after I graduated from college. So, I knew where I was headed the day I graduated from college, and I was truly excited about the opportunity to serve in such a way.

I arrived in South Vietnam on July 24, 1967, and I learned within several days that my first assignment was Lai Khe, with the 1st Infantry Division. What a great location and assignment. I also served in Chu Lai and Da Nang—all great assignments from my perspective.

There were, of course, some scary times. Shortly after arriving in Lai Khe, there was a mortar attack on the base. The only place we Donut Dollies could go was into a very thick-sided bathtub in the bathroom. Someone finally came to get us and took us to a bunker.

I was in Chu Lai during the infamous Tet Offensive of 1968, and we spent quite a bit of time in the bunkers. In fact, during the first night of the offensive, several trailers in our immediate area were hit, and ours suffered some damage. My first thought was to hide under the bed, which I did. Then, again, someone came and took us to the bunker.

Because I was so young, naïve and foolhardy at that point in my life, I saw these events more as an adventure than a life-threatening situation. I think that's how a lot of us got through the experience. I have also since learned that the war I was in from 1967–1968 was very different from a few years later, in terms of drugs, racism, and other characteristics. Drugs were just beginning to be a problem when I was there, and later were a major issue. Women I've talked with in recent years had more negative experiences than I did. Sometimes I wonder just how young and dumb I was.

My whole experience felt so much more positive. I grew up; I learned things about myself and what I was capable of—and what I was good at doing. It was a formative experience that set me on a path I've followed my whole career. I still work in the nonprofit arena, in volunteerism and community relations, and I think my year in Vietnam got me focused in that direction.

Of course, I fell in love many times. One in particular was more long-lasting, and while we never got married, we are still in touch periodically 30 years later—with a real affection for each other. I married a Vietnam veteran, but not someone I knew over there. My husband and I met in the anti-war movement while we were protesting together as members of the Vietnam Veterans Against the War.

Thirty years later, I am still so proud of what I did, and so appreciative of what it did for me. I would encourage my daughter to do the same thing, just as my mother encouraged me.

by Jackie Norris
American Red Cross, Donut Dolly, 1967–1968

Jackie Lively Norris served as an American Red Cross SRAO (Supplemental Recreational Activities Overseas), "Donut Dolly," from July 1967 to July 1968 in Lai Khe, Chu Lai, and Da Nang, Vietnam. She now has two children, a son and a daughter, both in their 20s. Jackie Norris is the Executive Director of Metro Volunteers, a volunteer resource center in Metro Denver, www.metrovolunteers.org

Proud To Be A Donut Dolly

During the Viet Nam war, the American Red Cross hired young women who were college graduates to work with the military in a program called SRAO (Supplemental Recreational Activities Overseas). We were affectionately called "Donut Dollies" by the GIs. Basically, we were morale boosters. There were about 110 of us in country at any given time, assigned in various numbers to about 21 military base camps. Some of these locations were in larger cities such as Cam Ranh Bay or Da Nang, and others were very small forward base camps where the action was more intense. We usually had some sort of recreation center for the men—some place they could go to relax a bit, talk to an

American girl, play games, cards, drink coffee or Kool-aid, and generally unwind for a couple of days before their unit was sent out again.

We always worked in pairs. Some girls stayed in base camp each day to run the Rec Center, while the others visited various units around the base camp or went out to the soldiers in the field. The object was to get them together, split them into teams and just...well...play games, sometimes adaptations of familiar television games. Sounds ridiculous, but the men loved it. We would split them into teams and get some competition going. Obviously, there weren't any stores around, so we scrounged the materials to make our props, and away we'd go in tanks, jeeps, or helicopters to the field where we'd stay for about an hour in each location before the helicopter would come pick us up and take us to our next stop.

We often visited six to eight locations a day. If the commanding officer felt it was too "active" or dangerous to gather the men together, then we would just go from bunker to bunker, visiting with the soldiers, and keeping a lower profile. We often just served chow, played cards, or talked with them about their homes, wives, girlfriends, trying all the while to raise their spirits a bit. Sometimes this was even more meaningful because we could talk to them one-on-one. We did this all day, seven days a week—just going all the time.

It's Your Thing
The Isley Brothers, 1969

I absolutely did not know what I was getting myself into, I suppose. I've always been the adventurous type and my father instilled a good deal of self-confidence in me, telling me I could do anything or be anything I wanted if I tried hard enough. Some of my friends were heading to Canada or burning draft cards, and many were involved in the antiwar protests, but I kept thinking about the enlisted men...why one man would choose to go and another wouldn't. Whether they went to Viet

Nam because they believed in what we were doing or not, I felt they were the ones needing our support. My mother had sent me an article about the SRAO program and closed her letter with, "This sounds like you." I applied, and three months later I was in Lai Khe.

We were sent to Washington, D.C., for two weeks of training, but nothing could "train" you for what was to come. These girls were, and still are, special. I came to find out all too soon that this was a good test of mettle. Not everyone made it through the one-year commitment, and if you couldn't "handle" it, you could go home. But what I experienced was a camaraderie with some of the finest women I've ever known. It took all our courage and initiative to hang in there, especially during mortar and rocket attacks. But the soldiers were wonderful. They were everything—what it was all about. And I don't regret one day, not *one*, of my time there.

Only The Strong Survive
Jerry Butler, 1969

My first assignment was with the 1st Infantry Division in a place called Lai Khe, a beautiful old French rubber tree plantation. This was a small, forward base camp about 45 miles northwest of Saigon. There were only four Donut Dollies, so two of us would visit some base units and run the Rec Center during the day, and the other two would do the rounds in the forward areas, visiting as many NDPs (night defensive positions) as we could in a day. We'd get up many times before light to be at the helipad on time for an early departure, and arrive back at dusk, tired but happy. It was something I started looking forward to each day actually. Then at night we'd all head for the Rec Center and play games or talk with the guys until about 10:00 at night.

In Lai Khe we had no hot water in our little house, and no flush toilet. I remember we had these big 55 gallon drums filled with water that we used for showering, and another drum of water that we used flushing the toilet. We'd dip a bucket in the drum and pour the water down the toilet. For the first few months we were taking malaria pills, which tended to bring on diarrhea, so you can imagine what fun that was!

After six months living with only three other girls in Lai Khe, I was transferred to Da Nang. It was hard leaving because I had been there so long and had attached myself to the 1st Infantry Division. The men and officers were attentive, responsive, and respectful. It had become my "home" in a very short time—so much so that I felt guilty leaving for the North. But Da Nang would prove to be a whole different experience.

In the week between leaving Lai Khe and my assignment in Da Nang, I went on R&R to Japan. Each night for seven nights, I filled the hotel bathtub up to the top with hot water and just soaked until my skin was all shriveled. I think it probably took the whole week for the red dirt of Lai Khe and Quan Loi to float out of my pores! It was heaven!

Living in Da Nang was like living in luxury compared to Lai Khe. There were about a dozen girls. We lived in a house in the city, and we had hot running water! Life there took some adjusting for several reasons, but mostly because I was suddenly with so many other women, and many of the units we visited were rear echelon units. It seemed more "stateside" and senseless to me. I did, however, visit many Special Forces camps, which I loved. It allowed me to see more of the Vietnamese people and see a completely different side of things. And there was more "night life" in Da Nang. There was always some place to go, but it wasn't the "me" I had discovered, so I asked to be transferred to a smaller base again.

Born To Be Wild
Steppenwolf, 1968

My third assignment, the Americal Division in Chu Lai, was once more a totally different experience. There, six of us lived in two air-conditioned trailers! And it was there that I remember one of the funniest things that happened to me: One day I answered the door and found a GI standing at the bottom of the steps. He just stood there with the oddest expression on his face and didn't say anything. So I asked what he wanted. The conversation went something like this:

Me: "Hi. Could I help you?"

Him: "Well…could I come in?"

Me: "Who are you looking for?"

Him: "Uh…well…I don't know…just anybody, I guess."

Me: "What do you mean?" (I realize how "slow" I was here, of course.)

Him: "Well…(looking down and fidgeting sheepishly now) you know…just anyone. I understand it's fifty dollars. (hope in his eyes here).

Me: (getting it finally!) "Fifty dollars? ARE YOU KIDDING ME?!!!?!?" I started cracking up, laughing at him, poor guy. "Are you CRAZY?!? Think about it soldier. Do you think if we wanted money for *that*, we would come half way around the world, live in a war zone with dirt and dust, have no conveniences of home, and dodge mortars and rocket attacks…for that? For FIFTY BUCKS?!?! Take off!"

He apologized of course and walked away with his head down and his tail between his legs and probably very embarrassed. I felt a bit sorry for him then. His buddies probably set him up, I imagine. Looking back on it now, I think it was pretty funny, but some of our girls had to deal with this kind of thing more seriously than I had in my experience. There were some very serious times regarding this kind of encounter, which infuriated us all, but they were not common. For the most part we were treated very respectfully. Still, all this experience did was make me miss Lai Khe even more. When I was offered the chance to go back, I jumped at it.

Angel of the Morning
Merrilee Rush, 1968

I returned to Lai Khe in September, 1968, to find things had, not surprisingly, changed. The women were wonderful, very friendly and talented. We had a good working relationship. But I also found that most of the soldiers I had know had either rotated home or worse, had been wounded or killed, some only days before I returned, which was very difficult for me to deal with.

One of these soldiers was a man I had played cards with many times. We were always sparring verbally, and always made sure we were on opposing teams in any game we played. It was just a friendly relationship we had formed along the way. A few days before I returned, his hand was blown off during a battle. A few of his men took me to see him in the hospital, and the first thing he did was smile at me and challenge me to a game of cards! His attitude and courage was infectious, and there was no way I could have cried at that moment. It would have let him down. So we all sat on his bed and instead of playing against him, I held his cards for him while he played. We just played as a team for the first time, and I knew we could both sense the special moment of it all. We did that daily until he was evacuated out of there. I never saw him again, but I'll never forget him or his bravery and attitude. It was times like this one that had such an impact on my life. And I realized that I was different things to different people. For some soldiers, I represented their sister. To others, a mother, and yet to others, a sweetheart. I've spent hours with GIs reading their "Dear John" letters and talking to them about their hurt, or about their children, or what their plans were when they returned to the "real world." I've laughed with them and held them while they cried. I'm sure most of us had those experiences as Donut Dollies.

Midnight Confessions
Grass Roots, 1968

And there were more humorous times as well, of course. One day I was working in one of the mess halls, making soup with some of the cooks. I'd been in country only about ten days. Up until then I'd thought, "This is really great! There are all these handsome guys, and I'm having a ball flying around in helicopters! War isn't so bad." But then these sirens started as I was happily stirring the soup, and everybody started running for bunkers. I just followed some guys and scrambled into a bunker myself, finding it a bit dark and chaotic. When somebody turned on a flashlight and I looked around, the first thing I thought was that this had to be a (television) episode right out of *McHale's Navy* or *Sergeant Bilco* or something! I looked around and surveyed my heroes. One soldier was armed with a long soup ladle, one with a stainless steel spoon and a rag, one with nothing in his hand, and the last with a weapon. "Ah," I said laughing in spite of the situation, "you guys are my protectors, and at least one of you has an M16."

"Yes, ma'am," came the reply, "but it isn't loaded!" This was my first mortar attack experience. There would be many more, of course, and none were this funny again. But I still can't help but laugh when I remember this one.

Can't Take My Eyes Off You
Frankie Valli, 1967

One day in our Rec. Center, I was playing cards with several soldiers when I became aware of someone looking over my shoulder. This was not uncommon really because there were usually only between two or four of us girls and many men, so they were always interested in what we were doing. We often had a dozen men just watching any game. But this was different. I was aware that this person behind me had sat there longer than usual. Then he made a comment, which made everybody laugh, and one of the men remarked, "That was a good one, Sir!" This was significant to me because we ran the Rec. Center only for the enlisted men. There were no hard rules of course, but it was understood that officers already had things a bit better and had their own clubs, so they were really a friendly "off limits" in ours. I didn't even have to look to know it was probably a lieutenant behind me who had come in without wearing his rank. Many of the lieutenants and captains were the same young age as the enlisted men, so it was an easy thing for them to blend in if they wanted. Consequently, when I heard the "Sir," I was prepared to let him know the jig was up and get him to leave, but I never got the words out.

When I turned, I looked into what had to have been the kindest eyes I had ever seen—big, brown and peaceful. There was a look of total recognition and silent understanding—defining and conclusive—as if I could see beyond his eyes to some place down the line. We just stared a moment, then smiled, and it was done. I remember being aware of the chatter and laughter around us and that I didn't blink for a long time. My mind's eye took a picture that I still see clearly today, and it's *that* picture I see whenever I get confused or "off balance." It just brings things back into focus somehow.

The Tet Offensive started soon after that, and we were unable to see each other. Everything was so chaotic, and the Donut Dollies were not allowed to go anywhere; our activities were suspended. So for about three weeks we couldn't do anything. Eventually, they evacuated us out of Lai Khe to Di An, a safer location. I was talking to my parents on a MARS call, letting them know I was all right, when Steve showed up. We spent the rest of the day and night talking until he was able to get a helicopter back to his unit; and when the girls finally returned to Lai Khe, he was back in the field. It would be weeks before we'd see each other again.

After things calmed down a bit, whenever he was back in base camp, he would come over with a friend and we'd all talk and find ways to laugh. We'd play games constantly, often finding our way to the bunker during a mortar attack and continue playing games there. Our bunker had become a very popular place in our "hooch" by then. After the first few nights of the Offensive, we were rocketed usually every hour, sometimes around the clock. It was so odd really. After a while we just became accustomed to it. It was as if they were just reminding us that they were out there and that we shouldn't get too comfortable. So we kept important supplies in our bunker such as playing cards, paper and pens, flashlights, pillows, a little food, and of course, bottles of wine. And it was there, during times in our bunker, that Steve and I really began developing our relationship.

All You Need Is Love
The Beatles, 1967

I was transferred a few weeks later in late April 1968, and I would only see him once more before he left country that following summer. When I was in Chu Lai, he found a way to fly up to see me for two days before going back to the States in July. I returned to Lai Khe until December 1968, and then I went home. But "home" had changed. It was very hard to relate to my parents or friends, and I felt so empty for leaving Viet Nam. "Home" had become hundreds of soldiers fighting a war thousands of miles away, and I just didn't feel comfortable in the U.S. So another Donut Dolly and I hitchhiked around Europe for about eight months trying to unwind I suppose, and find our place back "in the world." I didn't see or hear from Steve all that time. But when I returned to the United States in August 1969, I found him in Savannah, Georgia, just finishing flight school. We were married a few months later in November.

I believe we have a very special relationship due to our experience in Viet Nam. We share many of the same emotions and opinions about it all, which has been an important factor in our marriage. I counted the days we actually saw each other. From the time we met until the time we married, there were only about 32 days over a two-year period in which we actually saw each other. The rest of our relationship during that time was formed over field-phone calls, poems and letters (all of which are still kept in a special box). But those 32 days were marked with intensity. As in all relationships during the war, the men shed any facade that so many of us wear in the United States, and we learned about each other by sharing deeply from within.

These long years later, I know irrevocably that I am in the right place with the right person. The love Steve and I share has grown incredibly deeper and truer with each passing year, and it constantly amazes me that it all started on a rubber tree plantation in a Southeast Asian war zone. I am wonderfully blessed, and I have this picture in my mind that someday, when he and I are old and gray and watching sunsets, we'll be holding hands, still sharing that first "look," and we'll have great stories to tell our grandchildren.

Walk Away Renee
The Left Banke, 1966

Talking about Viet Nam is pretty therapeutic really. It was a rewarding, unforgettable experience for me. And leaving was probably the hardest thing I've ever done. When it was time for me to go home, I was so completely attached to the soldiers and involved with my job that I didn't want to leave. This was not an uncommon occurrence, and the Red Cross tried to prevent this by moving us around to other locations during our year there, which helped keep us fresh and challenged. But I stalled for a week before I actually left. I just hung out in the "Robin Hoods" (173rd Assault Helicopter Company) area, our aviation battalion. But I couldn't continue that, so a friend of mine, a major, personally flew me in a helicopter to Saigon. It was all they could do to get me in the helicopter, then even more to make me get out! Saying "goodbye" to those guys was incredibly hard. I'll never forget the feeling I had walking away from the helicopter and watching them hover and take off without me.

Those Were The Days
Mary Hopkin, 1968

How do I summarize my Viet Nam experience? It isn't any easier than trying to explain what we did there. It was such an intense time…such a challenge…and the single most defining time of my life really. I've seen things I don't care to remember, but can't forget. My memory isn't selective when it comes to Viet Nam; I remember it all—the sights, sounds, smells, fear, music, laughter, camaraderie, rocket attacks, the shrapnel in my bed, blood and death. It took all my ingenuity, creativity and courage. I found out who I was and what I was made of. Hopefully, I found a bigger "me," a stronger and deeper "me." I found the most courageous, honorable people I've ever met, and along the way, I found the love of my life.

Am I proud to have been a Donut Dolly? Would I go back and do it all over again? Would I put myself in "harm's way" and live that same experience once more? A thousand times, "Yes." You find the Huey, I'll meet you at the helipad.

by Patty Bright Fortenberry

Patty Bright Fortenberry was in Vietnam as a Donut Dolly from November 1967 to December 1968. She was with the 1st Infantry Division in Lai Khe from November 1967 to April 1968, where she met her future husband; the 3rd Marines in Da Nang from April to June 1968; the Americal Division from July to September 1968; and the 1st Infantry Division from October to December 1968. Patty's husband, Steve Fortenberry, was with 2/28 B Company Black Lions, 1st Infantry

Division, in Lai Khe 1967–1968 and 128th Aviation Tomahawks, 11th Aviation Battalion, at Phu Loi 1970–1971.

Patty is a flight attendant for Alaska Airlines and Steve is a captain for Japan Airlines. Both of their sons are pilots.

Visit Patty's Web site, American Red Cross Vietnam Donut Dollies, http://www.donutdolly.com, "a place to share e-mail and physical addresses, to enjoy connecting with old friends, also for making new friends with girls who were in country at a different time, but share the same, ever-haunting memories. All, of course, not bad memories. By 'haunting,' I just mean 'never ending' stories of courage and friendship, a thousand lost loves, and lots of laughter. We all have stories to tell, I suppose."
Patty Bright Fortenberry

Vung Tau
Photo courtesy of Patty Bright Fortenberry

"This was taken in Vung Tau one day. Vung Tau was an old French Colonial resort which was made into an in country R&R center. I'd guess though that less than 10% of the GIs got to go there. Actually, this was my first day off, and I flew down there with another Dolly and four helicopter pilots. It was such a change; we were gone from dawn to dusk

and were beat when we got back to Lai Khe, but it was worth it. This was just one of the men there on the beach who came up and talked to us. Times like these were interesting because you always wondered: Is this person really VC? Could be. I guess you could never be sure, even with some of the older children."
Patty Bright Fortenberry

Bob Hope, 1967
Photo courtesy of Patty Bright Fortenberry

"This was Bob Hope day. The Donut Dollies had worked on the stage the day before the show came in, and that's when Steve (Fortenberry) saw me for the first time. Some of the GIs got to come in from the field, and they went wild over Raquel Welch and Barbara McNair. McNair came out in a slinky dress and sang *I'm a Woman*. You can imagine the reaction. I'm surprised all the rubber trees didn't just fall down with the resounding din! Bob Hope himself was sort of lost in all the slobber over the women (who looked dynamite). It was fun to be there that day and watch all their stress turn to laughter for a few hours. That was a few days before Christmas 1967 in Lai Khe with the 1st Infantry Division. That Christmas season was, without doubt, the best Christmas I ever had."
Patty Bright Fortenberry

118   Angels in Vietnam: Women Who Served

Donut Dolly
Photo courtesy of Patty Bright Fortenberry

Patty Bright films 1st Infantry Division troops coming in from the field for the Bob Hope show, December 1967.

The Old Lady
Photo courtesy of Patty Bright Fortenberry

Mountain village people crowd around outside Da Nang at a Special Forces camp.

"The village people had just run up to us when we (Donut Dollies) arrived. They always did that, especially the children, but the adults were curious too about us. They were used to seeing American GIs, but not American women. So whenever we'd show up they'd come flocking. They would all sort of "inspect" us. They'd run their hands up and down our arms, feeling our arm hair; then some of the kids would touch our legs and lift up our skirt a bit…what? To see what we looked like up there I guess; I never really figured it out, but it used to make us laugh so much. They would follow us around the whole time, then the kids would wave goodbye. Most of the adults just stood and watched, expressionless."
Patty Bright Fortenberry

The Soldiers and The Children
Photo courtesy of Patty Bright Fortenberry

Patty Bright, center, with American troops and Vietnamese children outside Chu Lai in 1968.

"The people were just as interested in us as we were in them. Of course, we were actually there to play games with the guys, but sometimes that was not always possible. In this picture though, we had finished our time with the men and were heading back to the helicopter to travel to another location. We generally only saw the local people at Special Forces camps like this one, not fire bases. They wouldn't have been around there. I remember thinking how hard it was to tell the ages of these people. The young women looked so weathered and old...sort of used up...as if they had worked the land for years upon years...just worked the land and had children. I still wonder what they thought about us."
Patty Bright Fortenberry

Children are Wonderful
Photo courtesy of Patty Bright Fortenberry

"This picture was taken in Da Nang in 1968. It must have been one of our 'off' times because I'm in civvies. (My mom made my dress by the way. There was absolutely NO place we could get any western clothing so everybody read the Sears Catalog as if it were the Bible! I'm serious! You can't imagine how we loved opening a box from home no matter whose it was!!) American women were quite the novelty even in the cities, especially those without a military uniform on; they were quite curious about us and literally flocked around us and followed us everywhere we went when we got to town. Children are wonderful, aren't they? No matter what you look like, what you wear, bad hair day, etc., they make you feel like a million bucks—like Miss Universe or Superwoman. And we ate it up."
Patty Bright Fortenberry

Dauntless
Photo courtesy of Patty Bright Fortenberry

Patty's future husband, Steve Fortenberry, in 1968. Steve served with 2/28 B Company Black Lions, 1st Infantry Division in Lai Khe, Vietnam. He was a first lieutenant at the time of this picture.

When Did It Begin?

I can't remember when I didn't love you.
Was it last night when I was angry?
No. Not then.
I loved you.
Was it when I was lost in myself?
No. Not then.
I loved you.
Was it when you wandered around looking for adventure?
No. Not then.
I loved you.

I can't remember when I didn't love you.
Was it before the time we first made love?
No.
I loved you.
Before our eyes met in that villa so long ago?
No.
I loved you.
Before you rode floats waving in parades,
Before you rode horses through canyon streams,
Before you walked,
Before you breathed
I loved you.

And when I've breathed my last,
I'll love you still.

by Steve Fortenberry

CHAPTER 11

Once Upon A Time

*The best and the most beautiful things in the world
cannot be seen or even touched.
They must be felt with the heart.*
                                        Helen Keller, 1880–1968

We Smiled Anyway

I had graduated from college, was not getting married, and I needed a job. I interviewed with the ARC (American Red Cross) in San Francisco. After the interview, they asked me where I would rather go, Korea or Vietnam. I chose Vietnam—it was 1966, and I figured not many people would volunteer to go there. I had no idea what I was really volunteering for. And knowing all I know now, if you'd ask me today, I'd go again.

Most of us were recruited from college campuses. Requirements were for young women, minimum age of 21, single, with a college degree. In my case, my Mom worked for the Red Cross and told me about the jobs opening up in Vietnam. I flew to San Francisco and interviewed for the job—and was offered the job on the spot. Within six weeks, I had gotten my shots and was in Washington, D.C., for two weeks of training. From there, I was on a plane full of GIs with six other girls (we always called ourselves "girls"), and we were flying to Vietnam. Our tour of duty was for a full year.

When I went to Vietnam, I was the youngest girl in country. I had my newly earned college degree in sociology, was single, and needed a job—so I volunteered to go to Vietnam. I look back and cannot believe how innocent and naive I was.

Training

We only received two weeks training in Washington, D.C., before going to Nam—it was mostly on-the-job-training. And there was NON training in terms of protection against enemy fire. We were noncombatants and were "safe." Our training consisted of learning how to recognize the various branches of the military and their ranks, and how to behave like a lady in all situations.

My Job

I served as a Recreation worker with the American Red Cross (also known by some as "Donut Dollies"). Our job was to set up recreation centers before the USO and Special Services came in, and to write and conduct recreation programs out in the field for those guys who could not come in to our centers. In addition to "working" with the "well" guys, we also visited the hospitals and handed out activity books with puzzles, riddles, cartoons, jokes, etc., that we had written and put together, or we just went into the wards and spent some time with the wounded soldiers. Our job was to smile and be bubbly for an entire year—no matter what the situation.

Many times, I have been asked, "What did you do in Vietnam? Were you a nurse?" I don't think I would have had the strength to be a nurse in Vietnam, and I used to feel guilty telling people that I was there to play games with the guys. I never realized that what I did was important until I went back to Washington, D.C., in November 1993, for the dedication of the Women's Memorial at the Wall. And despite what many people have said, I feel the statue is a tribute to ALL women who served in Vietnam. There has to come a time when we all pull together, especially when we were so busy and leading such different and separate lives when we were in Vietnam. Maybe it is also wisdom with age.

Going to Vietnam

I was really excited! It was a whole new adventure. It was my first job after getting out of college! I had been raised in the military (my Dad was a pilot in the USAF), so I was never concerned for my safety. I just KNEW that the government would not send civilians into harm's way. Remember, this was April 1966, so there had not been a whole lot in the media about the war. In fact, I was not quite sure exactly where Vietnam was. But I was excited and anxious to go!

As the year progressed, my enthusiasm waned. My first six months were spent at Cam Ranh Army, which was a support area. Many of the guys there had come over to "fight the war," and instead they were unloading ships and doing other supply details. Morale was very low in this area. The ARC had a recreation center here, which we staffed seven days a week from early morning to late evening. In addition, we wrote clubmobile programs, which we took over to the Navy side and to some of the outlying areas where the guys could not get in to the center. We also visited the hospital and convalescence center at Cam Ranh Air Force. But mostly, our work was at the center, always thinking of new things we could offer (pool tournaments, Monte Carlo nights, luaus, talent nights, carnivals, etc) to keep the guys interested and to give them an alternative to drinking at their clubs or whatever else they could find to do. Remember, a lot of these guys were only 19 years old. They needed some "clean and safe" diversions from what was available.

Next I went to Long Binh where, although we had a center, we focused more on the clubmobile programs. We traveled a great deal—the guys were more appreciative of our being there—the work was very rewarding. But again, the job was exhausting, and when I was transferred to Cu Chi for my final couple of months, even though I wanted to be at a combat unit (no center—just clubmobile), I was tired. Plus here is where I really saw the wages of war—the looks in the guys' eyes when they would come in from the field. It got harder and harder to greet all the new guys—many of whom I knew would not make it back to the States alive. I would still be brave and smile every day, and when they would ask in amazement, "Why are you here?" I would just beam that smile and say, "Because you are here!" But inside, it hurt to know that I might be the last American girl he would ever talk to.

We were there because we wanted to be there. We were there to bring some joy and distraction into the lives of the guys, and we did it the best we knew how! We gave a lot of energy, and when we had no strength for another smile, we smiled anyway.

Returning Home

It was a very intense year. Even when we were not on duty, we were still on duty. We lived our jobs 24 hours a day—there is no way I could not leave a part of me there.

I was physically and emotionally exhausted. I really didn't know how to act. I would walk down a street and smile at everyone, because that was what was expected in Nam. Someone pointed out to me that I shouldn't be smiling at everyone—it wasn't right and people might get the wrong impression. I got very angry one day when I was in the grocery store. There was this huge long aisle of cereal boxes. It seemed like hundreds of different types of cereal. And it was more important to choose the correct brand of cereal than to think and worry about our guys who were being blown to bits on the news every night. Nobody seemed to get it that these guys were really dying and that was real blood. I got so very, very angry, and this was in 1967.

I felt lost. I didn't know what to do next. Get another job? Nothing could compare to the excitement and fulfillment I had while working with MY guys in Vietnam. The letdown was very, very hard.

I became very independent while in Nam. I learned that I could make decisions and do things on my own. However, when I got back to the states, I did not have the same feeling of worth that I did while in Nam. The self-confidence I gained in Nam was wiped away when I came back. I felt worthwhile in Nam, but I could not even find a decent job when I came back. My experience in Nam counted for nothing. I felt valuable in Nam, and the skills I needed there were not and are not recognized back here.

I was expected to fit right in, as if I had never been to "war." I was expected just to go out and get another job and get on with life. I felt as if I had to find a husband, have a family, and become the "educated" housewife that I had been destined to be. I did not feel as if I had many choices. I really felt I had to "conform" to the way I had been raised. I did not get a chance to decompress. I was more exhausted, physically and mentally, than traumatized by the horrors of Nam. Yet, even now, I still have dreams about going back because I am needed—and I go.

All jobs have paled in comparison to the satisfaction I got while in Nam. There was excitement and a real challenge to being a Donut Dolly!

by Sharon (Vander Ven) Cummings, American Red Cross SRAO (Supplemental Recreational Activities Overseas) "Donut Dolly"
April 1966–April 1967.

See more of Sharon's story at her Web site at Donut Dollies: Frequently Asked Questions, http://www.geocities.com/catellen/faq.html and at

Sharon (Vander Ven) Cummings, American Red Cross, SRAO, April 1966–67, www.illyria.com/rccummings.html.

**Once Upon A Time,
In Another World, And Another Time**
Photo courtesy of Sharon Vander Ven Cummings

"The Sandpipers" started as an informal group of Red Cross girls and GIs who used to pick and play folksongs at the American Red Cross recreation center in Cam Ranh (Army) Bay. This group developed into an actual clubmobile program as "The Sandpipers" and toured and performed for different military units (Army and Navy) and the convalescent hospital (on the Air Force side of Cam Ranh).

Performers (bottom, left to right): 1st Row: Skip Stiles, Sharon (Vander Ven) Cummings, Barry Curtis; 2nd Row: Tom Appleby, Bill Bates; 3rd Row: Bobbi (Hudson) Crocker, Sara (Yapple) Varney.

A Brief History of Red Cross Clubmobiles in W.W. II

In World War II the American Red Cross was asked by the U.S. Armed Forces to provide recreational services to the servicemen in the various theatres of operation.

The Red Cross clubmobile was conceived by the late prominent New York banker, Harvey D. Gibson, Red Cross Commissioner to Great Britain, who wanted to put a service club "on wheels," which would reach the serviceman at his camp or airfield. Also, by having a club on wheels, the Red Cross was able to get around the Army's request that servicemen pay for food. Everything distributed on a clubmobile was free.

The clubmobile consisted of a good-sized kitchen with a built-in doughnut machine. A primus stove was installed for heating water for coffee, which was prepared in 50-cup urns. On one side of the kitchen area, there was a counter and a large flap, which opened out for serving coffee and doughnuts. In the back one-third of the clubmobile was a lounge with a built-in bench on either side (which could be converted to sleeping bunks, if necessary), a Victrola (phonograph) with loud speakers, a large selection of up-to-date music records, and paperback books.

The American girls who chose this service were taught to make the doughnuts and coffee in the clubmobile. They were sent to a town near American Army installations, and they followed a routine of going to a different base each day, hooking up at a mess kitchen, making hundreds of doughnuts and preparing coffee, and then driving around the base, serving the men at their work. They also distributed cigarettes, Life Savers (candy) and gum, and had the loud speakers turned up for each stop.

In preparation for the invasion of Normandy, June, 1944, a smaller, 2-1/2-ton GMC truck was converted to a clubmobile, with the necessary kitchen containing doughnut machine, coffee urns, and the like. Close to one hundred of them were made ready. Red Cross girls who had worked on the larger clubmobile in Great Britain, were given driving instruction in order to manage the truck clubmobile.

Beginning in July 1944, as soon after the invasion that it was safe to send Red Cross personnel onto the Continent, ten groups of 32 Red Cross girls each, along with eight clubmobiles per group, a cinemobile, three supply trucks, trailers, and three British Hillman trucks, were sent to France to be attached to various U.S. Army Corps.

Each clubmobile group traveled with the rear echelon of the Army Corps and got its assignments from the Army for serving troops at rest from the front. The service continued through France, Belgium, Luxembourg and Germany, until V-E Day, May 7, 1945.

by Elma Ernst Fay U.S.R.C. (retired)

Elma Ernst was among hundreds of American Red Cross Clubmobile workers who served in World War II in Great Britain, France, and Germany from 1943–1946.

Look for Elma Ernst Fay's book, *Through The Hole of a Donut*. To read more and see pictures from the 1940s, visit World War II Red Cross Clubmobile at www.clubmobile.org on the Internet.

"Over the years many of us have stayed in touch with each other and have had wonderful reunions. Three of us meet six times a year. Occasionally others join us, and it is a wonderful way to keep in touch." Elma Ernst Fay.

CHAPTER 12

To Say Goodbye

The truest end of life is to know that life never ends.
William Penn, 1644–1718

Driving down Irving Park Road, one June Sunday in 1997, my twelve-year-old Chevy sputtered and nearly stalled at the stoplight on Western Avenue. Aged at three hundred thousand miles, it was choking but I couldn't afford to buy another car. I wanted to go back to twenty-five years earlier when my dad helped me pick out a brand new golden brown Impala. He was a pattern maker for General Motors and told the salesman how he had drawn the design for the sturdy doors. While I was deciding what accessories to get, the sales person asked if I would like a three or five-year payment plan to finance my new purchase.

I quickly responded, "Would it be possible to write a check for the full amount?" Glancing at my dad, it looked as if all the lights were turned on him. Even without showing his teeth, a smile flashed proudly. His oldest daughter had enough cash to buy a brand new GM product hot off the press. I saved the money during the year I spent as an Army nurse in Viet Nam.

Thirty-six years have passed since I made my papa so proud. I wondered what he would have thought of my clunky car complaining at the stoplight. Well, at least it was a General Motors vehicle and not "one of those flimsy foreign jobs that are nothing more than a death trap." I could almost hear his words when the radio announcer interrupted, "Today is Father's Day and the children whose dads died in Viet Nam are lined up, paying their respects at the War Memorial in Washington, D.C."

I shivered. Thinking about how my dad made it through W.W.II, I knew there was also a part of him that didn't return from the war. In 1945, his body was honorably discharged after serving two years in the Navy. It consumed food, eliminated by-products, aged, got fat, slimmed down, quit smoking, and got fat again. He drove his white and salmon colored Oldsmobile to work, supported his family, and taught me how to swim, but something in my daddy died in that war. It showed by the way he barricaded himself behind the Chicago Tribune. After supper, he read the news and stayed behind his paper fortress where he fell asleep.

Dad couldn't share his feelings about when his aircraft carrier was attacked in the middle of the Pacific Ocean, but I understood because I had a hard time sharing about my year in Viet Nam. My father didn't discuss his feelings for me, and I couldn't talk about mine until I learned that I could. By then it was too late.

At the age of sixty, dad retired from General Motors, and a month later the doctors found cancer inside his body. For a second opinion, he went to the hospital where I worked. I was happy to take care of him, but he never asked for anything. When I offered to give him a massage or to do anything that would make him feel more comfortable, he declined. I stopped asking. Just to give him a pitcher of water made me feel like I was intruding into his secret world. His room overlooked Lake Michigan. Attempting to ask him about the cancer, all I could say was how beautiful the lake looked as I leaned against the metal rail of the hospital bed. Dad wouldn't look out the window or at me. He stared at the television. The screen was blank.

After the second opinion confirmed small cell cancer of the lung, the W.W.II veteran had one dose of chemotherapy and said, "I'd rather die than go through that again." Then he was honorably discharged from an institution for the second time.

He went home to the middle bedroom of his ranch house in Darien, Illinois, where the windows faced west. You could watch the clouds and look at the sunset through those windows, but dad didn't see the beauty. On his second evening home, the sun went below the horizon taking that day and my father's sanity to the other side of the world. His soul got lost in time, and he was back on a battleship in the Pacific.

For ten days his body thrashed in bed. He kept taking off his pajamas. He pulled the tube out of his nose and refused water. He recoiled in fear when anybody got near him. By the third day, daddy didn't recognize his family anymore. He thought we were the enemy and commanded us off his ship. When I gave him pain shots in the wintertime of 1982, his face sneered and he yelled, "Get away." He slapped me with an unexpected force from someone who looked so weak in a skinny body.

On the ninth day, what was once my father daring me to dive into a river in Arkansas had become bones inside a bag of yellow skin with wide-open eyes that refused to close, steel blue eyes that once warmed me with a smile. He was haunted with fears that only his mind could see.

The family gave him permission to die, but the "goodbye" words got stuck in my throat. My uncle said, "You can go now, Frank, and we will see you later." My father didn't know he was dying and asked, "Where are you going?" We all had to laugh at the strangeness of it all.

My daddy was dying, and I couldn't tell him how much I would miss him when he was gone. On the tenth night we were all exhausted taking turns to watch him as he kept trying to crawl out of the rented hospital bed. The last time I was awake for so long was in Viet Nam when helicopters and ambulances came in with mass casualties. American and Vietnamese soldiers and civilians were carried in—bloody, wounded, and scared.

In my war, I didn't get to say "goodbye" to the friends who were killed, and I couldn't say "goodbye" to the ones who were alive. When I was shipped back to the States, my heart cracked in pain as I watched the 18th Surgical Hospital get smaller through the open back door of the C-130. "Go back down. I didn't say 'goodbye,'" I wanted to yell to the pilot, but I could only choke on the sobs in my throat as the men sitting across the aisle stared at me with unreadable faces. Not knowing it then, I had cheated the family I made during that year in Quang Tri out of their rightful choice because I told nobody when I was leaving.

The only way I could feel close to my father was to know that we had both experienced war. He was dying, and I didn't know what to do except take flight the way that his mind did when he was faced with the end of his physical life.

Running outside, the cold November air stung my eyes and froze my clothes as I walked my anxiety down the street. I smelled the smoke from the chimneys as woody scents filled the air on that bright, full moon night. Not believing, I yelled anyway, "If you are out there, God, you'd better hear me." Throwing my hell at the silvery white disc in the sky, I called out again. "Take him, God. Give him rest. We are all so tired." No one heard me, the mad daughter in Darien.

When I returned to the house, everybody was standing around his bed. Daddy had stopped fighting and the fear was gone. His eyes relaxed at half-mast, his breaths slowed down to a whisper. Dad surrendered. His war was over. Some moments after his final inspiration, Frank Sebek was honorably discharged for the last time.

I didn't cry. It took the passing of twenty-two seasons before the tears of grief could spill and nineteen years before I could gain insight into the lesson my father's dying was to teach me.

Five and a half years after he died, I worked for a near northside Chicago hospital. Checking the chart of a sixty-year-old man, I learned he was scheduled for a biopsy to rule out carcinoma of the lung. The man's eyes were closed until I placed the chart under the mattress of the gurney. He opened the lids and exposed shiny blue. I asked him if he was comfortable.

"Could you raise my head up, nurse?" He requested with a languid smile.

"Most certainly," I responded, and placed my arm around his shoulders for support while I raised the backrest. He thanked me and closed his eyes. I stood at his side for several minutes thinking that I would like to do more for him. A strange energy washed through me, and feeling a bit choked, I asked the boss if a break would be possible. She flashed black eyes and said that I had fifteen minutes.

Sitting in the locker room, I thought about my dad and realized that a stranger who might have lung cancer asked me to do more for him in three minutes than my father did during his whole illness. I cried for the loss of my father and felt ashamed of expressing the sadness. I went to the shower and turned on the water to drown down the sound of sobbing that seemed like it was coming from someplace else. Wearing green scrubs and dried up bloody shoes, I walked into the hot water and slid down to the shower floor.

Just as the waves of the ocean flow onto and off the beach, the pulse of sadness moves through our bodies. If we don't allow ourselves the power to heal through grieving, dreams may come to send us messages.

Around the first day of spring 2001, I had a dream that delivered a lifetime of information. I almost discarded the message until I shared it with a very wise doctor.

It was 1982 again, and I found myself at my father's deathbed. He was still restless. I thought he was cold so I pulled a dusty rose-colored blanket up under his arms and lay next to him. Hoping that the primordial energy from my body would calm him, I attempted to fill him with golden light, but he turned away from me. Daddy couldn't accept the comfort I wanted to give. I left him. Walking down the street, I met Dr. Sage and asked him what I should do.

"Hold a mirror up to him." Said the sage.

Then I woke up. When I shared this dream with the wise doctor, he asked me what the purpose of the mirror was.

"I think I would hold it up to him so he could see his face and know that he was dying. Then he could accept the truth, surrender and stop fighting." I said with the first logical thought that came into my mind.

"Would you like to hear what I think the mirror might mean?" he thoughtfully asked.

I tried not to show my eagerness, but I wanted a new point of view regarding the nineteen-year-old mystery that haunted me with relentless subterfuge in accepting intimacy into my life. I accepted his offer. He started philosophically feeding back some of my own ideology regarding the dying process.

"I think we have a responsibility to our children to show them how to die. A good death is life affirming."

I nodded.

"The mirror up to his face would reflect his own fear of a situation that was already terrorizing him. Perhaps, he was to see the mirror in the faces of those around him. See the pain in the faces of his family, the pain that his unwillingness to let in their love had caused them."

I thought how much like my father I was. Sitting behind a newspaper wasn't how I put up my barriers. I had more creative ways to isolate. I tried not to feel. There was no argument about how painful it was realizing that the only man I knew my whole life couldn't accept the love I wanted to give him, so I shared with the wise doctor how I thought I would die and boldly proclaimed, "I want to be in the woods surrounded by the beauty of Mother Nature and my energy will join the trees and flowers."

Kind blue eyes looked back at me. He ventured another point of view, "And what about dying in the arms of someone who loves you?"

Leaving the doctor's rooms, I wondered whose arms I would die in since I had no husband or children. The wise man had helped me get in touch with my loneliness. Forcing back tears as I drove home, I wondered if I could create someone who loves me. Would I ask for their help and could I hear their loving words? I would want to tell them to be happy and give them permission to go on living.

That is what I would have liked from my papa, his blessing to find peace in my life, reclaim my soul, and to not go on fighting the battle.

by Diana Sebek

See Diana Sebek's story, *My Visits With Jack,* chapter 23.

Lt. Sebek
Photo courtesy of Diana Sebek

First Lt. Diana Sebek is next to Highway One near Quang Tri, Viet Nam, 1970.

Diana Sebek became a registered nurse in 1968 after graduating from South Chicago Community Hospital. In 1970, she served as a combat nurse, first lieutenant, in Quang Tri with the Army Nurse Corps. Today, Sebek continues her nursing part-time while practicing alternative methods of healing. She teaches workshops on shamanism, therapeutic touch, and other spiritual methods for people wanting to include such into their lives and private practices. Diana Sebek is working on an autobiographical novel and is the author of *A Time to Honor*, a short story in the 1996 December issue of the *Monthly Aspectarian*. It can be found at http://www.lightworks.com/MonthlyAspectarian/1996/December/1296-09.html.

See Diana Sebek's Web site, A Shaman's Site, http://hometown.aol.com/chitownshamyneuz/Chicago_Shamanindex.html.

CHAPTER 13

Christmas in Vietnam

*Days were then full of health and happiness,
And suddenly you were exposed to a crazy war.*

*Remembering the times you didn't have today's pains,
Always looking back to how your life has changed.
To an honorable, brave, and honest Nam Vet, I salute.*
Frank Zamora

The Day It Snowed In Vietnam

The usual carols played in the mess hall at supper and the calendar said "December 24, 1969," but it didn't feel much like Christmas Eve. We were tired from a long day of flying many missions picking up infantrymen and recon patrols from field locations. We brought them back to the big airfield at Phan Thiet for the Christmas cease-fire. Gunship helicopters had escorted us because they were frequently needed, but today not a shot had been fired in either direction. It seemed that soldiers on both sides of this war were glad to allow the cease-fire to start one day early.

It had been a hot day, and even in the evening, after the withering sun had dipped below the horizon, we sat sweltering in T-shirts in the pilots' hooch. The air was somber. The usual discussions of recent close calls and superior airmanship were subdued by the subject on everyone's mind, but nobody would talk about: the recent loss of four pilots and four crewmen. We joked about the cease-fire and wondered how long it would last. One man predicted that the base would be hit with mortars just before midnight. It seemed that there was nothing to celebrate. One pilot tried to change the mood. "We have to do something happy! Let's sing Christmas Carols!" he said, almost in anguish. But no one started singing.

Mike Porter, my copilot, finally blurted out, "Let's take up a collection for the Project Concern hospital!" I thought back to the first time I saw that hospital at Dam Pao; I was copilot for Ted Thoman. A medic showed us a baby in desperate need of medical care, suffering from convulsions and dehydration. Flying that Huey helicopter at top speed, Ted soon had the baby girl and her parents at the hospital at Dam Pao. That "mission" made me feel good; it was the only one, so far, that was not part of making war. The memory was vivid because only hours before we had extracted a recon team under fire. The bullet holes in the aircraft had been counted, but not yet patched.

Mike shook my shoulder to wake me from my reverie. "Hey Jim, let's ask to fly the Da Lat Macvee (MACV—Military Assistance Command, Vietnam) mission tomorrow to take money that we collect tonight." Under his crewcut blonde hair, Mike's boyish face lit up, and I had to remind myself that he was among the older Army helicopter pilots; he was 22.

Mike's excitement was contagious. I jumped up, said, "Great idea, let's go ask!" and almost ran out the door. We stopped at the crew chiefs' hooch and asked Bascom if he would like to fly tomorrow. He and Dave quickly agreed, also wishing to escape the prevailing sadness.

Major Higginbotham, the company commander, was in the operations bunker. I explained our plan but he answered, "We don't have the Da Lat Macvee mission. In fact, there are no missions; there's a cease-fire tomorrow, remember?"

It had been Mike's idea, but the prospect of not being able to make this mission was too much, so I pleaded the cause, "Please, Sir, could you call battalion and see if some other company has Da Lat Macvee?" Macvee (MACV), the Military Assistance Command, Vietnam, was the U.S. Army unit of advisors to the Army of the Republic of Vietnam. One or two U.S. advisors were assigned to small military compounds in almost every large village. A Macvee mission usually meant flying the province Senior Advisor around to visit the villages. Macvee missions were a respite from the tension and danger of combat assaults or recon team missions, but had their own risks of weather, wind, and being without gunship escort. Flying near the beautiful city of Da Lat, up in the cool mountains, was an additional treat.

The CO picked up the phone and then started writing on a mission sheet form. He handed it to me and said, "Da Lat Macvee helipad, oh seven thirty; We took the mission from the 92nd." He opened his wallet, and handed me some money. "Here. Good luck!"

When we reached the gunship platoon hooch, three pilots looked on sadly as one man raked a pile of money across the table toward himself. We made our sales pitch about the hospital. The lucky gambler pushed the money toward us and said, "Here, take it! I'd just lose it all back to these guys anyway, Merry Christmas!"

Similar responses began to fill our ammo can with money of all denominations as we roamed among hooches and tents, collecting money from guys whose generosity began to make me a believer in the Christmas spirit again. At one stop, a pilot gave us a gift package of cheese. Food! We could take food! We decided to make another pass through the company area, asking for cookies, candy, and other things. As we left one hooch with our arms full, the men inside started singing "Deck the Halls," and soon those in other buildings were competing. Christmas Eve had arrived in this tropical land of heat and snakes and death!

When we reached the mess hall, the cooks were still there, preparing for Christmas Day. The mess sergeant said, "Do you have a truck with you? We have a surplus of food because so many guys went home early." One pilot went to get the maintenance truck while the rest of us checked dates on cans and cartons of food. Then we drove to the infantry mess hall where we accepted four cases of freeze-dried foods. The medic at the dispensary gave us bandages and dressings.

We tied down the pile of booty in the Huey. After returning the truck, the four pilots walked together back to our hooch. One looked at his watch and said, "Hey guys! It's midnight. Merry Christmas!"

My alarm clock startled me out of a deep sleep. A check with my wristwatch verified the time, but something was wrong. There was no shouting, no rumble of trucks, no roar of propellers and rotors. Mornings were usually bustling with the sounds of men and machines preparing for the daily business of war, but today there were no such sounds. I thought to myself, "Is this what peace sounds like?"

In the shower building, Mike and I talked about what our families would be doing today on the other side of the world. As all short timers do, I reminded Mike that in just two weeks I would be going home, my year in Vietnam over. My wife promised me another Christmas celebration, with a decorated tree and wrapped presents. I would also be meeting another Mike for the first time, my son, now only a few months old.

After breakfast, the others went to the flight line while I called for a weather briefing. When I reached the helicopter, Mike was doing the preflight inspection and had just climbed up to the top of the Huey. Together, we checked the main rotor hub and the "Jesus nut" that holds the rotor on the helicopter. Everything was fine; we were ready to fly. We took off and headed for the mountains.

It always felt good to fly with this crew; we were a finely tuned team. The rugged and muscular Lee looked every bit like a cowboy from his hometown in Bascom County, Wyoming; hence his nickname, "Bad Bascom." He was the crew chief of this Huey and did all the daily maintenance on it; it was his "baby." With Mike as copilot and Dave as door gunner, we had taken that helicopter into and out of many difficult situations, from landing supplies on a windy mountaintop to extracting recon teams from small clearings while taking enemy fire. The radio call sign of the 192nd Assault Helicopter Company was Polecat; we were Polecat Three Five Six and proud of it. This day was beginning to feel even better because we were going to use our combat skills for a mission that seemed so unrelated to war.

   I decided to climb higher than usual in the smooth morning air. As we left the jungle plains along the coast, the green mountains of the Central Highlands rose up to meet us. On the plateau, a thick blanket of fog lay like cotton under a Christmas tree. It spilled over between the peaks in slow, misty, waterfalls. In the rising sunlight the mountaintops cast long shadows on the fog. The beauty and serenity of the scene were dazzling. Had I noticed this before? I think I had, but today the gorgeous scenery wasn't a backdrop for the unexpected horror of war.

   The mess hall had been quiet. The airfield was quiet. The radios were quiet. We weren't even chattering on the intercom as we usually did. Our minds were all with different families, somewhere back home, thousands of miles away. Everything was quiet and peaceful. It felt very, very, strange. Was this the first day of a lasting peace, or just the eye in a hurricane of war?

   As our main rotor slowed down after we landed at Da Lat, a gray-haired lieutenant colonel walked up to the Huey. "Merry Christmas! I'm Colonel Beck. We have a busy day planned, my men are spread out all over this province, and we're going to take mail, hot turkey, and pumpkin pies to every one of them!" He handed me a map that had our cross-stitched route already carefully drawn on it. His distinguished look turned to a big grin as he added, "Oh, would you guys like to have some

Donut Dollies with us today?" Four heads with flight helmets were eagerly nodding, "YES," as the two young ladies got out of a jeep.

Donut Dollies were American Red Cross volunteers, college graduates in their early twenties. Although no longer distributing donuts like their namesakes of World War II, they were still in the service of helping the morale of the troops. At large bases they managed recreation centers but they also traveled to the smaller units in the field for short visits. For millions of GIs they represented the girlfriend, sister, or wife back home. Over the Huey's intercom, Colonel Beck introduced Sue, with the short, dark hair and Ann, a brunette, the taller one.

Soon we were heading toward the mountains with a Huey full of mail, food, Christmas cargo, and two American young women. For the soldiers who had been living off Vietnamese food and canned Army rations at lonely, isolated outposts, these touches of home would be a welcome surprise.

As we approached the first compound, Colonel Beck, by radio, told the men on the ground that we were going to make it snow. Sue and Ann sprinkled laundry soap flakes out of the Huey as we flew directly over a small group of American and Vietnamese soldiers who must have thought we were crazy. Several of them were rubbing their eyes as we came back to land. I will never know if it was emotion or if they just had soap in their eyes.

The three Americans came over to the Huey as we shut it down. Ann gave each of them a package from the Red Cross and Sue called out names to distribute the mail. After about fifteen minutes of small talk, Colonel Beck announced, "We have a lot more stops to make," and got back into the Huey. The soldiers stood there silently, staring at us as we started up, hovered, and then disappeared into the sky.

At the next outpost, Colonel Beck left us so he could talk privately with the local officials. The crew and I didn't mind escorting the Donut Dollies. It was easy to see how happy the soldiers were to talk with them. I wondered how Sue and Ann were feeling. Their job was to cheer up other people on what may have been their own first Christmas away from home; if they were lonely or sad, they never let it show. Throughout the day, the same scene was replayed at other small compounds. Some soldiers talked excitedly to the girls, while others would just stand quietly and stare, almost in shock to see American women visiting them out in the boonies.

Finally, with the official Macvee work finished, we were above the hospital at Dam Pao. Mike landed us a few hundred feet from the main building. Several men and women came out, carrying folding stretchers. They first showed surprise that we were not bringing an injured new patient, and then, joy when we showed them the food and medical supplies. Mike opened the ammo can full of money and said, "Merry Christmas from the Polecats and Tigersharks of the 192nd Assault Helicopter Company." One of the women began to cry and then hugged Mike.

A doctor asked if we would like to see the hospital. He talked as we carried the goods from the Huey to the one-floor, tin-roof hospital building. "Project Concern now has volunteer doctors and nurses from England, Australia, and the USA. We provide health services to civilians and train medical assistants to do the same in their own villages. We try to demonstrate God's love, so we remain neutral. Both sides respect our work, and leave us alone."

One of the women described a recent event. Two nurses and a medical assistant student were returning from a remote clinic in the jungle when their jeep became mired in mud. Many miles from even the smallest village, they knew that they would not be able to walk to civilization before dark. A Viet Cong foot patrol came upon them, pulled the jeep out of the mud, and sent them on their way.

There were homemade Christmas decorations everywhere, most made on the spot by patients or their families. Inside, the hospital was clean and neat, but stark; there were few pieces of modern equipment. The staff lived in a separate small building.

As we moved into one ward, a nurse gently lifted a very small baby from its bed, and before I could stop her, she placed him in my arms. He'd been born that morning. Although they had expected complications, the mother and baby were perfectly healthy! As I held the tiny infant, I started to tell the others that I would soon be meeting my own baby son, but the words got stuck in my throat. So I just stood there, marveling at the warmth and hope in that tiny new human being nestled peacefully in my arms. Would this child grow up in peace, or would this tiny life be snuffed out by a war that had already claimed thousands of Vietnamese and Americans? Would the deaths of my friends this past year help ensure for him a life of peace and freedom, or had they died in vain?

The staff invited us to stay for supper with them, and I could tell the invitation was sincere. However, the sun was getting low, and I didn't want to fly us home over eighty miles of mountainous jungle in the dark. I also would have felt guilty to take any food, even so graciously offered, from the most selfless people I had ever met. As we started the Huey, the doctors and nurses were about fifty feet away, still talking with Colonel Beck. The colonel took something out of his wallet and gave it to of one of the men with a double-hand handshake. He then quietly climbed on board.

There was no chatter on the intercom as we flew back to Da Lat. Mike landed the Huey softly. I asked him to shut down and got out quickly. Then we all stood there silently; I wanted to hug Sue and Ann, but I knew Donut Dollies were not allowed to hug. Instead, we all exchanged warm handshakes and Christmas wishes. Colonel Beck thanked us for taking him to the hospital. We, the crew of Polecat 356, got back in and flew away and out of the lives of our newfound friends.

Silence also marked the flight back to Phan Thiet. I thought of my family and friends back home and couldn't wait to see them. I also thought about the good friends I would soon be leaving behind, and other good friends who would never go home to their families.

I reflected on the rare nature of the day. I would always be able to remember Christmas Day in Vietnam as very special. Here, in the midst of war, trouble, and strife, was a time of sharing, happiness, love—and peace.

Epilog: I attended the 1993 dedication of the Vietnam Women's Memorial to place letters of remembrance from the Vietnam Helicopter Pilots Association. As friendly and helpful as 24 years earlier, other Donut Dollies were eager to help me find Sue and Ann, identified from a photograph I had taken at Dam Pao in 1969. One Donut Dolly finally exclaimed, "That's my sister!" and led me to Ann, and I collected on a long-overdue hug. Sue and I talked by telephone a few days later. I felt good to learn that Christmas Day in Vietnam was also special to them.

by Jim Schueckler.

Jim Schueckler was a 21-year-old helicopter pilot with the 192nd Assault Helicopter Company, Phan Thiet, 1969–1970. He is "still married to the same wonderful woman who saw me off to war." Jim and his wife, Judy, have "three children and two cute grandkids."

Schueckler is founder and Web master of the original virtual wall, The Virtual Wall, Vietnam Veterans' Memorial at www.VirtualWall.org

"Since March, 1997, the Virtual Wall has honored the 58,220 men and women named on the Vietnam Veterans Memorial, those who gave the ultimate sacrifice. Each name or photo on our index pages links to a personal memorial, either on this site or on personal Web sites elsewhere."

Jim Schueckler.

Project Concern International

In 1961, Dr. James Turpin founded Project Concern International to help the world's poor. In 1964, the Project Concern International facility opened in Dam Pao, South Vietnam. To learn more about Project Concern International, visit their Web site at www.projectconcern.org/contact.html.

Christmas in Vietnam, 1966

December 24, 1967

Last year Santa Claus arrived in a Huey.

That was the symbol we adopted for the Christmas we spent as Red Cross workers in Vietnam last year since the helicopter was the most dependable way of travel.

We tried to treat Christmas as lightheartedly as possible. Vietnam is no place to start remembering other, better things.

But there's a limit as to what you can ignore. So we hung Christmas decorations in the 100-degree-plus heat, and the GIs helped us make popcorn strings and trim the tree we had in our Red Cross recreation center.

We helped the guys wrap presents, and the crush down at the small base post office looked almost homelike as the deadline for mailing packages drew near.

We distributed the packages people sent from the States and salvaged what we could from the boxes of crumbled cookies and melted chocolate.

Cards came pouring in from school children and others. The guys used to scoff a little when they'd pick up a card addressed to "Our Brave Fighting Men." But they always read them.

As Christmas drew near, the pace quickened and our nine-girl unit was on the move constantly. We helped "Santa Claus" distribute ditty bags to men in the field, and we scrounged up decorations to send out to isolated units. We decorated mess halls for sergeants who doubted their artistic abilities.

And we noticed that the farther you went out in the field, the better the men responded to Christmas.

There were little Christmas trees stuck jauntily atop sandbags, and an APC (Armored Personnel Carrier) would thunder by with a shiny lettered sign saying, "Merry Christmas!"

We even had real Christmas trees. Enterprising businessmen, probably Japanese, had brought in shipments of trees to Saigon. We bought our tree for $10.

It was a strange sight.

Some stores, catering mainly to Americans, had put up fainthearted attempts at Christmas decorating in their windows. But to the Americans walking by sweltering in the heat, the snow scenes and heavily suited Santas seemed as alien as the moon.

People drank more.

I guess Americans can't really shut out Christmas from their minds.

The cooks outdid themselves on Christmas day and turned out turkey dinners with all the trimmings. It was amazing how good mincemeat pies and rolls made in field ovens tasted.

We flew all over the place, in helicopters, with our Christmas programs.

Christmas Eve, we went caroling in a five-ton truck.

A new group of infantrymen—I think it was the 196th—had just arrived in country. Their mail had not even caught up with them and they were sleeping on mud floors in their tents.

We roared up to the blacked out camp in our truck, singing carols. It didn't look like Christmas at all. They didn't have any trees or decorations.

General "Red" Ryder, as surprised as the rest of his men, gave us permission to walk through camp caroling.

So we went stumbling off in the dark through the muddy paths as the guys turned out more and more, startled by the singing. Everyone shook hands and yelled, "Merry Christmas," until his throat hurt.

Then, one very young GI came forward from the crowd. He was still pale, not tanned like the rest of us, and he looked a little sheepish. He suddenly put a small tin of candy into the hand of one of our cutest and most lighthearted girls.

"This is the only present from home I've gotten—I wish it were more," he said.

It was suddenly very quiet.

Then, she kissed him impulsively on the cheek. The guys roared their approval and joined in the singing.

We rode back alone in the truck to our billet. The young Red Cross worker kept looking at the small tin of candy and kept saying in amazement, "He gave me the only present he had."

She cried all the way home.

by Lindsey Stringfellow Weilbacher

Lindsey Stringfellow wrote the above article and the one that follows, *A Christmas Visit Remembered,* for *The Daily Advance* newspaper in Elizabeth City, North Carolina, in 1967, where she worked after returning from Vietnam. Lindsey was in Vietnam as an American Red Cross SRAO, Supplemental Recreation Activities Overseas, known as a Donut Dolly. She was stationed in Da Nang from June to November 1966 and in Long Binh from November 1966 to February 1967.

Lindsey Stringfellow Weilbacher, born in Virginia, graduated from the College of William and Mary with an English degree in 1964. She then spent a year in graduate school at the Yale School of Drama in playwriting. After returning from Vietnam in 1967, she began a career in journalism. Lindsey is married to a former Coast Guard aviator who is now an attorney. Edward and Lindsey have one daughter, Dorothy.

"I volunteered for Vietnam for several reasons. One, I wanted to be a writer and I thought everyone, like Hemingway, should be in a war in order to understand more about living and dying; two, I wanted to understand a bit about what my father went through as a Marine who didn't make it back from Okinawa; and three, I wanted to understand

what men were like in a wartime situation. I think I learned more about what women are like in a wartime situation. I also learned that for the rest of my life all my thoughts and experiences are like planets circling the constant sun of Vietnam. It was and still is the key to how I see the world."
Lindsey Weilbacher

The following is from Lindsey's book-in-progress, *Divine Hover*, based on the journal she kept in Vietnam. The title comes from graffito she saw on a wall in a helicopter hangar in Chu Lai, "To fly is heavenly— to hover is divine."

"It was raining when I ducked into that art gallery in Saigon trying to get away from the stares of both Americans and the Vietnamese. An art gallery in Saigon? But there it was: tiny and dark. I stumbled in, amazed at it being there in the midst of war. Went inside hesitantly, as if seeking something that was far away and receding quicker than I could ever recapture it. No one there, breathed a sigh of relief, went to the gray paint peeling walls. Mediocre tourist stuff, boys sleeping on backs of water buffaloes. Cranked out by the thousands and for sale on every Saigon street corner. But, on one dark wall a collage lit up that dark corner, touched something in my soul. I stared. An abstract. Impasto technique. Angry blobs of hot color paint applied with a knife. Tissue paper. No, maybe delicate rice paper applied in hunks and strips. Visceral strips. I stood there and over me washed the hot red morning suns of Vietnam; cool rice paddy greens. Here, an angry explosion of willy-peter white; there, orange defiance and metallic gray ramshackle bridges shining in the awful heat. And smells—oh lord the Quonset hut hospital ward smells. I fled from the shop. Later, thinking about the picture I tried to find that tiny hole in the wall place again but never could…Shortly thereafter I went home…"

A Christmas Visit Remembered

December 10, 1967

I didn't know Francis Cardinal Spellman (1889–1967)—don't pretend to have. I just saw him once from a distance like so many other people stationed overseas did. At Christmas.

The news of his death last Saturday didn't come as a shock. He was 78. Besides, he had told us last Christmas in Vietnam that he thought that tour would be his last.

He was right.

Every year since he became vicar-general of the U.S. Armed Forces in 1942, Cardinal Spellman went overseas at Christmas to visit, to say Mass, to assure Americans that they weren't forgotten at home.

Before he died of a stroke Saturday (December 2, 1967), he spoke of going to Vietnam again this year.

It was his third year.

Last year we got the news of his arrival a few hours before he would say Mass at II Field Headquarters at Long Binh, 15 miles northwest of Saigon.

They didn't announce his arrival sooner because the Viet Cong like to have time to arrange "surprises" for large groups of Americans gathered together.

"At 1400 Cardinal Spellman will say Mass at the amphitheatre."

That was the message. So we went. The girls in our Red Cross unit were not all Catholic; half were Protestant, one Jewish.

But Cardinal Spellman was somewhat of a living legend—like Bob Hope and Martha Raye, who practically lives in Vietnam.

The crowd gathered quietly. It was two days before Christmas and the temperature was 100 degrees plus.

The amphitheatre dug out of the red dirt was already packed with row after row of green clad soldiers, neat in their headquarters fatigues. A thousand of them.

Then a group of ragged-sleeved infantrymen, "grunts," arrived by truck. They had the "Big Red One" patch on their soldiers—1st Infantry Division soldiers who had run the short but ambush-lined gauntlet from Di An.

They stood together, battered helmets, M-16s slung over their shoulders, looking nervously at the crowd. Sweat stains showed around their heavy flak jackets.

The rest of us stared back.

Then the guys—the ones who didn't wear flak jackets—silently stood aside and gave the grunts their seats.

The dustoff helicopters came in bringing ambulatory and some stretcher patients from the nearby field hospital.

We stood at the top of the amphitheatre whose rows were made of sandbags and watched the helicopters far in the distance making lazy circles over a rubber plantation area. The sky was a lovely madonna blue.

The parachute canopy over the huge platform erected below for the Mass stirred slightly. The waiting crowd was quiet. Then the cardinal arrived.

He was very old and feeble.

We were amazed that he could make it up the stairs to the platform. Attendants helped him. The Mass began.

It was a strange cathedral for a cardinal.

No bells—no music. Just the lazy drone of the nervous helicopters. The headquarters flag snapped in the wind.

We knelt on the sandbags and wondered how the cardinal would be able to make it through the Mass. But he did.

When Mass was over, the cardinal was going to speak. They set up the mike. He swayed a second, then spoke in a firm, strong voice, totally unexpected from that frail body. He spoke again and again of America's love and pride for her fighting men.

He blessed God for allowing him the trip and his pleasure at seeing them. And then softly, almost thinking aloud, he said that he thought this would be his last trip.

Then it happened.

All those young men—all those hard young men who quite possibly wouldn't see another Christmas—suddenly focused their love and attention on the old, old man.

Some wept for him.

And nobody was ashamed.

After his blessing, boxes of religious medals were passed around so that each man could take one. They did.

There is a peculiar honesty among men who have little.

Cardinal Spellman gave a lot.

by Lindsey Stringfellow Weilbacher

CHAPTER 14

Christmas in Vietnam

*The cost of war is measured in
blood, sweat and tears,
as is the price for freedom.*
                                    Jim F. McColloch

In My Heart Forever

I only met two (American) women during my three tours as a medic with the First Cavalry. One was in 1967 in the spring, at An Khe. The woman, I can't remember her name, was a Red Cross volunteer from New Jersey. Being from New York City, we had something in common. B Company 2/5 had a bad time, and after our return to the base camp we made a few hours to go to the Red Cross day room. Her ability to draw out the hidden terror in my soul and make me forget and feel human again for just a couple of hours burned her image in my heart forever. I wish I could have found her to say thank you.
James P. Dempsey.

See *I Can Still See Her Face* by James P. Dempsey, chapter 3.

Boosting Morale

In 1968, nearly 500 American Red Cross workers were stationed throughout Southeast Asia, boosting the morale of the troops.

In addition to bringing a touch of home in the way of games and smiles, the American Red Cross workers aided the servicemen with emergency leave and brought them information from home, such as the birth of their sons and daughters. Of all the services provided to the military personnel by the ARC, just being there may have been one of the biggest morale boosters of all.

The following story relates one of the myriad services provided by the American Red Cross workers in Vietnam.

A Year To Kill

The arrival of our baby was very near and I waited anxiously, expecting each day to hear from the Red Cross the good news that I was a daddy. Since the lag time for mail was nearly three weeks, it did nothing to write letters of inquiry. Consequently, I was nearly consumed with worry on the tenth day after Annie's due date. Finally, a messenger arrived with the news that the Red Cross representative wanted to talk to me.

On the way to the Red Cross office, I felt as if I were ten feet tall while trying to decide a nickname for my new son. I planned to give him the name I inherited from my grandfather, but I knew that two men with the same name in the same household would be confusing, so it was important that he have a good nickname.

The closer I came to my destination, the more proud I became, knowing I had fathered my dad's first grandchild and a son, to carry on the family name. By the time I reached the door, I thought I was going to explode with anticipation.

I composed myself and regained my military bearing before I knocked on the door and entered smartly at attention when invited to enter. The Red Cross officer was all smiles as she began to read the telegram, and I dared not look at her for fear I could not keep from laughing with joy at the long awaited good news.

"We are pleased to inform you of the birth of your daughter born this date," the telegram began. I was shocked at the birth of a daughter because I expected a son. My mouth dropped open, my eyes popped wide, and I weakly exclaimed, "You're kidding!"

The Red Cross woman, perhaps thinking I was unaware of my wife's pregnancy, immediately stopped reading and began to counsel me, saying, "These things sometimes happen when husbands are away."

"But it's not possible," I blurted, still surprised and not realizing what she was thinking.

My comment reinforced the woman's concerns, and she stepped from behind her desk walking toward me while she tried to calm and console me. Just as she invited me to sit and talk about it, I realized what she was thinking and began chuckling. This caught her completely off guard, and she looked at me as if I was crazy, until I explained why I was so surprised.

We had a good laugh together, and I left feeling very proud of my new role as father, even if my daughter was ten thousand miles away. Although it would be months before I could see her, I had a new daughter, and I went straight to the malt shop to celebrate.

by Jim McColloch, from *A Year To Kill*.

To read the entire book, see McColloch's Web site, *A Year To Kill, A Vietnam War Novel* at http://vietnam67.home.att.net.

Jim McColloch, B.B.S., Th.M., Th.D., is presently the pastor of the First Baptist Church of Turley, Oklahoma. He is also owner of Jimmy Mac Music Company, which can be viewed at http://jimmy.mac.home.att.net on the Internet.

McColloch was 22 years old during his tour in Vietnam with the 9th Administration Company, located in Camp Bearcat, Mekong Delta. Bearcat was the name given to the 9th Infantry Division's base, built by the 9th Division.

"I went to RVN as a Pfc. (private first class) and was promoted twice. First to Spc. 4 (Specialist 4th Class) and then to Spc. 5. My MOS when I arrived in RVN was 11B20 or light weapons infantryman. My MOS was changed to 73C20 or finance clerk when I was promoted to SP/5. I was in country from May 1967 until May 1968.

"Annie and I are still married. We have two daughters, Jana and Jina, and one granddaughter."
Jim McColloch

Jim
by Julie Parker

CHAPTER 15

Post Traumatic Stress Disorder

Mournful and never-ending remembrance.
Edgar Allan Poe, 1809–1945

Ambushed

I call out
My voice
Caught in the
Vortex of
Inner space

Asking Why

Unending echoes
Ricochet across
My mind

As Vietnam
Once again

Ambushes
My soul

by Penni Evans

Read about Penni Evans and her poetry, *Sisters,* chapter 1; *Souvenirs,* chapter 18; *My Brother,* chapter 26; and *Folded Flag,* chapter 27.

Flashbacks

"For 20 years I had pushed things back into my mind until a simple remark started a chain of flashbacks. Terrible for me and very frightening to be thrust back in time with the same sounds and, heaven forbid, the smells....I still can't stand cannon or mortar fire or fireworks or maggots."
Eileen P. Wolfe, New Zealand, nurse, New Zealand Surgical Team, Qui Nhon, Vietnam, 1968–1969. Reprinted with permission, *The Vietnam Scrapbook—The Second ANZAC Adventure,* Mike Subritzky.

A Soldier's Prayer

Dear Lord
Please let me have regular dreams like others do
Not these nightmares of memory
Let my dreams be filled with light and joy
Not smoke and terror
Let me hear the laughter of children
Not the screams of men dying
Let the birds fill the air with song
Not the sounds of bombs and bullets
Let the rivers run pure and clear
Not red with blood

Let everyone be healthy and whole
Not missing limbs and faces
Let the earth look as you made it
Not scorched and cratered
Let me wake up smiling
Not searching for the enemy
Let the sweat on my pillow be from summer's heat
Not the sweat of fear and anxiety
but dear Lord most of all
I beg you
Please don't let my children or their children
pray to you as I am doing tonight.
Amen

by Maria Sutherland

Maria Sutherland, Cottam, Ontario, Canada, is a contributor to the IWVPA, International War Veterans' Poetry Archives, www.iwvpa.net on the Internet. Although she is not a Vietnam veteran, she was still deeply affected by the war.

"I was very young when the Vietnam War happened, but I remember watching it on television with my dad. My dad was a Dutch veteran from W.W.II, and from 1945–48 he fought in a "police action" in the Dutch East Indies, now Indonesia. Vietnam really affected him because they were very similar. Quite often after he watched the TV, he would get out his wooden box with his photographs from Indonesia.

"I am not a vet, have never had to face the trials of war, and wrote all my poems based on what I've seen, heard and learned from veterans." Maria Sutherland.

See more of Maria Sutherland's poetry at http://msbeliever. tripod.com/WWII.html, A Tribute To My Daddy and All Veterans Lest We Forget. See Maria Sutherland's poem *Why?* in chapter 17.

Memories Penetrating the Shroud of Death: PTSD
The Shroud of Lost Innocence and Life

We left our homes fearful, uncertain and
cautiously willing, some of us did.
Knowing war through Battles of History, mostly unread,
of movies and television news not fully explained;
short stories of moments of agony plucked out of time.

Movies of heroes welcomed home,
stories of bloodless victims, no cries for mom,
no sounds of pain and agony, no smells of burning flesh:
these…impressions of a sterile war presented
by glory-building movie moguls.
Wars whose lines were drawn by intent or strategy.

No talk of pain and life everlasting
when men walked bent from wounds of bouncing betties,
claymores, punji sticks, cages, and mistakes.
Bullets that seared the soul and fragged the spirit.
No stories of life everlasting with legs and arms left behind,
eyes that do not see and hearing lost;
of life viewed from below in wheelchairs of metal and foam.

This War…met only in person and known from the inside.
Who had that sterile war from days past?
Not our men whose youth was lost.
Nor our women whose innocence was lost.

Little Women, ideal in their nursing zeal
whose skills were turned to iron and feelings to steel.
Ha! What feelings? Stomped to death by fear, pain and
suffering of male, mirrored images of youth,
slight of frame, development twisted by
backpacks, helmets, and M-16's…and death.

Little Women whose smiles became veiled by
knowledge of hard times present and to come.
Smiles veiled by pain of families in absentia,
surrogate mothers who could not love as they would,
hold as they could.
Withholding for fear of crumbling and finding pieces
of themselves on the floor near the youthful men they met.

Was this nursing? Was this War?…YES!!

he box in the attic of my mind
stuffed full of memories of regrets of deeds insufficient,
wishes not fulfilled, tasks beyond my abilities of this age,
weary actions blundered and saved by grace…and
Wisdom, come too soon.

Wisdom not softly layered and welcomed but
Exploded into being by knowledge of blood, guts and war.
Assault on our beings, this war.
Torn of flesh and privacy invaded by men,

bullets and ugliness.

Memories in a box, covered in a shroud.
Lift the lid a little and move the Death aside
to find the Life that was there before
Innocence denied.

by Nancy Quirk Lilja

See Nancy Q. Lilja's poetry, *Veteran's Day* and *Dear Little Boy of Mine*, chapter 6.

Julie

Gulping in hot stale air, Julie rubbed a hand across her sweaty brow. She sat up in the queen-size bed, pushed the burgundy and green quilt away from her, and pulled her knees into her arms, embracing them. A spiraling lock of damp auburn hair streaked with gray fell over her left eye as she squinted at the digital clock on the chair that she used as a nightstand. She had found the chair at a flea market, painted it green and declared it a bedside table. She thought the chair looked shabby-chic, eclectic, or whatever those decorating magazines were calling it these days.

A bright green "2" glared back at her out of the plastic shadow box on the shabby-chic chair. She swiped at the hair over her eye, then tugged at one crumpled strap of her tank top. She owned a half dozen lovely nightgowns, but what if she had to run from the house in the middle of the night due to a fire or incoming…well, fire anyway. She didn't want the neighbors to see her in her silky finest.

Two a.m. It's always two a.m., Julie thought. *Always two.* She rolled her long legs off the side of the bed and reached over the back of the nightstand-chair with both hands. Forcing the window down, she made a mental note to take a sleeping pill tomorrow night. *Or tonight,* she thought, *it's tonight, it's two a.m. It's too late to take a pill now, or too early. Too two.*

Her bare feet softly padding on the wood floor, Julie made her way into the kitchen. By the glow of a plastic night light in the shape of a seashell, she found her way to the thermostat. Flipping on the air, she heard him behind her.

Russ slipped his arms around her waist and pulled her close, her back to his bare chest. "It's hot tonight. I see you've decided to squeeze the piggy bank and go for some air," he said with a slight grin, amused with himself for his choice of words.

Julie wriggled away from him, irritated that he was awake and intruding on her thoughts. *How can you always be thinking about sex,* she thought. "I can't sleep when it's so hot," was all she said. "I've got to get some sleep." She grabbed at the refrigerator handle and yanked it open. The shock of the bright interior light made her tighten her forehead down toward her eyes. She pulled out a carton of milk and slurped from the opening. She could feel him staring at her as she placed the milk back on the shelf. The air conditioner kicked on with a clunking noise.

"What?" she snapped, an "11" firmly planted between her scowling eyebrows as she brushed past him.

"I'm worried about you is all," he said following the backside of her blue flowered bikini panties with his eyes. *She is so beautiful,* he thought.

"Well, don't be," she snarled.

Don't be what, he thought, *in love with you? Think you're so beautiful all the time?*

"Maybe you should see somebody," he said instead.

"See who? About what?" she asked with irritated curiosity.

"Take a yoga class, try transcendental meditation, get an exorcism, see a psychiatrist, I don't know," he said, feeling his face flush in the darkness.

She turned to face him, opening her mouth to spout a denial, a witty comeback, a squeak of indignation. Instead, she stared at him, her face softening. She slowly lifted her shoulders backward and straightened her back. "You mean about my nightmares?" she asked quietly.

"More like night terrors," he said. "Yours and mine. You're putting me through this too, ya know."

She turned as the tears began to well up in her eyes. By the time she reached the bed, she was audibly sobbing as a maelstrom of emotions flooded down her face.

"Ju-wel-ee," Russ began. She loved the way he sang her name, making three syllables out of what should be two. He sat down on the bed beside her and stroked her back.

Leave me alone. Everyone, leave me alone, she thought. But aloud, she only sobbed. She liked the comforting feeling of her husband's hand rubbing up and down her spine.

Russ crawled into bed beside her. Julie wiped at her nose with the back of her hand and buried her face deep into the pillow. She could feel the air conditioning taking the stuffiness out of the room. *I wonder what this month's electric bill will be,* she thought as she drifted off to sleep.

Later that morning, Julie stumbled into the bathroom. Looking in the mirror, she said aloud, "Thank you Goldie Hawn for showing us what 50 should look like." She rolled her eyes in sarcasm and turned away from the mirror. She was off today from her job at the hospital, and she knew what she was going to do with her free time. Flipping on the computer, she thought about her letter as the computer hummed and whirred into service. Searching for the e-mail address of the book author, she began:

"No one knows I went to Vietnam. No one that knows me now, that is. I've never told anyone, except for you. My husband knows, but we don't really talk about it. And I've never told my two children who are now in their 20s. I guess I just wanted to wipe the memory from my mind, but that didn't happen. That year plays in my mind like yesterday's movie.

"When the kids were younger, I'd be sitting in a PTA meeting listening to someone complaining about this and that, and in my mind I'd be quietly saying, *I was in Nam, and what you're saying just isn't worth getting so worked up about.*

"People see me, and they see a mom, a wife, a nurse. Not a nurse in the middle of a war. I can't even watch war movies—they are too painful.

"As the years passed, I thought perhaps I did want to talk to someone, but who? My husband knew, but he hadn't been over there, and he wouldn't understand, I thought. I was like an alcoholic—only another alcoholic would understand.

"I started going to a doctor for symptoms that I thought were surely Nam related. It turned out to be menopause. Time passes. I can't believe I'm in my 50s. I finally asked the doctor for a referral. He linked me up with a therapist who specializes in PTSD, Post Traumatic Stress Disorder. He told me about your Web site and that you were writing a book about the women in Vietnam. I'm still not ready to tell my neighbors or my co-workers, but I thought it might be healing to see my words in a book. I'll show this to my children. Thank you for telling my story."
Julie (anonymous), a Vietnam nurse.

Story by Jan Hornung with Julie's permission, from several correspondences.

The Dam Burst

For 30 years I said that Vietnam did not affect me like others. I weathered it well. I was doing what nurses do. I was raped in Vietnam (ha—which didn't affect me). I had it very deeply buried until I saw a program interviewing others. I was on a discussion list then, still saying no not me. Well, my walls gradually got chipped away.

I started counseling and the dam burst. My PTSD, I guess is with memories that don't go away, triggered at most unusual times. I came home emotionally numb and shut down and went through the motions of life and what is expected. That rape did affect my personal life, hence the marital problems.

I do have nightmares although less frequently now. I had 30 years of not sleeping well. Took me hours to go to sleep, up often, and by morning exhausted and sleeping late. I have a little bit of everything that I have been able, I thought, to control. And not until I started counseling, did I learn exactly what my problems were and why. I just thought it was me.

Starting counseling was like pulling a cork out of the bottle. What came out cannot be put back—you have to deal with it, and is not easy.

by Nan (anonymous), Vietnam Nurse.

Midnight Movie

A quiet night in the barracks,
around midnight he starts it again,
he's yelling about some damned ambush,
and calling some Viet woman's name.

He always yells out he's sorry,
so sorry for all of the pain,
but every night around midnight;
he kills her all over again.

His life's in a kind of a freeze frame,
he can't move on from the war,

and every night just after twelve,
he's back in the Nam once more.

Back with the old 'Victor' Company,
back in that same Free-Fire-Zone,
and no bastard told those young Kiwi Grunts;
they patrolled near a wood cutters home.

When the Lead Scout signals it's Charlie,
the Platoon melts quietly away,
the 'Immediate Ambush' signs given,
and the Safety Catch slips onto 'play'.

There's five in the group in pyjamas,
as black as a midnight in May,
and the Killing Ground moves into picture;
then the Gun Group opens the way.

Black figures are falling around him,
now he's up on his feet running through,
and they're sweeping the ground where they dropped them,
as he 'double taps' a screaming torso.

At the Re-Org his fingers are trembling,
the Platoon Sergeant gives him a smoke,
then it's back to the bodies to check them;
and his round hit a woman in the throat.

There are blood trails leading behind them,
and entrails are spilled on the track,
but the woman who screamed once is silent,
two rounds exit right through her back.

The jungle seems silent and empty,
as they dig down and bury the mess,
then it's check ammunition and weapons;
and don't dwell on the past just forget.

Another night in the barracks,
and Jimmy is yelling again,
it's that same old Vietnam movie,
that's spinning around in his brain.

He always yells out he's sorry,
so sorry for all of the pain,
but every night around midnight;
he kills her all over again.

by Mike Subritzky, The Kiwi Kipling

See Mike Subritzky's poetry, *Sister,* chapter 8; *Soldier's Farewell,* chapter 28; and *bird of a single flight,* chapter 29.

PTSD

Doctors referred to "irritable heart" in the Revolutionary War, "nostalgia" in the Civil War, "shell shock" in World War I, and "combat neurosis," "combat fatigue," or "combat exhaustion" in World War II. "Feigning illness" as well as "combat exhaustion" were common terms used during the Korean War.

Whatever the label, Post Traumatic Stress Disorder has been around long before the Vietnam War. Psychologists agree, it's human nature to experience reactions such as intense fear to traumatic events involving death or injury. These reactions or symptoms may continue or even first occur decades after the horrific events.

The symptoms of PTSD are numerous, and not everyone that endures a traumatic event such as war displays any or all of the symptoms. Some of the symptoms are tension, sleep problems, nightmares, flashbacks (memories and feelings of past events), social withdrawal, emotional detachment, irritability, mood swings, anxiety, depression, and even physiological reactions such as headaches and stomach aches. Alcohol and drug abuse may also be a part of PTSD.

Friends and family members may notice a change in the person's behavior with the onset of PTSD symptoms. These changes may include panic attacks and other indications that the person does not handle stressful situations as well as he or she once did. Others may also notice the person is more withdrawn and not interested in activities that he or she once enjoyed.

Many doctors emphasize that the symptoms of PTSD are expected reactions to traumatic situations. It is treatable, and many veterans have found relief from PTSD with a doctor's help, talk groups, and other forms of therapy.

Until the mid-1970s, many medical professionals thought time was all the war veteran needed for the symptoms of "combat exhaustion" or "shell shock" to disappear. We now know that time alone is often not the cure for the stressful reactions brought on by traumatic events experienced two or three decades ago.

Congress authorized the Veterans Administration to establish Vietnam Veterans Readjustment Counseling Centers in 1979. Five years later, the National Vietnam Veterans Readjustment study estimated that a little over one-fourth of Vietnam veterans suffer or have suffered from PTSD symptoms of one form or another. Many Vietnam veterans received treatment in the 1970s and 1980s. Through the 1990s and into the new millennium, veterans continue to come forward, seeking help for PTSD from doctors and therapy groups. It's never too late for veterans to find peace from PTSD.

CHAPTER 16

A Woman Looks Back At War

*Change is Mandatory,
Stress is Manageable,
Misery is Optional*

Janis Nark

I never dreamed as a little girl that I would know about war, let alone be intimately involved in two of them, but all that changed junior year of nursing school. That was when the recruiters from all the services came around—the Army, the Navy, the Air Force. They were all in their Class A uniforms with their medals and ribbons and decorations. Oh, they were an impressive bunch. They were articulate, they were intelligent, they were well-traveled, and they wanted us bad. It was 1968, and most of us were woefully naïve about what was going on in the world. They made us wonderful promises like the moon and the stars and condos on the beach. They promised us more concrete things like good pay, status as an officer, and travel.

Travel certainly perked up my ears. I had visions of being "The" nurse in the dispensary in Garmisch, Germany, and skiing the Zugspitze everyday, and taking care of soldiers who had broken their leg skiing or gotten frostbite—to which they replied, "Not a problem. You can go anywhere in the world you want to go. You just give us three choices; you're guaranteed one of them."

I thought, "I'm not stupid, I know there's a war going on."

I said, "I'm not stupid, I know there's a war going on."

And the recruiters replied, "Don't worry, Vietnam is strictly voluntary. Even the nurses that want to go can't get there. It's a very choice assignment."

We believed them. But of course, the hook for most of the young women—ladies, they always called us ladies—was, "There are 2000 men for every woman in the Armed Forces."

That got our attention. So, I signed up. I raised my hand, and I joined on what was called the Army student nurse program. After I finished nursing school, I went down to Fort Sam Houston for basic training. Now I don't know what you've heard about basic training, but in 1970, basic training for nurses was a lot of fun. It was grand adventure. We learned how to land navigate, how to read a compass, how to eat C-rations, how to salute, and how to suture. We learned military history, and we learned how to march. I love to march; it's like everybody dancing, all doing the same thing at the same time. You haven't lived until you've seen a platoon of nurses try to do an about face in high heels.

Then they issued us our uniforms. I have always stood tall. Mother Nature and Mother Nark made me that way, but I never stood as tall as I did the first day I wore the uniform of my country. We were developing a common identity, unit cohesion, esprit de corps—and it was all very purposeful.

There were a hundred nurses going through basic training. The recruiters hadn't lied. There were thousands of young Army officer men down there going through medical services corps school and helicopter school. In my little platoon of 30 nurses, in class one day, I remember our instructor going to the front of the room. He stood there on a little riser, and he looked at us and said, "How many of you had recruiters that promised you that you wouldn't have to go to Vietnam?" And in my little class of 30 nurses, 29 of us raised our hand. And he said, "Well, they lied. The truth is, six months from now you will be in Vietnam, or you will be in Korea, or you will be some place so god-awful, you will wish that you were in Vietnam or Korea."

I looked around at all those other nurses, at all those shocked faces, and expressions, and I thought, "Well, he is obviously talking to them, because I'm going to Germany."

At the end of basic training, I got orders for my first duty station. And it was at Madigan General Hospital at Fort Lewis in Washington State. I had never heard of Madigan General Hospital before I got my orders. This should have been my second clue about recruiters' promises.

It was at Madigan that I saw my first young soldier die, and that took a piece of my heart that I will miss for as long as I live. It was at Madigan that I learned how good we were getting at the job we had to do—the job of saving young soldiers lives.

Our medical evacuation system was so good in Vietnam that it was not unusual for a soldier to be wounded in the field and lose consciousness, be medevaced by helicopter, taken to the rear, sedated, stabilized, put on a jet, flown across the ocean, and be bussed to my facility, and literally wake up in my hands. We got busloads of air evacs in every day from Vietnam, and I would look at all of them and check them over. I'd check the cast and the dressings and the IVs and the tractions, before I would assign them a bed.

About once a week, a soldier would look up from his litter, and he'd look at me, and then he'd look around, and he'd say, "Well, either I'm home or I'm dead 'cause you sure look like an angel to me." Talk about your job perks.

I was at Madigan for exactly six months when I was ordered to go to Vietnam. My instructor at basic training hadn't lied. I was 21 years old.

All wars are bad, but Vietnam was particularly horrible in the types of casualties it produced—gunshot wounds, frag wounds, huge chunks of their young bodies just blown away. And so many amputations. I could have never imagined how many amputations. Because of the jungle environment and the enemy weapons, every wound was contaminated. And because our evacuation system was so good, soldiers that would have died in previous wars, made it to our hospital more grievously wounded than we'd ever had to deal with before.

Like most of us that served in Vietnam, I stayed for a year. I cared for the sick and for the wounded and for those that would die. And when I came home, I didn't know what to do with all the emotions, the memories, my personal pain. So I did what so many others did—I took all those memories and I buried them, deep. So deep that I thought that they could never hurt me again. They stayed buried for over 20 years. And for 20 years, I didn't talk about Vietnam. And for 20 years, I didn't cry. I know now that I was terrified that if I started to cry, I could never stop.

In 1982 the initial healing ground was laid, in the form of the Vietnam Veterans' Memorial—The Wall. The women, just like men who served, were drawn to it. The healing power of that sacred place is evident to all who have been there. We could go to The Wall, and mourn and cry and reach out for comfort if we chose…and yet it was so easy to be invisible there. Women simply weren't recognized as veterans.

Veteran's Day 1993, the Vietnam Women's Memorial is dedicated in Washington, D.C. Thousands of women vets attend, and we are overwhelmed. We lead the parade—the nurses, Red Cross workers, entertainers, women who worked in administration, logistics, and intelligence. The streets are lined with people applauding and crying. A vet sits high up in a tree yelling, "Thank You! Thank You!" A man in a flight suit stands for over two hours at attention, saluting as the women pass by. People hand us flowers and hug us. One GI has a picture of his nurse taken "July 1964." He is trying to find her.

We find each other. We know, at last, that we are not alone; that we are not crazy or paranoid, but that we have a lot of work to do in order to heal. We talk to each other and find comfort as well as pain in our words and our tears. Words and tears, that now, finally we share. Now, after so many years, the process has finally begun—and we hold each other close, and say, "Welcome Home!"

by Janis Nark, printed with permission from her audio tape, *A Woman Looks Back at War*.

Janis Nark is a retired U.S. Army Reserve Lieutenant Colonel. She served in the active duty Army as a second and first lieutenant nurse in Cam Ranh Bay, Vietnam, 1970–1971, and again during Desert Storm as a lieutenant colonel. Janis Nark shares her life's stories as a professional motivational speaker helping others to find "control in chaos." *A Woman's Journey To War And Back* is one of her humorous as well as poignant speech topics.

Find out more about Janis Nark at her Web site, http://www.nark.com. Look for her book about her Vietnam experiences, *Scattered Memories, A Woman's Journey To War And Back*. Her story also appears in *A 4th Course of Chicken Soup for the Soul: 101 Stories to Open the Heart and Rekindle the Spirits*.

Contact Janis Nark by e-mail: janisnark@aol.com, phone: 828-652-2155, or FAX: 828-652-4547.

CHAPTER 17

Veterans Resource Network Association

The rewards of service to country come in many forms.
Janis Nark

Are you a Vet?
Four little words with so much meaning

Whenever I visit Washington, D.C., I'm always drawn to the Vietnam Veterans' Memorial and the Women's Memorial that honors those who served and those who died in Vietnam.

More than 11,500 women served in Vietnam in capacities ranging from intelligence and air traffic control to supply and logistics. And, of course, there were the nurses. I know, I was one.

It's true, we all volunteered to be in service to our country, but many of us with our recruiters solemn promise that "of course, you won't have to go to Vietnam…it's strictly voluntary…even the nurses that want to go can't."

Still, when our orders arrived, sending us to war, most of us believed in our hearts that we were needed, that what we were doing was important and that it was our duty to go.

We went to our jobs, faced the perils of enemy fire, the horrible heat and humidity, disease, insects, isolation, long work days and sleepless nights dealing in life and death. And, every day we managed to pull ourselves together, dab some perfume behind our ears and do it all again.

We learned a lot about ourselves. We discovered our strengths and tried to survive our weaknesses. We were ordinary young women trying to function in the most extraordinary circumstances.

After a year, we came home. We knew we had changed, that our lives would never be the same and that we could not explain any of it to the folks back home. For as unacceptable as it was for the guys to talk about the war, no one wanted to acknowledge that women had been there. The underlying message was very clear: Nice girls do not go to war.

We came home quietly, went back to our homes, our families, our jobs and never spoke about the war to anyone.

I go to the Wall and the Women's Memorial now, but that was not always the case. For more than 20 years, I never volunteered the information that I was a Vietnam vet. I, like many vets, believed I was alone—that no one knew where I had been or what I had done or what I had seen or how I felt.

It wasn't until I allowed myself to be in the company of other veterans that I discovered I wasn't alone. In fact, I had a whole lot of company: men and women who served in Vietnam, in Desert Storm, in Panama, in Somalia, in Mogadishu, and places many Americans have never heard of; men and women who served proudly, honorably and passionately. The ones who did their duty, came home, kept their silence and may still believe they are alone.

It is for these and other veterans that I joined the board of a new organization, the Veterans Resource Network Association (VRNA). Our job is to recognize, to honor and to bring together a group with a common past to forge a more productive future.

The Veterans Resource Network Association is designed to educate and counsel veterans about their rights to benefits from the Veterans Administration, deliver valued benefits and services from the private sector, and enhance the lifestyle of members through healthcare and financial services. We also want to help veterans locate and talk to their buddies and to other veterans over the Internet and, most important, inform Americans about the role veterans have played in keeping our country independent, safe, and free.

Today, there are 25 million veterans here in America, and only a small percentage are now members of any veterans' organization. We are not here to replace the existing veterans' groups but have found a willingness on the part of veterans to join an organization if it offered the right kinds of services and benefits. We believe we have met that need.

The goal of the Veterans Resource Network Association is to reach out to those veterans from all branches of the military, the National Guard, and the Reserves who have served this country so well for so long and who want to be recognized for that service.

For too many years, too many veterans have felt they were alone and they were forgotten by society, while still believing they did the right thing. They served their country well and now we want to rekindle that pride—to help them find strength in their numbers and answers to their questions.

It is our way of saying: Thank you and welcome home!

by Lt. Col. Janis Nark (USAR, retired), reprinted with permission, *Veterans Resource*, vol.2, no.1, spring 2001.

The Veterans Resource Network Association is on the Internet at www.vrna.org or write Veterans Resource Network Association Member Services, 112 E. Lincoln Ave., Fergus Falls, MN, 56537, or call 1-877-848-VRNA (8762). Janis Nark, a Vietnam nurse, is a professional motivational speaker, and she is on the VRNA Board of Directors. Read her story, chapter 16.

Why?

I did as my country asked me
although I was but a boy
I took my rifle in my hand
and to jungle I did deploy.
Nam was so very different
than all I had ever known
and this war wasn't like the ones
I use to play at home.
But I remember grandpa's stories
of the happiness when he got back
so I held my head up high
and continued on the track.
I was one of the lucky ones
and got a seat on the plane
I couldn't believe the condemnation
and my country's disdain.
as tears of disbelief and pain
blurred out that hissing crowd
I had to close my ears and heart
to the insults shouted so loud.
I only did my duty
I fought instead of ran

so why are people ashamed of me
and refuse to shake my hand?

by Maria Sutherland

See Maria's poem, *A Soldier's Prayer*, chapter 15.

CHAPTER 18

The Healing Continues

*Mankind must put an end to war,
or war will put an end to mankind.*
        John Fitzgerald Kennedy, 1917–1963

Souvenirs

Sometimes they were small items
Pinned on jackets or hats
Other times they were photographs
Of those we once were

At times they were items
Captured on the field of battle
Or bought in the stalls of the abundant markets
Or in the bars and clubs by Saigon warriors

Many times they were shipped home to be forgotten
Where they remained in closets and footlockers
Sometimes they were even hung proudly on walls
Or displayed on a special shelf in the den

But they also were the nighttime sweats
The startled reactions and flashbacks
Brought home against our will
They are the voices from the past

They are the faces that never change
Souvenirs brought home which are unwanted
Uninvited they stay with us and are as important
As those tangible ones that came home in our luggage

How to sort through and decide what to keep
What can be thrown away without guilt and pain
But flashbacks aren't given the choice of being
They just are and come without fanfare or warning

Souvenirs of the soul we left behind
Lost in that time and place
Yet staying with us in thoughts and actions
Can they ever be cleaned and polished for display

by Penni Evans

Read about Penni Evans and her poetry, *Sisters,* chapter 1; *Ambushed,* chapter 15; *Souvenirs,* chapter 18; *My Brother,* chapter 26; and *Folded Flag,* chapter 27.

Psyched

It was October of 1967, and I had been in Vietnam a few weeks as a Red Cross Donut Dolly. I was 21, just out of college and full of all the idealism and guilelessness of youth. Our job as Donut Dollies was to visit guys at firebases, day rooms, LZs, hospitals, wherever we could present some type of recreation program and/or visit awhile. We gave them a reminder of home. Took their minds off of the war. The loneliness. The fear. A pretty daunting job for 21 year olds who were grappling with the same things. But we were sincere in our efforts and made many a soldier forget the war for just a little while.

I was visiting an evac hospital at Long Binh on this particular day, and I somehow wound up in the psych ward. I had wandered from one Quonset hut to another and by mistake had gone into a wrong ward. Sometimes nurses walked us to a ward and checked in on us from time to time. Usually there were nurses on each unit doing their nursing things. But hospitals were busy places and physical wounds got more attention.

The guys were in beds up and down both sides of the walls. They had on military-issued blue hospital pajamas. Most of them were lying on top of the covers, feet sticking up, sweltering in the heat. You could see that their feet were cracked and peeling from jungle rot. Most everybody got jungle rot at one time or the other from the constant wet and sweat that was part of living in Southeast Asia.

Somewhere in the back of the ward a fan droned. I could hear helicopters whirring overhead and occasionally an F-4 coming or going. At night, mortar fire would make its way into sleep. But this day it seemed the silence was what I heard loudest. It was hard enough going into a hospital unit, but in this one no one was listening to the radio. No card games were going. No teasing back and forth across the aisles. A few were reading. A few smoked. Most just stared at something unseen.

My usual schtick was to ask, "Where are you from in the real world?" and tell them that I was, "from L.A.—Lovely Atlanta." That usually brought a smile and got us to talking. Some of these fellas responded, some I could tell didn't want to talk.

The one soldier I remember, the one I will always remember, was a fella who was just staring off into space. His eyes were fixed on something invisible to me. I have tried and tried to remember more about him. Wasn't he the one with those big, sad brown eyes? No, no, he was that black guy, wasn't he?

I asked him, "How ya' doin'?"

His response was, "Why did my buddy have to die?"

The silence got louder and louder. It roared. I wanted to run. I wanted to say, "You aren't supposed to ask questions like that. We aren't supposed to talk about death. Why can't you play by the rules?" I looked at him through tears, knowing I couldn't answer him. Could not soothe him. Could not comfort him. I said gently, "I don't know why." I moved on to the next bed.

That day and visit and the overall powerlessness of the moment have stayed with me. Through the years I've asked myself over and over why did he have to die, what could I have said, if only…

I now know that this unremembered face was every soldier. Every Red Cross girl. Every nurse. I am no longer naïve and innocent, but have found peace knowing he asked the question we all asked, and that I gave him the right answer. The answer all us of have to live with.

by Pat Hewatt
American Red Cross, Donut Dolly, 1967–1968

Pat Hewatt went to Vietnam in the fall of 1967. She served as a recreational specialist in the Supplemental Recreational Activities Overseas Division of the American Red Cross, better known as a Donut Dolly. Her first assignment was with the II Field Force at Long Binh. She lived on Cong Ly Street in the city of Bien Hoa from October 1967 through January of 1968. The two-story French Villa, known as the Pink Palace, was home to 14 women and had one bathroom. She watched Long Binh under attack during the Tet Offense from the roof of the villa.

Her second duty station was at Chu Lai with the Americal Division from January through May. Chu Lai was on the South China Sea and was constantly under mortar and rocket attack. Lastly, she severed with the 4th Division in Pleiku from June to October of 1968.

Seasons of Siege
Vietnam Twenty Years After

I
The nameless, faceless
rank and file that
thunders through my dreams
calls red alert
to already cautioned sleep.

One by one I wave
a sleepy farewell
to those round-eyed boys
gone to fight a killer
that still sleeps in my bed

II
What camouflage can
disguise a heart
whose beat
is tapped out by bones
on shell case droppings,
metered by staccato mortar,
martyred by the shell-shocked,
tone-deaf third chairs
of last year's high school
marching band?

III
We danced on the edge of an open grave.
Slipped 'round mounds of dusty red clay.
Hot and humid
clashed with Cutty Sark.
Perfumes and after shaves mingled
into that inevitable tropical sweet sweat.
You in your khaki's
me in some yellow-daisied flounce
sent from home with love and fear.

A two-day stand down at Long Binh
was a shoddy farewell from this earth—
RX, PX, a steak and some beer.
And the dance.
Then back to Pineapple Plantation,
that fatal fruited LZ
that flashed a napalm dawn. And death.
You returned to Long Binh—
but to Quartermaster this trip.
No khaki. Green.
And three days ago we danced.

Today I feel the earth splitting
just so long and just so wide
six feet of Georgia clay at my side.
My toes are tapping last notes
as I wait in my daisied dress

Who will dance with me?

IV
I froze staring at your
slicked back hair
black where it once was blonde

I saw your eyes
stitched closed
where once they were blue
Your mouth
stuffed quiet with cotton
jaws set, lips pursed forever

Where are you now, Alan
twenty years alive. Twenty years dead.
Life couldn't hold you
Death didn't flatter you

V
I'll kiss your lips
and free the words still there
if you are unable to speak

I'll clasp your hand
and gently lead you
when your footsteps make no path

I'll hum you songs
whose words have faded
but whose melody lingers

I'll do all this and more
if you'll tell me just one time
what it's like to be dead

by Pat Hewatt

Parts is Parts

(ICU at the 24th Evac hospital)

Hospital runs were the worst.
Families and countries were already torn apart
and here, ICU-ed bodies
like peeled oranges split into—
(a piece for you, two for me)
with pulpy fragments dangling
were sticky with juice.
A cruel puzzle, unsolved
but clamped, cut and tied with #00 suture.
Reality held at bay by Demerol—
IV problems already a part of the solution

I've seen arms
bulging with muscles
and fastened to bodies
with waxen flesh
that moved as awkwardly
as Billy Jones' first slow dance.
Others hung like grapes
only coming to life

when pruned and pressed by others
Some were spares—forever out of socket

Stomachs were laid wide
with tube moving life along
in and out of metered machines
whose clocks were running
and running out.
Dialysised daydreams
floated in their own poisonous fluid.

All of these things spread before me
like Frank my biology frog.

One legged Arthur Murrays
would always remember their two-step.
Chrome and spoked centaurs
were coaxed and counselled
to roll with the punches.
All bandy-legged heroes
who footed the bill for war.

Visionless eyes that let no
light dance on rods or cones
had retinas detached at the heart.
Some eyes flickered of devil things
unknown unless you've gone blindly
to the bottom of the river Styx
and there, opened shutter-wide,
saw and were conquered.

Some days I'm back at the 24th
back on the ward where
the guy asked why I let his buddy die.
Been home 20 years
and I still don't know.

by Pat Hewatt

I think Donut Dollies saw more because we were out in the field all of the time and we were in much greater danger. The nurses, however, are really the unsung heroes. They saw the horror and gore we (Red Cross) didn't see that much of. They had to remain "present" with young men as they died. My heart leaps out to them and what they did.

I am not altogether sure why my poetry is soulfully more connected to these women—the nurses. I know there is a sad, dark place in my own soul that connected me with them. Tucked in between the photographs and fatigues, were PTSD, suicidal depression, addiction—the by-products of that war. I knew then I would never see my country the same way after Vietnam. There are wounds that remain open for many. I felt like we lost credibility and that, like us, our country did not come out whole."
Pat Hewatt.

Pat Hewatt is the author of *Seasons of Siege,* a book of poetry. Read more of Pat's poetry at www.donutdolly.com, American Red Cross Vietnam Donut Dollies. Since Vietnam, she has worked as a copy writer and editor, and she is now Director of Communications at a state psychiatric hospital. "I have volunteered for the last 10 years in mental health advocacy. I live with my dog, Riley, a German Shepherd that I adopted from a kill shelter. I told him he was going home with me to live the life of Riley—thus the name."
Pat Hewatt

Do You Know

Do you know what it's like
to find yourself in a foreign country away from all loved ones?
Do you know what it's like
to eat C-rations, craving for a home cooked meal?
Do you know what it's like
to write a letter thinking you may not be alive when the reply comes?
Do you know what it's like
to hold a buddy in your arms and witness the pain he feels?

Do you know what it feels like
to take a human being's life? Knowing this you must do or die?
Do you know what it's like
to return home and your friends act as if you have been on vacation?
Do you know what it feels like
to be greeted by a friend who asks, "How many people did you kill?"
Not how many people did you save? Or I'm glad you're alive.
Do you know what it's like
to see a mother given a flag to honor a son for his dedication?
Do you know what it's like
to read of four protesters' deaths and how they were honored?
Do you know what it's like
to see people burning the flag you fought for in a demonstration?

Do you know who fought for freedom of the press?
Do you know who fought to give you the right to a fair trail?
Do you know who works the most hours but gets paid the least?
Do you know who gets a tear in their eye when the melody Taps plays?

If you know, you have the heart of a soldier.
Remember! Remember them all, that shed their blood for us.
Thank! Thank them all, that guard our freedom today.

by Johnny Hutcherson

    Johnny Hutcherson arrived in Vietnam in 1968. He was a 20-year-old helicopter door gunner. "Some say the Vietnam War was for nothing and 58,000 died for no reason. All I know is I went because President Johnson told me to. I feel in Vietnam, the soldiers fought for each other. We had to and we still do!"
Johnny Hutcherson.

Nightmare of a Soldier

Can't you hear their crying,
how can you not feel their pain;
when their blood still runs heavy
each year with the monsoon rains;

I keep hearing these voices calling me,
from somewhere far away;
scared to death, they sound so familiar
as I hear them say;

You're safe now at home,
you left our souls here in Vietnam;
come on back and finish
this job you left undone;

Can't you hear their crying,
how can you not feel their pain;

when their blood still runs heavy
each year with the monsoon rains;

Now someone said it's for freedom,
and for freedom some must fall;
but what they got was deserted
and their names on cold stone wall;

Can't you hear their crying,
how can you not feel their pain;
when their blood still runs heavy
each year with the monsoon rains;

Can't you hear their crying,
how can you not feel their pain;
when their blood still runs heavy
each year with the monsoon rains.

Song by Doc Hollywood

Doc Hollywood was in Vietnam from 1969–1970 with 1st Infantry Division/1st Medical Battalion as an Army combat medic. Like many of the young men who went off to the war, he was only 18 years old at the time, a private first class. Today, Doc Hollywood has four children and 12 grandchildren.

"Many of the songs I have composed were sort of a form of therapy for myself," Hollywood said. Although he wrote the above song through the eyes of a man, he said that he could write "a song through the eyes of a female nurse in Vietnam, but I wouldn't think she would see things much differently than I saw them and felt them. They were soldiers, just as much so as we men were. The contributions they made were as equal or surpassed those made by male soldiers."

CHAPTER 19

My Name is Karen

*The more one does and sees and feels,
the more one is able to do,
and the more genuine may be
one's appreciation of fundamental things
like home, and love,
and understanding companionship.*
                    Amelia Earhart, 1897–1937

My name is Karen and I am a Vietnam veteran, having served in the Army. I was in country during 1969 and 1970. I was not a nurse in Nam, although I became one when I returned. I was one of about 500 WACs (Women's Army Corps), who volunteered and was accepted to serve in Southeast Asia. I served in Long Binh and Saigon but also traveled to various locations such as Cu Chi, Da Nang, Bien Hoa, etc. I was stationed with MACV (Military Assistance Command, Vietnam) where I worked six and a half days a week, 10–15 hours a day. On my half day off, I volunteered at an orphanage, an experience that will forever be with me.
Karen Offutt.

And The War Goes On

Don't show them you're afraid.
Smile—get on the plane.
Go on over there, wherever "there" is.
You'll probably come back.
I don't feel like I'll come back.
I'm scared 'cause ahead is the unknown.
My family is crying. They're making this worse.
Go home. Let me do this. I have to.

Long flight. I am tired.
Already miss my brother—My best friend.
I'll show my parents I am strong and brave and, and,
And can do anything a boy can do.
Plane full of men—no women—what am I doing?
What am I trying to prove?
You know it won't be good enough anyway.
You'll die and it still won't be good enough.

They'll say, "We told her not to go."
"We told her to marry, stay home and sew,
Raise babies, take care of a man."
Act like a girl! What's wrong with you?

Finally, I am here, but I don't know where.
I want to go home but I can't.
Need to sleep and try to figure this out.
Pick a bed, any bed, not that bed, this one.

Monsoon rains pouring outside and in the room.
Hitting metal pans with giant "plunk," "plunk," "plunks"

Everything is hot and the earth red as blood.
Click your heels together and you'll be home.
You are home, silly girl. Rest now.

What's wrong? Being hit with powerful concussions,
as though a giant's fists are pounding the walls.
My bed is shaking and I'm afraid.
More afraid than I've ever been.

There is nowhere to hide…to run to.
Someone says there's a bunker somewhere.
What's a bunker? Where is it?
I'm lost and new here. Why won't anyone help me?
I am paralyzed in my little bed. It continues all night.

I wait to die. Well, this is why you came.
Give your life for your country.
Make them proud, as they drape the flag
Over your empty casket, because you're in pieces
Somewhere in a place far away from home.

Pray. Tell God to let your family know you loved them.
Prepare to die. I am 19. I haven't learned how to live.
And I don't know how to die.
How do I do this right? Can't I do this one thing right?

Fall asleep from the drumbeat. It pounds steadily,
Louder than my heart. What music is that?
It's a rocket and mortar
Symphony. It's the music of war.

How can I sleep while someone is trying to kill me?
This is insane.

I awake and it's morning. The music has stopped.
I am alive. I am dead. I am a kid. I am old.
Home Ec, Honor's Biology, Basic Training,
All of it worthless. No class prepared me for this.

Naked children playing in mud.
Beer can and cardboard houses.
Children selling their sisters to the soldiers.
Working 9–5, what a way to make a living.
Just like a song, only this is real.
Children touching my skin, teenage girls feeling my eyelashes,
GIs taking my picture.
Strange sounds, penetrating smells that will never leave.

Snipers firing, barely missing my head.
Don't flick your lighter—it'll explode.
Don't pick the kids up—they may be booby trapped.
Claymores and barbed wire, mama-sans and black pajamas.

Time to go home, but I am home.
I don't want to leave. I'm on the edge of life and death.
Fear and excitement mix. Pride and guilt intermingle.
I'm confused again—still.

Parents meet me at the airport. Seems they think
I've been on vacation. They have suffered they say.
Mom shows me her white hair and her limp from
Where a tumor is pressing on her uterus.

I feel guilty. I have failed again.
I haven't brought them honor—only pain.
Why didn't I die there?

Maybe I can go back and try again.
What am I afraid of? Of not measuring up?
Of not doing life right even though there
Seems to be no "right" way of doing it?

Afraid to die but wishing I could, quickly, painlessly.
Scared of not being loved. Frightened of the dark,
When all the bad people out there
Wanted to hurt someone with their war toys and evil hearts.

Afraid of myself and the rage inside.
Afraid of the dark side of myself,
The war words that can come from within
To push others away so that I am alone
As I deserve to be. Alone and afraid. Afraid to live, afraid to die.

That year of war changed me. Made me see the evil in mankind.
Took my youth and trust and naiveté,
Grounding them into the red mud of Vietnam.
You can't see the scars…I look as good as new,
But they're there—inside.
Vietnam is alive and well.
And the war goes on…

by Karen Offutt

Read more about Karen Offutt and her poetry at her Web site, http://walkwithme.netfirms.com, Walk With Me.

"This site is dedicated to all my brothers and sisters who served thanklessly in the Vietnam War, to all of us bearing physical and emotional scars, those who have given their all, those who have taken their own lives rather than live with the memories of that Hell, to all those

suffering from Agent Orange who will never be recognized, including my own three children (twin sons and a daughter) and one granddaughter, all born with cancer, epilepsy, or Attention Deficit Hyperactivity Disorder. To my children and (two) grandchildren, who are my life, I say, I went to Vietnam with honorable intentions. I am sorry for the pain it has caused you."
Karen Offutt.

Soldier's Medal

In January 1970, I was to be given the Soldier's Medal for heroic action. My paperwork states I was the only American woman to pull many people from a hamlet fire. I mention this not because I consider myself a hero but because I never received the medal. I was told at that time that "women just did not receive the Soldier's Medal." I was given a Certificate of Appreciation instead. It shows the inequities of being a female in the service, even though I went to Vietnam knowing I might very well never return. I do hope that things have changed for women in uniform today.
Karen Offutt

Update: On April 7, 2001, at 2 p.m., after Karen Offutt's speech at The Moving Wall in Florida, in a surprise ceremony, she was awarded The Soldiers Medal.

> The citation reads:
> Soldier's Medal
> Karen I. Offutt
> (Then) Specialist Five, United States Army
> For heroism not involving actual conflict with an armed enemy: Specialist Karen I. Offutt, Women's Army Corps, United States Army, assigned to Headquarters Military Assistance Command Vietnam, J47, distinguished herself by heroic action on 24

January 1970 while in an off-duty status. Observing a fire in Vietnamese dwellings near her quarters, she hurried to the scene to provide assistance. Without regard for her personal safety and in great danger of serious injury or death from smoke, flames, and falling debris, she assisted in rescuing several adults and children from the burning structures. Without protective clothing or shoes she repeatedly entered the buildings to lead children that had re-entered their homes to safety. She continued to assist the Vietnamese residents in removing personal property and livestock, although danger increased until fire-fighting equipment and personnel arrived. Specialist Five Offutt's heroic action reflects great credit on herself, the United States Army, and the United States mission in Vietnam.

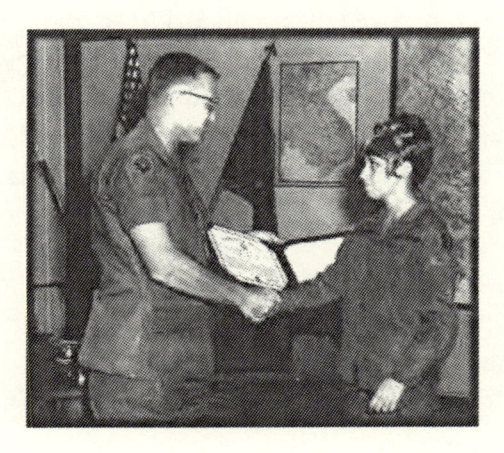

Certificate of Achievement
Photo courtesy of Karen Offutt

Karen Offutt receives a Certificate of Achievement from General B.G. Bautz in 1970.

CHAPTER 20

Seeking God

Our deepest fear is not that we are inadequate.
Our deepest fear is that we are powerful beyond measure.
Nelson Mandela, 1918–present

God, a Soldier, and a Red Cross Worker

Thirty years ago, I was serving in a military field hospital in Vietnam. My year's tour of duty was almost over. I was physically and emotionally tired. I'd been living with death and dying patients for a year. I was ready for it to be over. I wanted to go home.

I was in the office one day when a nurse called over from the hospital ward. He said he had a patient that should have been recovering from spinal surgery, but was not. The patient was going to be a paraplegic, unable to walk for the rest of his life, but he was healthy and had come through the surgery easily. The young man should have been awake and talking by this time, but the nurse said instead he was just lying in his bed, unresponsive to any stimulus. His vital signs were quickly deteriorating. The nurse was afraid they were going to lose the patient. He

203

wondered if the Red Cross could come over and do something. I hadn't a clue what the nurse thought a person employed to provide recreation for long-term hospital patients could actually do to help. I was hot and tired and crabby.

I doubted I could be of any use, but I dutifully plodded over to the ward. I found the patient. I pretended I was just visiting on the wards and had just happened to stop by. I started chatting away like we were at an informal party in someone's back yard. Perhaps it was a whiff of perfume, perhaps it was surprise to be addressed in such a manner, perhaps he had been raised to be polite and just didn't want to appear rude; whatever it was, I knew I was on the road to success when I realized we had made eye contact and he was watching me.

I kept talking away. I saw his picture album on his bedside stand. I got it out and started looking through it all the while talking away. Finally I asked him a direct question. Was this a picture of his girlfriend? He nodded. Hurray, I thought. I kept talking. Who was this I asked? He began to talk, slowly and haltingly. He identified pictures of his parents, his dog, his younger brothers and sisters, and his fiancée, who were all waiting for him to come home.

The conversation began to die out, and I felt rather frantic that the young man was not quite out of the woods. I silently prayed to God for some help. I raised my eyes and at that exact moment a young soldier was walking toward us. The young soldier worked in the hospital post office. He said he had needed a break and just decided to walk over to the ward and deliver this package to this patient in person. The box was obviously a care package full of cookies and goodies from his family. The corporal from the post office and I didn't have to work hard to make a big deal over the care package. Everyone got excited over care packages from home.

I asked the young patient if he minded if I opened the package for him. He nodded and watched as I unwrapped homemade chocolate cookies, only slightly worse for their trip from the states and a rather round about route through Vietnam before finally catching up with the patient. When the young patient reached out for the cookie I offered to him, I knew he was going to make it. Of course I knew that the fellow had too many tubes in him to be able to eat cookies, but I acted out my part and I went over to inquire from the nurse if he could eat cookies. The nurse with a very puzzled look said, well if he just waited, they would take the tubes out and he'd be able to eat food within the hour. I took that as my cue to leave. I told them I'd be back for cookies later and had him promise to save me some. I knew he'd be fine.

God must have had a plan for that young man. That young man's parents must have been praying for him. His fiancée must have been praying for his safe return. His younger brothers and sisters must have prayed that their older brother would come home. God used whoever happened to be available to save the life of that young man. When the doctors had done all they could, and the young man realized he would be paralyzed, he lost the will to live. God heard the prayers of the young man's family.

God creatively used whoever was handy and would respond to help give that young man the will to live. I know that God used the nurse on duty, God used me, and God used the young corporal from the post office to create a will to live and to restore that young man to his family.

In our humanness we get weak. Sometimes fatigue stalls us in the midst of our work. We want to do good, but our intentions fall by the wayside. God gives us another opportunity each and every day to do the work we are sent to do. God's will and plans for each of us is endlessly creative. God will use us as instruments of grace to accomplish the plan God has in mind for us and for others. God is still in the business of saving, raising, restoring, and empowering each one of us. Let us keep the faith. God has a plan for our lives.

by Rev. Nancy Landauer

Reverend Nancy Landauer is a Methodist minister in Monterey, California. At the time of her story, 1969, she was a 22-year-old American Red Cross worker in Vietnam. "I occasionally tell Vietnam stories in my sermons," Nancy said.

I was hired by the Red Cross when I was a senior in college at Hamline University in Minnesota. I wanted to travel, and the guidance counselor suggested that the Red Cross was sending people overseas. I heard her talk about Japan, England, and Spain. I chose not to hear her explain about Vietnam. However, by the time I had spent six months at William Beaumont in El Paso, Texas, I had been listening to others talk about their experiences in Vietnam and I wanted to go. I didn't agree with the United States' position in Vietnam, but I felt like I could be of service to the troops without agreeing to the war effort.

I had no idea (at that time) that I would go into ministry. I never even went to the chapel services while I was in Vietnam. I had an interest in religious studies in college, but I never thought of organized religion as a career choice.

I was at William Beaumont Hospital in El Paso, Texas, for six months, then I was at the 24th Evacuation Hospital at Long Binh, Vietnam. Later I served at Fort Sam Houston, San Antonio, Texas, on the burn unit for a year, and then six months at Fort Riley, Kansas. I ended my Red Cross career at Lettermen Hospital in San Francisco.

I was not a nurse. I was a recreation worker. We planned games and activities for men who were hospitalized. Back then, men coming home from the war could be hospitalized for months, even years.
Rev. Nancy Landauer

God, I'd Really Like To Know

As day breaks, the same question floods my mind.
If I die here, will I go to heaven? God, I'd really like to know!

Another day in the Nam.
Sun's up. Same smells, same scenery, same haunting question;
will I make it through today, one more day in the Nam?

The order is given to "saddle up."
The likelihood of death is just a rice paddy away
and once again the question comes.
God, I'd really like to know.

by Rick Lewis

See Rick Lewis' poem, *Becky Died,* chapter 2.

Parade of Fear

Fear is a powerful force in our lives. Sometimes fear urges us to make changes in our lives and put forth extra effort. I remember back in college, I really wanted to graduate, but I wasn't interested in putting forth a lot of effort to get good grades. I remember fall term my freshman year of college, I was shocked to realize that my mid semester grades indicated I was getting Ds and Fs. It was purely through fear of flunking out that I grabbed my books, headed for the library, and began studying in earnest. Fear of failure isn't necessarily such a bad thing. It can motivate us to get going and accomplish what we need to do. Fear motivates us to seek protection when we are in danger. It prompts us to take precautions ahead of time so that we won't be placed in dangerous situations.

In 1970, I was working for the American Red Cross. I was stationed at the U.S. Army Medical Center in San Antonio, Texas. Summer is always hot in San Antonio, but that summer seemed especially hot. Racial tensions were high. There were race riots in other cities, and San Antonio simmered that summer, seemingly about to boil over into its own riot. San Antonio was a city clearly divided into the haves and the have nots.

At the top were a few white families who had become extremely wealthy from oil and cattle. At the bottom were the Hispanics and blacks who had little.

Years ago the wealthy whites had seceded from the city. The small section of town where the wealthy whites lived had become incorporated into their own little town. They paid for their own police, fire, water, and sewer. The rest of the city of San Antonio suffered with inadequate police and fire protection. They lived from year to year with an antiquated sewer system. Each spring the sewers overflowed, homes were lost, and several people, always the poor, were swept away in flash flooding.

At no time were these inequalities more obvious than during the summer celebration called Fiesta Week. The Fiesta Parade was the occasion that the white debutantes, in their dresses made specially for the occasion and costing $5,000 dollars or more, were driven slowly down the street perched on the back of convertibles. Huge crowds gathered for the three-hour parade.

The Red Cross had brought five busloads full of GIs. They were all men patients at the hospital, primarily in various stages of recovery from wounds received in Vietnam. We military personnel claimed the steps of the post office for seating. The post office offered a little shade, the wide steps accommodated all five busloads, and we were up high enough where we could see the parade more easily. We had patients in wheelchairs, crutches, and on stretchers on wheels. Suddenly, as I looked down to the corner where there was a standing room only crowd, I saw a chair go flying in the air. A second chair flew up ten feet in the air, and the riot began.

"Run!" someone screamed. Right, I thought, let's run with a couple hundred disabled veterans. But the doors to the post office were open, and everyone who was mobile pushed, pulled, or shoved someone who was not. In a matter of minutes we were all safely inside the post office. The last person into the post office looked back. "They're coming this way," he yelled. I panicked. "Lock the doors," I yelled. Several innocent people were killed in the crush on that street corner that afternoon. We were truly afraid.

Very few emotions in life are as strong as fear; very few experiences are as awesome and full as those moments in life when we feel genuinely afraid. Mary Magdalene and the disciples discovered an empty tomb and the doors where the disciples meet are locked in fear. Mary heard her own name being called by her beloved teacher and friend, she told the other disciples, and the doors of the room were locked for fear. I can't help wondering. When I hear this resurrection story, were the doors locked because Jesus' followers were afraid of death, or were the doors locked because the followers were afraid of resurrection life?

Resurrection life, which leaves tombs empty and grave clothes laying about the tomb, is not always a glorious and joyful thing. It raises puzzling questions not easily answered. Resurrection life, which calls us by name and urges us to bring a message of life and hope to others, is not always welcomed with open arms. Most of us feel pretty preoccupied with our own lives, earning a living, getting ahead, having a little fun in life. Very few of us feel an automatic urge to jump up and say, Me Lord, Send Me! Resurrection life, which holds out hands that have been nailed and a side that has been pierced, is seldom what we would boldly choose for ourselves. When we look at the wounds and the pain, we are apt to pause and wonder if there might not be a more comfortable although possibly duller way to live? When violence and hatred threaten us, we run, we lock the doors.

Resurrection life begins wherever one heart opens to another, wherever righteous attitudes are built, wherever goodness triumphs over the instincts of hatred.

What about you? What about me? What doors have we kept locked out of fear? What doors do we need to open? Who do we need to share a message of hope with? Where do we need to create a space for God's righteousness in the midst of fear?

by Rev. Nancy Landauer

The true story, above, as told by American Red Cross worker Nancy Landauer, depicts a single, horrifying incident in 1970 that provoked fear, anger, confusion, and unease in several Vietnam veterans and Red Cross workers in America, not Vietnam. Now a Methodist minister, Rev. Landauer told the story from the pulpit of her church nearly 30 years later through her eyes of religious wisdom and insight. The story was condensed from a sermon, April 1998.

I Only See Blue Pajamas

Hatred is difficult to overcome. When we see attitudes of hatred that will lead to violence, we may feel disgusted, we may feel frightened, we surely want to turn around and walk away. When we look in our own hearts, we know we have our own prejudices and biases that rightly or wrongly we cling to out of ignorance or perhaps out of fear of the unknown. It is difficult to develop an open heart, a heart that can be changed by another. Creating room for God often means letting go of our own dearly held biases, or it can mean reaching out a hand of love and caring.

The day I arrived to go to work in San Antonio, I met another young woman who had also just arrived to work for the Red Cross. In the morning we went through our Red Cross orientation together, and in the afternoon we set out to look for apartments to rent. We each rented an apartment in the same apartment complex. We drove to work together every morning, and we became the best of friends.

My new friend's name was Jalah. She was born and raised in the black ghetto section of Dallas. She had come from what I thought of as a stereotype background. Her father had deserted the family. Her mother worked as a maid for white people to support and raise her two daughters. Fortunately for Jalah and her sister, they graduated from high school and were ready for college during Lyndon Johnson's economic push for what he called the Great Society. Both Jalah and her sister got scholarships for college from Johnson's Great Society programs.

After college it took Jalah a year to find a job. When at last she was hired by the Red Cross, her hometown paper thought it was such a marvelous event that they ran Jalah's picture and a story about her new job. Jalah told me that after that story ran in the newspaper, she received bags full of mail for a month. People in the black community were overjoyed and proud of her success.

The racial tensions that erupted in a riot that summer were certainly felt at Brooke Army Hospital at Fort Sam Houston where we worked. Jalah worked on a large orthopedic ward. Most of her patients were black, but she also had quite a few white patients. White and black patients didn't mix. They kept to their separate side of the hospital ward. Jalah was an outgoing person. She spent time chatting and getting acquainted with both white and black patients. One afternoon a particularly aggressive group of black patients surrounded Jalah after she had come on the ward. They were angry. They thought she had spent too much time with white patients. They said she was a disgrace, only they didn't say disgrace, they used harsher words, humiliating words. Jalah rose to the occasion. With a smile on her face, she defused the situation.

"Why, when I come on this ward I don't see no black, and I don't see no white. The only color I see on this ward is blue pajamas," she said.

The soldiers couldn't help but smile. They relaxed. They began to understand that Jalah was a professional doing the job she was paid to do. Jalah created an opening for peace and acceptance and tolerance. Jalah created a space for God on that hospital ward.

by Rev. Nancy Landauer

Contact Rev. Nancy Landauer by e-mail at nland@montereybay.com.

CHAPTER 21

Nightingale Mom

Sometime they'll give a war and nobody will come.
                              Carl Sandburg, 1878–1967

Phyllis Nelson graduated from nursing school in 1945, at the end of World War II. "I would have gone into the Army as a nurse upon graduation, but the war ended," Phyllis said. She married Eddie Nelson, an Army career man, and lived at various bases in the United States and Germany for the next 20 years. The following is Phyllis' story about her nursing experience with the Vietnam veterans at Fitzsimons Army Medical Center, Denver, Colorado.

The War Comes Home

Eddie returned from Korea in 1967 and retired from the Army later that year. I had begun my nursing career again on August 1, 1966, at Fitzsimons Army Medical Center (known as FAMC), assigned to the Orthopedic Ward on the fifth floor. I was told that many amputees transported back from Vietnam were transferred to FAMC and the job would be very demanding.

I was assigned to be the dressing nurse. The ward was short of staff and all beds were full, so I knew there was plenty of work ahead of me. I went to the dressing room, set up my dressing cart, and started my nursing care. At each bed, I assured the patient I was there to do the best I could for them. Some had only one limb missing; some were multiple amputees. There were many in very serious condition. The one thing I am most proud of is that not a single amputee ever died on my shift, though many were barely hanging on when they first came to FAMC.

As time went along, many patients became attached to me. I was old enough to be their mother, and in time they started calling me Mom or Ma. That was very touching to me, and I was very proud to have them call me Mom and fully put their trust in me. It wasn't long before I was helping remove shipping casts from patients and putting amputees in traction as well as doing my dressings. Shipping casts were casts that were put on in Vietnam and stayed on until the patients arrived at Fitzsimons. This situation could get ugly.

I remember one time I was helping to remove the shipping cast from a patient's leg when we discovered his wound full of maggots. The doctor's eyes almost popped out of his head and slowly he slid to the floor—he had never seen this before and it was a little too much for him. Actually, maggots eat only dead flesh, so while it looked bad, it wasn't hurting the patient.

Some of the patients stayed in the hospital as long as several years, and many came back for yearly follow-ups, so I have kept in close contact with "my boys" over the years. When they came back, they always asked for Mom or Ma. If I wasn't working that day, they would stop by the house to see me. Now, after being retired almost 20 years, I still see some of my boys. Some travel here to Colorado to see me, and some we visit when Eddie and I are in their areas.

As patients started healing and could travel, the doctors would allow them to take leave. We had a station wagon and would take patients to the airport and be there when they returned. We also treated them to pizza from time to time. One day, our son-in-law had a party at his restaurant for all the patients who could leave the hospital plus some of the doctors. Everything to eat and drink was on the house. There were wheelchairs all over the place and we all had a grand time.

In all my years of work, all the patients were wonderful—they accepted their losses and got on with their lives. To see these men race down the corridors doing wheelies almost made my heart stop, but they rolled with the punches! While in the hospital, some learned to ski on one leg, some rode horses, and others took oil painting lessons taught by a retired colonel. One amputee even became a skydiver, and landed in the nearby Cherry Creek Reservoir for pick up. One bought a plane and did a lot of flying. I have photos of most of them, since I always had my camera with me and ready to capture unusual happenings or just a photo of one of my boys.

In April 1981, I was forced to retire due to arthritis in my joints, which made it hard to walk and keep pace with the grinding work on the ward. I reported to Civilian Personnel to start the retirement paperwork, which I thought would take six months for approval. They took one look at me and retired me effective that day! I was in shock when that happened, thinking I'd have to struggle on a few more months. It was very difficult to leave the ward after 16 years of working with the amputees whom I dearly loved.

During the winter of 1991, I received a letter from a former patient of mine, who said that he and another former patient wanted to submit my name in nomination for a Nightingale Award, a prestigious nursing award. They sent me paperwork to fill out, which involved telling my life story and about my nursing experiences. I told Eddie that it was wonderful to be considered for such an honor, since I had been out of nursing for 10 years. Many of my former patients were asked to write a letter about the care they had received from me at Fitzsimons, and most answered with glowing reports.

There were 229 names submitted for the six awards. After considerable time spent reviewing all nominations, 15 nurses were selected as finalists. The Nightingale Awards dinner took place on May 9, 1992. Our daughter, Cheryl, and son, Gary, and his wife, Janice, were at our table, as well as the two former patients who had handled all the paperwork leading up to this moment.

After dinner they started the program. The first five winners were called, and we were sitting on pins and needles awaiting the sixth and final name. Finally the announcement was made: "The winner is Phyllis Nelson!" I thought my daughter was going to pass out from screaming and jumping up and down. She was the most excited person in the room. I'll never forget the thrill of this moment, and thinking of the two men who did the groundwork and of all my boys for their touching letters that led to this honor.

Here is the final write up for the award. While I was not technically an Army nurse, as the statement says, I worked in Army facilities as a civilian and did the same work.

> Join the Army and see the world. That's what PHYLLIS NELSON did. As a Civil Service nurse, she saw Louisiana, New Jersey, Indiana and Frankfurt, Germany. And she saw Vietnam, as that war came home to Ward 5 East, Men's Orthopedic, Fitzsimons Hospital. That was not a pretty sight.
>
> In war, things blow up, frequently under, beside, or on top of human bodies. Human bodies are surprisingly sturdy but not built to withstand being blown up. Consequently, repair is long, difficult, frustrating and ugly. But that's what Army nurses are for. So Phyllis did her job, which it's best not to describe.

In addition to her job, she cooked, sewed, wrote letters, shopped, and took her boys out for pizza. And always she taught that it's possible to be a whole person, even if missing a few body parts.

Actually, she wasn't a nurse so much as she was a housemother. She has alumni all over the country who call her "Mom." They owe a debt of endless gratitude to a doctor whose children Phyllis babysat when she was herself a child. He thought she should be a nurse. She agreed but couldn't afford the expense of education. He arranged for her scholarship, thus ranking among the world's most successful mentors.

Phyllis says she learned her philosophy of caring from her patients: Never give up, work hard to get well, and get on with your life.

And that's what I've always tried to do.

by Phyllis Nelson

CHAPTER 22

FYI

Real joy comes not from ease or riches or from the praise of others, but from doing something worthwhile.
                              Wilfred Grenfell, 1865–1940

For Your Information

Between 1954 and 1975, Vietnam was divided into Viet-Nam Cong-Hoa (Republic of Viet Nam in the South) and Viet Nam Dan Chu Cong Hoa in the North. On April 30, 1975, Saigon fell to the Communists. Saigon became Ho Chi Min City and North and South Vietnam reunified as Cong Hoa Xa Hoi Chu Nghia Viet Nam (Socialist Republic of Viet Nam).

In 1969, over 200,000 Americans participated in an anti-Vietnam War demonstration in Washington, D. C.

The first two Americans to die in the Vietnam conflict were military advisors in 1959.

The United States spent over $140 billion on the Vietnam War.

Vietnam Veterans made up nearly 10% of their generation.

From 1960 to 1964, the U.S. had military advisors in Vietnam; 50,000 personnel served during this time.

In April of 1968, 543,482 personnel were in Vietnam—peak troop strength during the war.

The youngest American soldier to die in Vietnam was 16, the oldest was 62.

The average age of the fighting soldier in Vietnam was 22.

In addition to the United States, Australia, New Zealand, Thailand, Korea, and the Philippines also sent military forces to the aid of South Vietnam. Australia, New Zealand, and the U.S. were the only nations that paid their own way.

Operation Babylift

In the spring of 1975, thousands of South Vietnam refugees fled their country as the North Vietnamese gained control. By the end of that year, 132,000 South Vietnamese refugees had emigrated to the United States. Thousands of others found their way into Europe, Australia, and Canada.

In early April of that year, President Gerald Ford authorized thirty flights of children out of South Vietnam. Known as Operation Babylift, approximately 3,500 children were evacuated to the United States, Australia, and some European countries where the babies and children were adopted by waiting families.

The two million dollar project met with tragedy April 5, 1975, when a C-5A Galaxy, military transport plane, crashed outside of Saigon. Over 300 children and adults were on board; nearly half died in the crash caused by an explosion.

Where is Vietnam?

Today's communist government of the Socialist Republic of Viet Nam is divided into 58 provinces with Hanoi as the capital city. Although Viet Nam's land area (325,360 square kilometers) is a little bigger than that of New Mexico in the United States, it stretches along the Gulf of Tonkin, Gulf of Thailand, and the South China Sea next to China, Laos, and Cambodia for 2,152.5 miles in Southeast Asia. Over 78,773,873 people inhabit Viet Nam today.

What They Said

"These people who say that we ought to withdraw from Vietnam are wholly wrong, because if we withdrew from Vietnam, the Communists would control Vietnam."
President John F. Kennedy (1917–1963), president of the United States 1961–1963, stated September 1963.

"This is not a jungle war, but a struggle for freedom on every front of human activity."
President Lyndon B. Johnson (1908–1973), president of the United States 1963–1969, stated August 1964.

"I do not find it easy to send the flower of our youth, our finest young men into battle. I have seen them in a thousand streets, of a hundred towns in every state in this Union, working and laughing and

building and filled with hope and life. But as long as there are men who hate and destroy, we must have the courage to resist."
President Lyndon B. Johnson (1908–1973), stated July 1965.

"We should declare war on North Vietnam....We could pave the whole country and put parking strips on it, and still be home by Christmas."
Ronald Reagan (1911–present), president of the United States 1981–1989, stated October 1965.

"Let us understand: North Vietnam cannot defeat or humiliate the United States. Only Americans can do that."
Richard Nixon (1913–1994), president of the United States 1969–1974, stated November 1969.

"The Vietcong are going to collapse within weeks. Not months, but weeks."
Walt Whitman Rostow (1916–present), chairman of the policy planning council of the State Dept. 1961–66; and special assistant to President Lyndon B. Johnson 1966–69.

"In a war, it is natural that there are losses and sacrifices. Our people are determined to fight on. We will endure all sacrifice for ten years, 20 years or longer, until complete victory."
Ho Chi Minh (1890–1969), president of North Vietnam, 1954–1969.

"If the United States now were to throw in the towel and come home and the Communists took over South Vietnam, then all over Southeast Asia, all over the Pacific, in the Mideast, in Europe, in the world, the United States would suffer a blow. And peace—because we are the great peace-keeping nation in the world today, because of our power—would suffer a blow from which it might not recover."

President Richard M. Nixon (1913–1994), stated March 1971.

"A cease-fire, internationally supervised, will begin at 7:00 p.m. this Saturday, January 27, Washington time. Within 60 days from this Saturday, all Americans held prisoners of war throughout Indochina will be released. There will be the fullest possible accounting for all of those who are missing in action. During the same 60-day period, all American forces will be withdrawn from South Vietnam. The people of South Vietnam have been guaranteed the right to determine their own future."
President Richard M. Nixon (1913–1994), stated January 23, 1973.

"I viewed it (Vietnam War) as a genuine tragedy."
Henry Kissinger (1923–present), Secretary of State, 1973–1977.

Who Was Ho Chi Minh?

Ho Chi Minh, born as Nguyen Sinh Cung in 1890, was the first president of North Vietnam from 1945 until his death in 1969.

He left Vietnam in 1911, living and traveling in London, France, Moscow, Hong Kong, and even the United States. During his travels, he changed his name to Ho Chi Minh, "He Who Enlightens." Ho Chi Minh was a founding member of the French Communist party in the 1920s, and founded the Indochinese Communist Party in Hong Kong.

After returning to Viet Nam in 1941, he organized a Vietnamese independence movement, the Viet Minh and led the fight for Vietnamese independence from France. He continued his fight for communism until his death.

Why Vietnam?

We have today concluded an agreement to end the war and bring peace with honor in Vietnam and Southeast Asia.
             President Richard M. Nixon, January 23, 1973

By early spring of 1973, the United States had pulled out the last remaining American troops from Vietnam. It had been almost 10 years since the government had informed the United States public that we could resolve this Vietnam conflict in a matter of weeks.

Why were we there? Why had it taken so long, over a decade, to bring our Americans home? Volumes have been written on the history of Vietnam and the American involvement in that war. Many myths as well as false assumptions have been printed over the years. As former President Richard M. Nixon said in 1985, "No event in American history is more misunderstood than the Vietnam War. It was misreported then, and it is misremembered now."

In short, in the summer of 1964, North Vietnamese attacked U.S. Navy vessels in the Gulf of Tonkin. The bottom line was, as President Lyndon B. Johnson announced in a televised speech, we were going to send troops to Vietnam. Although the United States had already given over $1 billion in aid between 1955 and 1961, President John F. Kennedy tripled this amount in 1963 and increased the number of U.S. military advisers in Vietnam from 700 to over 16,000. Now, in 1964, President Johnson was going to send military force. Over the next decade, over 58,000 Americans going to Vietnam would not come home alive. Over 11,400 of those men were under 20 years old.

The United States government's stated objective as to the independence of South Vietnam and President Lyndon B. Johnson's quote, "This is not a jungle war, but a struggle for freedom on every front of human activity," did not go over well with most of the American public. Protests in Washington, D.C., demonstrations on college campuses, and a general attitude of opposition toward the war prevailed through the late 1960s and into the early 1970s. Many Americans turned their anger on the veterans returning from their Vietnam tours—veterans who had gone to war because their country sent them. To these courageous men who obeyed the call of their country, dodging the draft was not an option. According to the Veterans of Foreign Wars, only 25% of those sent to Vietnam were actually drafted. Compare this to World War II in which 66% of the military force was drafted.

The Tet Offensive in January of 1968 convinced General William Westmoreland, the U.S. commander in Vietnam, that the end of the war was not in sight. President Johnson began Vietnamization—reducing the American troops in Vietnam and letting the South Vietnamese take more responsibility for their own conflict. Finally, the United States and North Vietnam signed the Paris Peace Agreement in January of 1973. This agreement provided a cease-fire and the withdrawal of all remaining U.S. military forces from Vietnam. It also included the return of U.S. prisoners of war. The war continued without the Americans until the fall of Saigon in April of 1975 when Saigon became Ho Chi Minh City.

There is no simple answer to the question, "Why?" For two and a half million Americans who were there, perhaps "why" is no longer a question they ask. "How do I live with these memories?" might be a more grounded question. The Vietnam veterans have endeavored over the past few decades to make successful and happy lives for themselves and to come to terms, each in his and her own way, with a one year tour of duty, longer for some.

For many, however, that one year does not stay in the past. It returns again and again in dreams, in nightmares, in recurring movies in their heads. Living with these memories is harder for some than others. Vietnam veterans have found ways to cope with their horrific war memories through therapy, religion, veterans' groups, and for some, writing.

Writing novels, stories, and poetry is a healing way for veterans to share their experiences with other veterans, their families, and friends.

Not all of the memories are bad. Some veterans recall the happy moments, the shared camaraderie, and the knowledge that they were doing something important for those who needed them most.

Note: Statistics used in this book were provided by the Office of Reports and Statistics, Veterans Administration, Washington, D.C., Combat Area Casualty File, Center for Electronic Records, National Archives, Washington, D.C., and The Veterans of Foreign Wars.

CHAPTER 23

Love Stories and Poems

O lyric Love, half angel and half bird
And all a wonder and a wild desire.
                    Robert Browning, 1812–1889

Although there was nothing romantic about the Vietnam War, there are love stories from that time. Such as Patty Bright and Steve Fortenberry who met while Patty was an American Red Cross Donut Dolly and Steve was serving with the 1st Infantry Division in Lai Khe in 1967 (chapter 10).

James "Mike" Hopkins, and Deanna (Shlee) Hopkins met years after the war, but it was through both of their work regarding Vietnam that they had the opportunity to meet at all.

A Moment

A gentle kiss upon my cheek,
From a lover so discreet;
Slow has been his love to show,
He does not know I love him so.
From my sleep I awake,
To be held in his embrace;

I never thought that I would find,
Someone so caring and so kind.
I thank God for you every day,
That he placed you in my way;
I was lost in this dark life,
You bring the sun into this strife.
My heart has hope, lost joy in measure,
Each day I discover you are a treasure
That never did I think I'd find,
You take the hurt from this world of mine.
Best friends we are, as well as lovers, too,
You watch over me; I do the same for you;
One we are, and think and speak the same,
Hold me now, forever, and speak my name.

by Deanna Gail Shlee, 1996, to James Michael Hopkins

Deanna's Love Story

I marvel at how destiny works—if not for my keeping my dream of going to college alive for 28 years, and finally attending college, and touching a computer for the first time in my life, and finding the Internet, and Bill McBride (the creator of Vietnam Veterans Home Page, VVHP, http://vets.appliedphysics.swri.edu/), I would not be here.

My Vigil at the Vietnam Wall and the VVHP Web site certainly had a lot to do with my journey. And, this journey led me to Mike (James M. Hopkins), my husband.

I had worked on the VVHP Web site for awhile as editor, but then I had to go back East for the summer (as I usually did to stay with my daughter and help her with her three children when they got out of school, as she was a single, working mother). I was then also Squad Leader of the VVHP's Remembrance Section, and I turned it over to someone else, Roger Herrick, to handle the e-mails and material coming in for that section while I was gone.

That summer, Mike wrote to the Remembrance Section contact e-mail point (which had changed from me to my "stand in," Roger) and submitted material to start this Gallery of his now on the VVHP. I had no idea this was going on because I was gone with no computer contact.

I returned home in the fall (I was living in Arizona then) and went back online in Remembrance. It was a sheer accident that Mike thought I was Roger when he e-mailed the Remembrance Section again on something, using Roger's name! I e-mailed back, copying Roger, saying he had made a mistake, and that I was copying his comms to Roger to handle.

Mike e-mailed me back that if he had to make a mistake, he was glad it was with me—the flirt! We started to e-mail back and forth all day and into the night, and Mike would also call me long distance from Texas.

The following summer, when I told him of my annual trek, he invited me to stop by on my way for coffee. Well, that cup of coffee turned into a week. He slept on the couch in the family room and gave me his bed in the master bedroom. After a few days at his home, and we had come to know one another better, he would brew a fresh pot of coffee in the mornings. He would bring me a cup before I got up and set it on the nightstand by my bed. He had already painted the "cup of coffee" some time before I even knew him. It fit perfectly with the time of the poem. (James M. Hopkins also is an artist.)

This time, however, I had a "computer, will travel" in the back seat of my car; and got online when I got back to my daughter's with a local provider there. Mike and I continued to e-mail and call on the phone. He e-mailed he wanted me to stop by again on the way home (to Arizona) to talk about and see if there was a future for us. At the end of summer, I did just that! We have been together ever since and finally married—a very successful Internet Romance!

by Deanna Gail Shlee Hopkins.

Deanna Shlee Hopkins is the author of *My Vigil at the Vietnam Wall*, copyright 1989. She was awarded first place for non-fiction in *The Traveler*, a literary and creative arts magazine for this article. See *Vigil* at http://vets.appliedphysics.swri.edu/dgs.htm for a complete copy of this article that has been read at National and Regional Collegiate and University Honor Conventions and Leadership Conferences. See http://vets.appliedphysics.swri.edu/history3.htm for a history of the Vietnam Veterans Home Page.

More of the Hopkins' Web sites are:

A Circle of Friends at http://gecko.gc.maricopa.edu/~dgshleeh

"*Circle* was created to publish writings by our 'circle of friends' about any subject, not just Vietnam War related."

James M. Hopkins

Deanna's Stories—Life's Flavors at http://gecko.gc.maricopa.edu/~dgshleeh/dsstorie.htm is "Special moments of life, thoughts about our future, wishes for what could be."

Deanna Shlee Hopkins

Love's Good Vibrations

I feel your loving vibration,
A delightfully caressing sensation,
Suddenly a sacred silence
Pleasured stillness…
An omen of carnal presence
Of sweet honeyed revelation
Portent of spiritual manifestation
That shatters the soul,
Permeates being whole…

Sultry fevered wine,
Worldly yet heavenly divine
Within and without me
To the very core of me
Don't you see,
Your loving word
Sanctified in a celestial sword
Pulsates
Vibrates
Soothing me
Comforting like unto waves of the sea.

In sweetest fragrant bouquet
I lay,
All cares dissolving
Broken by light of morning
Mid aromatic scent
Of heaven sent
Rejoicing
In sweetened dawning…

Love's cadence flows as ethereal poetry
Immodest rhythms harmony
Of purely unblemished love
Holy from above…
An act of supreme devotion
Fulfilling Godly consecration
Heavenly procreation.
Fluttering on gossamer wings
In true art the heart truly sings.

Enjoy the balance of divine symmetry
Immaculate chemistry
Played out in dark somber night,
Delicate delight…
Shimmering light…
Bearing sweetness of French pastry
Noblest gallantry.

Dark till that fate laced hour,
Light of life sweet thrills empower,
Softest whispering hearing,
Flailing human hearts beating
Love at times looms so distant,
So devilishly persistent,
My soul capturing
The sacred inspiring
Endearing being possessing
Consecrating…

In sanctified communion
Comes deeply spiritual union,
Your longing heart meets mine,
Aspiring to share the divine,
Shoved against me breathlessly,
Suddenly passionately,
In true loves dance of desire,
That sets souls on fire
Causing spirit flows
Of divine rapturous throes…

I close my eyes and you I feel,
Your body delicious hurtings heal

All around me real,
Tenderly vibrating
With sweet ecstasy,
In chivalry
Pleasuring me.

I find myself suddenly
Consumed with divine deviltry
sacred idolatry
At your thrilling embrace
Fragrant lace,
Racing in my blood of torrid pace.

Your sweet nearness blossoming
Senses coming alive exciting
Pumps a captivating perfume
Cupid's arrow shot with sweetest doom.
Pricking my skin with its longing,
Enthralled in silent belonging.

In the presence of your holy essence
Sharing life's delicious effervescence
Searing my brain.
Drive me nigh insane.
You are the harmony of life's song,
For which I fervently long.

Your beauty brings me to my knees
Singing sweetest melodies.
I drink your kisses
Drunk with the wine bliss is.

Drinking in abiding ardor
Delectable honeyed nectar
With abandon so sweet,
Lacking of discretion indiscreet.

I hunger for your coy innocence,
Shining radiance,
Mesmerized by charms
That totally disarm
Besieged by you,
Captured by you,
Already missing you.

Your chanted mantra lulls me,
Entices me to be,
A flowing stream in dream I see,
Erotically innocent
Expressive love amatory
Inflammatory,
Imprisoned in being magnificent
Mesmerizing my soul,
Hypnotizing a spirit's whole.

The seed of you,
The immaculate power of you,
Forever is planted in my being.
I want to spend a lifetime
You always seeing.
I want to live with you,
Walk with you,
Talk with you,

Grow old with you,
Die with you.

by Gary Jacobson

Love and War

He was always in such command of himself; one of those rough and tumble sort of guys, charismatic—drawing you in like gravity. The kind of man people love in spite of themselves. We met in his mess hall one day in December 1967, a few days before Christmas. He just came through the chow line with some of the other officers, looked directly at me and smiled. I just slopped the food on his tray, not taking my eyes from his gaze, feeling the instant, electric rapport. Zap! Just like that. No denying what had just transpired.

He kept a very tightly run outfit, riding herd on his men if they were anything less than disciplined troops, but he was also sensitive to their needs. Known for being smart and tactically savvy, the men just seemed to have an understanding about him, and I think they would have followed him anywhere.

We'd see each other every now and then after that day, talking for hours, sharing things from deep within, shedding the facade that we usually hide behind when forming relationships in the States. That's rather the way it was most of the time with all the soldiers over there. Nobody pretended, and nobody spent precious time with small talk and meaningless chatter.

Some of the time he'd show up at the Recreation Center without wearing his rank. This was significant because we kept the Rec Center only for enlisted men, and he could just slip in if he didn't wear his rank. He'd come in, wearing a huge grin and watch me squirm, knowing full well I wouldn't say anything. And he'd pull me aside and make sure his unit was on our schedule for the next day. Even if it wasn't, I'd wind up making changes so we'd be there. And, yes, it was partly because he wanted to see me, but also because he knew his men would only be in base camp a couple of days, and he knew they'd like having the Donut Dollies there. It was always hard to tell him, "No." To this day I remember that magnetic pull he had. I just wanted to say, "Yes," to him. He made things make sense to me.

One evening at an officers' get-together, we were holding hands, having a good time, when another officer, new in country, engaged him in conversation. They had been in Germany together and started reminiscing about the good times they both had there with their wives and children. It didn't take long for the light bulb to go on and the red flag to start waving, so I walked out. He caught up to me, explaining that his "marriage was over," etc., which I didn't believe. Getting involved with a married man started looking like a possible merry-go-round ride to me, and I wasn't about to set myself up as a home wrecker. It changed the relationship, and I suppose, looking back on it, that I was pretty stunned and hurt. I was young, naive, and thought I loved him. He had this ability to just draw me in.

The night before his unit was to go back to the field, two of his men showed up in a jeep at the Rec Center and "kidnapped" me. He had instructed them to, "Go get her, bring her back, and don't come back without her." I wasn't about to go along with them, so they literally picked me up, put me in the jeep, and drove off. Once back at their unit, he met me, and we spent the rest of the night together until he had to move out in the morning. There we were, on a rubber tree plantation, in the middle of the war at the onset of the Tet Offensive, and I was having a very romantic evening, just as if things were normal. However, there were a few exceptions. Instead of the latest "hot" car, this date was in an Army Track. I was wearing my "high fashion" blue uniform, and he was in combat boots and jungle fatigues perfumed with that indelible smell that never leaves your memory. Sounds ridiculous.

A few days later, two of his men showed up to tell me he had been hit during a firefight, and they took me to the hospital. Seeing him there, this mighty man, full of the fire of life, now resigned to a hospital bed, and tubes running in and out of his body, shocked me. To say that I suddenly "grew up" doesn't come close to describe the moment or the inexplicable feelings I had. But that's the best I can do. It all came together, and the "little girl" left me forever that day.

I read once that "Our souls are written in our eyes," and I believe it. I looked into his eyes that day and saw him…saw HIM…saw the pain and disappointment, the shock and unbelief, his battle, determination, his steel and courage, and the recognition of a future he had not planned on. He let me go then. I saw the look in his eyes and knew he was releasing me…letting me go…facing "Reality" square in the face and challenging it to get the best of him. Even in his pain he had more a grip on things than I did, and he knew what he had to say. They had told him he would be sent home, that he might not walk again, and I just couldn't believe that. I couldn't accept it. And my guess is, he wouldn't accept it either.

He basically told me that I needed to move on with my life, that he would never be a "whole" man again—the kind of man I would need. I fought that for a long time until he finally told me to "Get the hell out of here." I knew what he was doing, but I knew also he was right. I remember that moment vividly. I knew it was pride and pain, and his acceptance of reality speaking, but I turned my back then and walked out of his life, not allowing him to see my tears. I knew I'd never see him again. I was horrified with the reality of war and how personal it had become, and I was confused and hurt. But I also knew he was correct about life going on. I had a job to do…a job I loved. I knew I would keep going, knew his sheer mettle would see him through, but I also knew he would not be in my future.

I'll remember him and that moment all my life. I don't know whether or not he made it, and I'll probably never find out. I hope he went home to his family and is living a full and rewarding life just as I am. However, I'm sure it's best not to try and find him. We had an intense relationship, full of beautiful thoughts and moments caught somewhere between hope and rocket attacks. But some stories are best left to a beautiful memory. While that doesn't make them less precious, I realize that it's best to leave past loves alone, that we can wear them out in the effort to recapture them. We are wiser to leave them suspended in memory rather than demean it all by trying to bring them into the "Present." I knew when I walked away from him that I was leaving the "Past," and that the "Future" would hold something different for us both. As things turned out, the "Future" for me would be unbelievably wonderful, and come surprisingly sooner than I could have ever imagined. But I will treasure those days of my life, and my memory of this soldier's radiant smile and laughing eyes, and know that I experienced "Life" fully in those months of war—a time I would not trade for anything, and a memory of something beautiful that I will remember forever.

by A Vietnam Donut Dolly

An Affair To Remember

Lovers are like lilies
Wafting on fragranted breezes
In mystical fields Elysian
With heady bouquet of ambrosian
Far and beyond mortal fate
When souls find their mate
Find a true love affair
Gloriously remember times exceeding fair

Interwoven in sublime rhyme
Forever will knotted souls intertwine

Till the very end of time
Symbiotic relationship preordained to be
Interlaced for life meant for eternity
Star crossed destiny
Formed of celestial moods
Truly a love worthy of the Gods

Bless me with divine love exceeding tender
Perfect love to stand the test of time render
Pure love to confer immortality
Sanctified love most Holy
Yet rife with worldly pleasure
Beyond Idyllic measure

Doves fly from this mortal utopian
Revel in love's distilled Amazonian
Bearing bonds of tender strength
Love's accord on the same wavelength
Ever holding the invisible embrace
Forever enjoined in illusory lace

Even if true love is a million miles away
Chimerically in absence hallucinatory
Far and across the forever sea
Forever human heart's panacea
Walks in dreamy love's perfumed shadow
A true love abiding always at your elbow

Ever sparkling in fireworks phantasmagoric
Reaching in love to stars meteoric
A man and woman's spirit truly blends
Life partners bliss earth transcends

Minds of one thought
Desires together in sweet union wrought
Each worshipping the other more than self

In grand love monolithic
Eclipsing gender's gulf
Each is greater than the other
Eternal father, blessed mother
True love larger by far
Than the sum of its parts
A scriptural, tempestuous, earthy love
Fire and wind imparts
Given spiritually endowed hearts…

A love kissed by immortal essence
Veracious beneficence
Quietude's tranquil silence
In orbit around you spiraling care
Unwavering devotion genuinely share
Above rainbows whimsy perspective
Love for you
Just you
Love's central objective!

by Gary Jacobson

Read Gary Jacobson's story, *Gary's Angel,* chapter 7; read Gary's comments regarding September 11, 2001, *A Stronger America,* and *My Fellow Americans,* chapter 29.

My Visits With Jack

It is a festive night, this 1990 New Year's Eve, in a room full of people, music, and effervescent decorations. A floor length, black velvet dress elegantly covers my throat and arms while one elbow is propped at the end of a cherry wood bar. It is almost midnight, and the cloaked figure of the grim reaper is about to appear.

He stands in the doorway, the portal where all energy flows into and out of the room. Wearing the khaki uniform and gold insignia, Jack's black hair, deep blue eyes, and ready arms are balanced above a strong, healthy body. He glides toward me, streaming in golden light.

The countdown is launched as desire mounts to the midnight hour. My breath stops as our souls meet in the embrace of a lifetime—promises of ecstatic love that only one with a body can feel. His arms and hands slide over my second skin of burnished black, pulling my back, legs and head to him. In consensual union, an untapped womanhood awakens through a shared heart beating in our bosoms.

Whispering into each other's ears, lovers embrace for the first time in a physical caress. Our mouths meet and we swallow the other's essence. Shaking with the quake of the earth's joining together, midnight rings. As I hold his handsome head in both hands, the skin melts from my lover's face. Like petals from a flower stem, his muscles fall to the floor; only a skeleton remains in my arms.

A voice murmurs in the breeze, sweeping through the portal where he first stood. I awaken with the memory. "What did he say?"

I was extremely uncomfortable during the humid Midwest summers, but nothing in Chicago's weather could compare to the Southeast Asian climate. During the first month of my year in Quang Tri, Viet Nam, the influence of war was eating away at my ego strength. Plagued with homesickness during that hot January in 1970, my twenty-two-year-old body was totally out of its element with a mood that tipped the scales toward madness. It was just as wet outside my skin as it was inside, and I fancied that I would rather be a fish living in the South China Sea.

One auspicious day, my disposition was relieved from its corporeal discomfort when Jack walked through the emergency room doors of the 18th Surgical Hospital. He was with two other Australian soldiers. The regal men in their khakis and side-flipped slouch hats charmed everybody as they strode toward the desk where I was writing the roster assignment. I stood tall, attempting to look slender in spite of the water fill. A lumbering silence was broken when Brian Lawrance, the tallest of the three, introduced himself, and the other medical advisor, Mr. Clooney; and then, I shook hands with Jack. His touch offered a sense of comfort, reassuring this unsullied Army lieutenant with his firm and sustaining nature.

Brian suggested a visit to the adjacent children's hospital, and the nurse in charge said it would be a good idea for me to accompany them. While we walked, Clooney and Brian talked as I fell under the spell of their nostalgic native dialect. Jack was in country longer than his mates, and his swimming blue eyes under the thick dark brows captivated me. I wanted to know more about him, but I felt uncomfortable asking personal questions. He, however, seemed to return my fascination. Noticing our connection, Clooney posted his male pride and started to tell stories. When he revealed that Jack was married with children back in the Down Under, I turned quickly and picked up the pace to the corridor ahead.

The sight of children with frightful wounds and missing limbs made me angry. Jack picked up on the upset and asked questions about my home and how people in the U.S. felt about the war. His awareness of American geography and attitudes was more than what I knew about Australia. I enjoyed the discourse and attempted to glean knowledge from the more mature man. There was a slump in the conversation inside the Vietnamese part of the hospital as we watched the American RNs guiding the native nurses and healthcare givers in procedures.

Cultural differences were apparent with the lack of hygienic techniques. Families camped with the patients, and they cooked next to the beds. Spills were not cleaned.

Mama-sans tended to their children and smiled as we passed. At first, I thought they had no teeth, but then I saw black stubs. The teeth of the younger Vietnamese women were white, and I mentioned this to the Australian trio. Jack said that a lot of the Southeast Asian people were in the habit of chewing Betel nut.

"So the women add bugs to their diet?" I asked with uninformed amazement.

"The men chew it too, Di," said Jack with a resonance in his chest, using the shorter version of my name. I warmed at the familiar way he referred to me.

Clooney quipped, "The whole family gets a set of the pearly blacks, eh?" He laughed at his own cleverness, attempting to gain more power in the pecking order.

Brian returned the conversation back to civility stating that Betel nut elevates their moods but first stains red the teeth and gums. He named the plant Areca Catechu, stating that it grew like a vine everywhere in the South Pacific Islands. I was impressed with the knowledge of the Australian advisors for the ARVN (Army of the Republic of Vietnam).

I worked twelve-hour shifts, 0700 to 1900 hours, with one day off a week if we were lucky. Mr. Clooney visited frequently. Skilled in war medicine, he demonstrated ways to take care of injuries and cleanse wounds that I didn't learn in nursing school. When it was quiet on the frontlines (an oxymoron because the frontlines were everywhere), he would sit around with the medics and crack jokes. Clooney loved being the center of attention, and with each visit, he gave me a piece of clothing or a cosmetic from Hue City or Da Nang that made living conditions a little less miserable. He made me feel special, and I could overlook his ragamuffin sense of humor.

My visits with Jack were different. When he stopped in for a "cup o' java" after dinnertime, we exchanged polite conversation about the weather and safety of my unit.

"The children's hospital cares for Viet Cong kids, too, Di. Nothin'll happen to ya' here." I wanted to die when he said my name with his deep voice and accent. As I cared for the wounded men, he watched me with a far away look in his eyes. During those evening visits, his words never spoke the stories that I wanted to hear. There was so little time. He had to get back to the compound where the AATTV (Australian Army Teaching Team, Vietnam) was headquartered in Quang Tri City. The gate that closed the city off from Highway One went down at 2100 hours, and the Vietnamese soldiers often got trigger-happy. When I mentioned my concern to Jack about him getting shot, he placed his hand near where mine rested on the ER desk and gave a little smile. It seemed like nothing could touch him.

Brian was a friendly soul for the Americans, and we threw him a party at the club. Jack didn't come, and I questioned the advisors about him. Brian was indispensable to his mates, and Clooney became abrupt with my queries. He was getting jealous, and I didn't want to alienate a friendship that was taking a comfortable turn. In honor of the Australians, I painted a big red kangaroo opposite the white Ankh sign on the wooden façade of my hootch. The call sign over the radio waves for the Aussies was "Zulu," and I became known as Little Australian with the radio name of Mini-Zulu. They had honored me back, and I was learning that the war wasn't so bad as I settled into knowing people and making friends.

In the early part of April, there was a get-together for Army officials at the Australia House. I was invited to Da Nang, and I obtained an in country R&R for three days. My hopes to travel with Jack were crushed when he flew down, while Clooney and I took the scenic route in a jeep. We stopped at the Hai Van Pass, a picturesque elevation that overlooked rice paddies and the distant South China Sea. It was beautiful looking toward the ocean, but the mountains behind were cratered with pockmarks from earlier fallen bombs. I remember having seen a photo in the *National Geographic* from the early '60s of this same place where Clooney and I had stopped. The verdant low mountains were lush before the war ruined the countryside and scarred the face of our mother earth.

A few miles outside of our destination, we stretched our legs and gazed at the far-away sea. When Clooney slid an arm around my waist saying, "C'mere and give us a kiss," a shot rang out. I paid no attention to being fired at as I wondered how to discourage any further advances from him. The shots got louder, and he rushed me to the jeep. It almost overturned, rounding a curve. However, it was a mixed blessing, that sniper fire, as I didn't want to kiss Clooney and was more in a hurry to get to Da Nang. Strangely, I felt little fear as I sensed safety with thoughts of Jack being so near.

At the Australia House, the wall-to-wall accents were agonizingly beautiful, and I felt overwhelmed being the only woman in a large room full of alien men. Jack was nowhere to be found, and Clooney took me to a room to freshen up. I was to bunk alone, but he dropped his bags next to an adjacent bed. Staring at the duffel, I asked him where he was going to sleep. He said that the men's quarters were down the hall and suggested I rest before dinner. There would be speeches and toasts, and I learned later, the pomp and circumstance of the ANZAC (Australian and New Zealand Army Corps) spirit.

Clooney helped me off with my boots, and I removed the holster. I felt like Annie Oakley when I unbuckled the forty-five he had given me to wear for the trip. After placing the gun on a cabinet, I lay down in my fatigues and fell into a hypnogogic trance. In the middle of dreamland, he spooned in behind my back and got no complaint about the massage when his fingers masterfully took control. Hands can do an awful lot, and he proved his prowess of how to satisfy a woman. In my altered state, Clooney could have been any man, Jack, or George, my fiancé from whom I had to end the engagement after leaving for basic training. He wanted me to get pregnant as soon as possible to leave the Army. I was so sorry to have to break his heart, but Uncle Sam owned me before he did. Upon reflection of that painful time, I believe I made the right choice. I now think it's immoral to create a child and expect it to be responsible for the happiness of the parent's lives.

Clooney could have been Larry, my high school sweetheart or even Bob, a Medal of Honor winner, who courted me at Fort Knox. He said he would keep in touch as he left for another assignment in New Jersey; but after several letters, I learned from an acquaintance that he married a schoolteacher. I also learned from the force of the Universe that balances the energies of light and dark. The affair with Bob broke my heart in 1969, but the poetic Muse visiting Southeast Asia in April 1970, rewrote my life and altered my personal course of the war. Even though Clooney and I didn't engage sexually in the biblical sense, I fell mystically in love with a man the way a virgin would on her honeymoon.

Wanting to look less conspicuous in a room full of soldiers, I didn't wear civilian clothes to dinner. So, I laced up my boots, and he locked both our weapons inside the cabinet. The Muse had also vexed Clooney as an aura of magnetism glued us together. During that meal, he was not the prankster; even though awkward with the newfound familiarity, he was a perfect gentleman.

Toasts and speeches lived in their moment. Jack was at a nearby table as I sat in a blissful, awakened state of the new me. I wanted to be next to him, but he sat with the higher-ranking soldiers. When we made eye contact, he looked quickly away and I felt another energy. It was a heavy burden. Jack had to have sensed my transformation, and obtusely, it seemed like I had cheated on him. The sea of heads between Jack and myself became a protective barrier that helped to suspend my guilt.

The Muse drove back to Quang Tri with Clooney and me. She wrote the romance part about the lady lieutenant who careened with a sexy man inside a cozy jeep on a rainy day. The once sassy Aussie got no complaint when he'd say, "C'mere and give us a kiss." Upon return to duty, the sensations of ecstasy wore off as war with its death and destruction again became real. Clooney remained attentive, but I missed Jack. My shift changed to nights, and when I politely asked about Jack, Clooney said that he was out on a long reconnaissance mission advising the ARVN soldiers. During the nights, I often sensed a caliginous figure. Feeling Jack behind me, I turned to see no one there.

The monsoons started early that year, and some of the men who came in suffered from exposure and hypothermia. It was so different from the hot season when they were overheated and needed cold intravenous injections or had to be sprayed with a hose while standing in front of a large fan. Casualties picked up toward the middle of April. Helicopters were nonstop as they unloaded their victims, and around 0400 on April 17th, a cloaked figure walked in through the emergency room doors. This time, it was Jack. Nearly tripping over bloody bandages, I rushed to greet him. He pulled the poncho hood back, and I saw the familiar glint in his eyes when he tried to cover up a smile. "I thought you were out in the bush!" I said with a fatuous grin on my face.

"Hi, Di. I just stopped in for a cup o' java," he said, his voice throaty.

"Oh Jack, I would love to visit but..." I stammered, wanting to hug him through the cold and wet poncho, "...but these guys need so much."

He nodded knowingly. I went back to a wet soldier lying on a stretcher who was so cold that it was hard to get an IV into him.

I glanced up several times and saw Jack holding a paper cup to his lips sipping coffee. He watched me like he had so many times before, and I wondered why he would come to the emergency room so late in the night. He wasn't seeking medical attention. A little after the end of the shift, I looked for Jack but he was gone. There was so much I wanted to know about him and never had the chance to ask. Figuring that he went back to the bush, I followed the planks back to my hootch.

The morning sky had few clouds. I hoped for a sunny day since Clooney had noontime plans for us to take a jeep trip to one of the fire support bases. I sat on my cot staring at the picture of a gold, red, and black tunnel I painted on one of those rare days off. The white swirl at the center was pulling me into it when fast footsteps clanked on the planks between the hootches. They stopped at my door and a voice announced, "Lieutenant Sebek, you are needed in graves registration."

"What do they want? Nobody was sent from the emergency room last night," I said with a bit of a complaint in my voice.

"I don't know ma'am. He just told me to get you."

Before I could ask who "He" was, the unlaced boots were clopping back to the hospital.

"Does someone want to see me?" I asked the sergeant at the desk. The tables in the funereal anteroom of graves registration were empty.

"In the back, there is someone we think is an Australian," said the dark blond haired man who led me through a door. I attempted to search his face for the joke that Clooney was playing on me. I imagined the morose trickster hiding in a body bag just to jump out with a gift and ask for a kiss. Behind the door, there was a body bag on the floor. Thinking what a fool I was to fall for such a cheap trick, my body jolted as the sizzle of the unzipping rattled my sleepless nerves.

Inside was my dear Jack. His face was turned away, and I couldn't see his smile. He didn't move. I screamed, "Go get an ambu bag, we have to breathe for him." My knees bent in my want to resuscitate.

The sergeant pulled a chair under me before I fell to the floor and stated, "He's dead, ma'am."

Death punched me in the sternum.

"Do you know him?" Quietly asked the sergeant.

I sucked the breath back into my lungs, the breath that I wanted to send into Jack and make him live again.

"This soldier's name is Captain Jack Fitzgerald of the Australian Army. Please call the MACV (Military Assistance Command, Vietnam) compound in Quang Tri City, and tell them he is here."

I stared and noticed there was no blood, only a hole in his right temple. There was no insignia or identification on his uniform. My grief was too distant to feel. The Muse said to be glad that it wasn't Clooney, and my rage wanted to break the neck of an invisible enemy. When the bag was zipped up, I sent a part of my soul with Jack.

The only thing that existed was the sounds my boots made on the planks as I walked back to the one room with the red kangaroo that I slept in for the rest of my service in the war. Clooney attempted to make me forget, but I could talk with Brian about Jack. He offered a shoulder. As I washed his khakis with my tears, he spoke to me in the true ANZAC spirit about soldiers who were proud to live and die as a part of the corps.

Now, at times, I wonder if Vietnamese children play among the ruins of the military post. Do they look up at the red kangaroo and wonder? Does the Muse take them for magical rides on the tail of a mysterious animal? Twenty years after I left Viet Nam, Jack whispered to me in the dream. I think he was giving my soul back and said, "Thanks, Di, I don't need it anymore. It's time to move on."

On April 28, 2001, three days after ANZAC Day, Brian Lawrance died in Perth, Australia. He had lived a happy, full life, and his loved ones surrounded him when he passed on. I like to think of him being in the dreamtime with Jack and all their mates who served in the Australian New Zealand Army Corps. Brian is terribly missed, and I pray for Jack's family. I would like to comfort them with the knowledge that he was near somebody who cared during the last hours of his life.

by Diana Sebek

ANZAC Day

ANZAC Day, April 25, commemorates the Australian and New Zealand Army Corps soldiers' mateship, unity, courage, self-sacrifice and loyalty. Originating with the ANZAC who fought and lost their lives on Gallipoli Peninsula during an eight-month siege that began April 25, 1915, during World War I, Australians and New Zealanders pay tribute each April 25 to their military men and women. In recent times it has become the national day of remembrance for all Wars, including Vietnam as well as Peacekeeping Operations.

CHAPTER 24

Vietnam Light

*To be successful in business,
you will either need to find a need and fill it,
or find a hurt and heal it.*
          Dr. Robert H. Schuller, 1925–present

The following story contains excerpts from Ann Caddell Crawford's in-progress online book, *Vietnam Light.* In 1963, Ann traveled with her three children to live with her husband, Roy Crawford, a United States Army officer stationed in Saigon. The next year, Ann, Roy, and their three children returned to the United States. In 1967, Roy once again received orders to Vietnam. Due to the escalation of the war, Ann and the children lived in Bangkok during this tour.

Vietnam Light
Memoirs of an American Family in Vietnam
Circa 1962–1968

From Part I:

The year was 1963. The brand new World Airways Boeing 707 320C jet aircraft circled the Saigon Airport, known as Tan Son Nhut. As my three kids, all pre-schoolers, and I peered out our window and saw the purely agricultural countryside with Saigon not yet in view, I suddenly felt very nauseous. What in the world had I gotten us into?

From Part II: Where's Roy?

Roy took us to our temporary new home in Saigon at 117 Tran Qui Cap. It had two bedrooms and they were air conditioned!! In fact, I had never been in a room cooled to 65 degrees before when the temperature outside was near 100 with an equal amount of humidity. We were exhausted. When we woke the next day, Roy was really SUPER NICE to us...flowers were everywhere and he had not one but two household helpers there to assist us with everything. Somehow, he seemed just too solicitous.

"What's up?" I asked.

"Gosh, I don't know how to tell you this, doll,...but I'm on orders for several weeks TDY in Hawaii! I leave in just a few days." His office promised they would look out for us, but we didn't have a phone. The last word of warning Roy gave me was, "Whatever you do, stay in town, do not cross any bridges or you will be out in the boondocks, and it isn't safe!"

Two nights after Roy left, elements of the Viet Cong threw grenades into the Marine general's home just a few doors down the street! What a welcome. That kind of shook me up but I still had my chores to do, one of which was to register Roy, Jr. at the American Community School near Tan Son Nhut. He and I got in a cyclo (a pedicab where you ride in front and the man pedals a bicycle in the back). The maid told him where we wanted to go. We headed out Cong Ly Street, when all of a sudden I saw a bridge.

"Stop, stop, stop," I yelled, and waved my hands; there was no time to consult my Vietnamese dictionary. He did stop, and there we stood on one side of the bridge; the poor cyclo driver didn't know what he had done wrong! And, I had no way to explain it to him. After about twenty minutes, a U.S. military sedan came by and stopped.

"What's the matter, lady? Can we help?"

I told him Roy's last words to me before he left for Hawaii and that I had just been in the country a few days.

"Oh," he laughed, "don't worry about this bridge, he probably forgot about it…but lady, don't cross any other bridges, you hear?"

With that, I thanked them. Roy, Jr. and I sheepishly got back in the cyclo and rode about ten more minutes to the American school. I still had no way to explain my actions to the cyclo driver. I often wondered what he thought!

Now, this story goes on and on. I will tell you all about my life as a military wife who found herself and her young children in Vietnam during this historic time. There are many incidents both funny and sad, which will be fodder for my memoirs, *Vietnam Light*.

In short, during the first tour, I became accredited as a correspondent working part-time for several news agencies such as *Copley News Service, Newsday,* and the *Stars and Stripes*. Due to the nature of my being in the command as a military wife, I chose to write feature stories and illustrate them with my own photographs. In addition, I researched a book during our first Vietnam tour, which was published in 1966 by the Charles E. Tuttle Company of Rutland, Vermont, and Tokyo, Japan. It had been my intention to write about our unusual life in Vietnam, but Mr. Tuttle encouraged me to do the book, "Customs and Culture of Vietnam."

"It is badly needed and will be popular for years," he advised. "A memoir may only sell a few thousand copies," he said.

I took his advice, but did not particularly like the idea. I wanted to do something that was FUN!

Thirty-one years later, I have decided to write the memoir that I wanted to do back then. Over the years, I have published over 100 editions of helpful travel books for military families. There are deadlines every day. I figure that the only way I can write this book is to write it on the Internet…one story at a time. This book will continue as long as I have stories. Presently, it is unedited and written straight from my heart. Keep coming back to our Web site at http://www.militaryliving.com. Click on the Vietnam Connection and follow our lives in Nam under *Vietnam Light*.

From Part III: Who is Pulling This Short Tour Anyway?

During both tours, it was very easy for me to fly around the country as a correspondent, and my work was well received back home. I was definitely not the typical wartime correspondent covering "hard" news. I never covered the war in the jungles where many other correspondents were killed.

In fact, during the second tour, when we were in Nha-Trang when it was hit hard during the Tet Offensive, my main goal was to get out and back to Bangkok. Having a family definitely made a difference to me. Even so I've always been somewhat of a "chicken."

There were many hardships during our first family tour in Vietnam. After all was said and done, however, that first Vietnam tour became our favorite in 28 years of military service for Roy. Even though Roy's hours were long at work in Vietnam, it was still a great tour. And, we became "an old coup hand" in the process. We experienced three coup d'etats with all that goes with them while we lived there on our first tour.

We left Vietnam at the end of 1964. My book, *Customs and Culture of Vietnam*, was published in 1966. The very next year, Roy got orders for Vietnam again.

From Part V: Stop! Don't Drink That Water!

One thing we had to do every day was to purify our water and vegetables before eating them. The children had to be taught not to drink the water out of the faucet even when brushing their teeth. I was really afraid of the diseases I had read about which thrived in third world countries, so I considered this to be one of my first priorities.

My husband's office had given me a packet of information which showed where some of the U.S. military facilities were located. The kids and I managed to find the Navy health clinic, which was located adjacent to a small Special Services library and across from the American facility, the Capitol Kinh Do movie theater. Like our home, there were no real compounds at the time. American facilities were placed right in Vietnamese neighborhoods.

At the clinic, I asked how to purify the water and to make vegetables and fruits safe to eat. They gave me a pamphlet which gave instructions for boiling regular water for about twenty minutes and adding a teaspoon of Clorox bleach to each large pan of water. It then had to be filtered and put in jugs. We always kept a supply of purified water in the refrigerator. Vegetables and fruits were soaked in purified water with a small amount of bleach added. This solution was used to scrub the individual pieces and then they were washed with purified water.

I was so concerned about our children's health that I boiled the water twice as long as required. The vegetables and fruits tasted a lot like the smell of clean laundry washed with a whole cup of bleach. Just getting the food sanitized took a mighty long time each day.

From Part IX: Paranoia Pays Off

After a couple of weeks in Nam, paranoia set in. One thing I learned right away was how to avoid having a grenade catch you by surprise. Always sit with your back to the wall where you can see what is coming in the door! Even now, over thirty-five years later, I am still very uncomfortable if I have to sit with my back to a door.

When the Viet Cong tossed a grenade in Marine Major General Richard Weed's home, we learned the sound of a "bomb." The general's home was about a block or so away as the crow flies from our house. As I recall, not much damage was done. It may as well have been a warning shot across our bow! After that, we practiced hitting the floor and getting under whatever we could until the danger passed. This would be the first of many such sounds we would hear over the next two years.

In a way living in Saigon reminded me of World War II and the air raids held in my hometown of Birmingham, Alabama. As a child I thought that was so exciting. I decided that I would make this current situation a game with the kids. We had our own little drills with different scenarios called "What would we do if…" When the Navy bus picked up our two eldest children for Sunday School, they practiced looking for "bombs" under the bus before they got on.

The grenade tossed into the yard of the general's home made me even more anxious about the children's safety. I was greatly concerned that being the only "round eyes" on our street might make us a target, too. I was especially worried because I had no telephone.

by Ann Caddell Crawford

Ann Caddell Crawford is the founder of *Military Living Publications*. Started in 1969, it is still a family owned and operated business. Today, Ann's son, R.J. (Roy, Jr.) is the president of the company. (R.J. was in first and second grade in Saigon.) *Military Living Publications* is the largest publisher of military travel books, maps and atlases. View *Military Living* online at http://www.militaryliving.com.

Readers can enjoy Ann Caddell Crawford's *Vietnam Light, Memoirs of an American Family in Vietnam* at the Military Living Web site. Ann adds chapters periodically to the ongoing story.

Read Ann Caddell Crawford's book, *Customs and Cultures of Vietnam*, first published in 1966, at the Military Living's Vietnam Connection also at www.militaryliving.com. Ann's writing took her all over South Vietnam. While in Quin Nhon in 1967, she was able to visit her husband, Major Roy Crawford, who was the executive officer of the 41st Signal Battalion. Ann was doing some features on the local U.S. military hospitals in that city for *Copley News Service* at the time. See feature on Web site, militaryliving.com, *Viet Cong Get Good Surprise*.

To contact Ann C. Crawford, e-mail her at militaryliving@aol.com.

Jack and Kathy
Photo courtesy of Ann Caddell Crawford

What to do? No TV, no VCRs, no Video Games or Game Boys…BORING! That's when Ann called in a cyclo to ride two of her kids (Jack and Kathy) around her walled yard at 164 Phan Than Gian, Saigon.

Roy and the President
Photo courtesy of Ann Caddell Crawford

My son, Roy, Jr., met the new President of South Vietnam in a chance meeting in Saigon in February 1964. I had met General Khanh at several press conferences after he overthrew General Duong Van Minh in a bloodless coup d'etat. Recognizing me and seeing my son, he stopped and came over to chat. This meeting led to an exclusive interview with Mrs. Khanh, which was published worldwide by *Copley News Service*. My children were great icebreakers in South Vietnam and actually helped me a great deal in my work.
Ann Caddell Crawford

CHAPTER 25

Return to Vietnam

You can't go home again.
Thomas Wolfe, 1900–1938

My Thirty Year Anniversary Trip
Vietnam: August 1969–August 1999

When I was in elementary school, I remember writing more than once about what I did on my summer vacation. It never seemed that I ever did anything terribly important or exciting. As I continued on through junior high school, high school, and college, I no longer received writing assignments that involved chronicles of my uneventful, singularly uninteresting summer vacations.

The summer of 1969, though, was different, although no one ever assigned me to write about it. That was the summer that a human being walked on the moon and the summer of Woodstock. It was also the summer I graduated from the UCLA library school with a master's degree in library science and volunteered to go to Vietnam as a librarian with Army Special Services. Although I didn't realize it then, what I did that summer changed my life not just for the next year, but for all the years that followed. Now thirty of those years have passed, and it is

September again, so I am writing about my summer vacation just like I did in elementary school. This time, however, it was exciting and important, for me anyway, as I returned to the places where I spent a year in 1969–1970: Saigon, Cam Ranh Bay, Dong Ba Thin, and Nha Trang.

On August 16, I arrived in Taipei for four days of papers and presentations discussing new information technologies in libraries. Then it was off to Bangkok for another week of meetings at the annual conference of the International Federation of Library Associations. This was the business part of the trip.

I had never been to Taipei and I still feel as if I was never there. Except for a dash across the street to the Chiang Kaishek Memorial, a large walled compound with a plaza reminiscent of Tiananmen Square featuring a Lincolnesque statue of Chiang Kaishek inside a towering memorial hall, and a whirlwind visit to the National Palace Museum, every moment was spent in the sleek and modern auditorium of the National Library. I am particularly sorry that I was not able to see more of Taiwan, since the devastating earthquake that shook the island a month to the day after my departure, will surely have changed it greatly. I still don't know how the National Library staff and collections fared.

I have been to Bangkok many times since my first visit in 1969, but there were still some surprises. It didn't seem that it could be possible, but the incredible traffic and resulting pollution were worse than my last visit in 1992. The Thai hope that an elevated train, which was being tested while I was there, and a subway system that is under construction, will alleviate some of the congestion and improve breathing for the general population. The mass transit projects are certainly changing the face of Bangkok, the elevated railway in particular casting Sukhumvit and Ploenchit Roads into shadow. I was also surprised to discover a large and bustling Starbucks Coffee Shop on Ploenchit Road sandwiched between the J.W. Marriott and Holiday Inn Hotels.

Some things are still the same though. The hotels used by so many servicemen and women during R&R trips are still in business and thriving. I stayed at the Florida in 1969, and it is still there along with the Miami, the Honey, and the Ambassador. Even the names, chosen most likely to appeal to homesick American soldiers, have stayed the same.

On August 28, meetings and business completed, I flew on Thai Air from Bangkok to Ho Chi Minh City/Saigon. Vietnamese use both names almost interchangeably. As the plane landed at Tan Son Nhat Airport, the Muzak system was playing *Raindrops Keep Falling on My Head* by B.J. Thomas. It was a strange sensation. That was the very song that was popular when I landed at Tan Son Nhut Air Base on August 30, 1969. I remember hearing it on the radio again and again during the two months I spent in Saigon, blaring from the radio tuned to AFVN in the snack bar at the Meyerkord BOQ, as the rain pounded down on the tin roof. I was somewhat surprised to see the revetments, corrugated metal enclosures for airplanes and helicopters, still in place along the runway at Tan Son Nhat. Some held the rusty hulks of planes and choppers, but brand new modern versions nestled inside a few.

Driving into Saigon along the street we knew as Cong Ly, I was struck by the new construction and renovation, completed and in process, of both buildings and infrastructure. There was far less barbed wire hanging over walls and roofs. Large, modern, glass buildings surrounded the downtown area around the Cathedral and the old Presidential Palace now the Reunification Palace. Prominent on the river front at the end of Nguyen Hue was a large glass structure with Citibank emblazoned across the top. Sadly, the flower stalls down the center of Nguyen Hue between the river and Le Loi have been displaced to make room for skyscrapers and large, modern hotels. The flower market was a charming piece of old Saigon, even during the war, but times change and now they have been moved to an area where the real estate is less valuable.

I stayed at the newly enlarged and totally renovated Caravelle, now known as the Delta Caravelle, Hotel. The old dining room and roof bar is still a bar, but little else is recognizable. It is a five star hotel with CNN and HBO, a fitness center loaded with weights and treadmills, gourmet restaurants, and a lovely swimming pool. While I was there *Good Morning, Vietnam* was playing on late night television.

I walked to the places I remembered from 1969 and which I had gone back to 'visit' on my two previous trips in 1992 and 1994—the Meyerkord, the building where the Headquarters Area Command Special Services library had been located; the Rex Hotel, the Cathedral; the Splendid BOQ. Amazingly, they were all still there. The Meyerkord looks a little worse than it did on my last trip in 1994. It is now a school, the Ho Chi Minh City Institute of Science and Technology, and the bookstore is located on the site of the snack bar. Somehow this seemed fitting to me. The buildings where the library and the Splendid were located appeared to have undergone some renovation and really looked quite nice. The Rex had expanded into the space that used be occupied by the Rex movie theatre, the site of many bombings in the sixties. Next door was an expanded Federal Express office, larger than the previous location in the main post office. The Rex roof bar and the rooftop swimming pool looked much the same as they did in 1992 and 1994 and not a whole lot different from how they looked thirty years ago in 1969. A Parc Hyatt sat partially completed on the site of the Brink BOQ behind the Continental Palace Hotel.

Saigon was clearly undergoing a transformation fueled by the influx of loans and investment capital. It was no longer the Saigon of 1969, and I found myself saying Ho Chi Minh more and more. This too seemed fitting.

Bright and early the next morning, August 29, the guide and driver from Vido Tours collected me at the hotel, and we set off on the eight hour drive north on Highway 1 to Nha Trang.

Flashback: On August 29, 1969, at the Ontario, California, airport, I struggled, laden with luggage, up the steps into the Western Airlines plane that flew me to San Francisco where I caught to a bus to Travis Air Force Base to board a Braniff Airlines (contracted to the Military Air Transport Service (MATS)) flight to Saigon. Dressed in my brand new dark blue uniform complete with straight skirt, hose, black pumps, white gloves, and hat, I was totally unprepared for what I was about to encounter. In 1999 I was far better prepared, clothes-wise and otherwise.

As we drove out of Saigon toward Long Binh, I immediately noticed that the road had been improved and widened since I had traveled on it on the way to Vung Tau in 1994. The road improvements were still in process, and a large section of road on the outskirts of the city was under construction. Motorbikes seemed the most popular mode of transportation, displacing the bicycles, but not yet displaced themselves by automobiles. New businesses alongside the road included a mini-Disneyland amusement park and a water park.

Long Binh was a great surprise. In 1994 the area around the old USARV (U.S. Army, Vietnam) headquarters was barren and empty, with only a very few of the USARV buildings being used by the Vietnamese military. In 1999, it was a different place. An export or foreign trade zone had sprouted up on the land bordering Highway 1 below the hill where USARV headquarters had been. The area was bustling with activity, although the Saigon English language newspaper had mentioned that the rapid growth had included neither sufficient nor adequate housing for people from the provinces moving to the area to work in the new factories. On the corner, directly below the former location of USARV, where Highway 1 turns left toward Saigon, was a large supermarket attached to a mall. The guide said that this was a favorite spot for Saigonese to come on Saturday to do their grocery shopping. Motor bikes swirled around us with passengers holding tight to the morning's purchases.

We left Long Binh heading north through Xuan Loc on the way to Phan Thiet. The guide mentioned that his father had spent three years in a re-education camp in Long Thanh just outside Xuan Loc. He pointed out the site as we drove past. Highway 1 was newly paved and widened here also, leaving room for most traffic to move fairly rapidly. The road was filled with motorbikes, bicycles, and Saigon Tourist buses packed with Vietnamese on their way to a weekend holiday in Nha Trang. Recent floods had destroyed several bridges along the route, however, and passage over the temporary structures serving as interim bridges was reminiscent of the bus ride from Hanoi to Haiphong in 1992, when all traffic crossed rivers on railroad trestles. The guide volunteered that the flooding that had destroyed the bridges was the result of deforestation in the mountains.

Along the road were an amazing number of huge Roman Catholic cathedrals, far outnumbering and dwarfing the more modest Buddhist, Cao Dai, and Protestant temples and churches. The size and number of cathedrals reminded me very much of Quebec, where a large, Gothic cathedral was the centerpiece of every small town and village. There were also many, many graveyards, cemeteries, and tombs, often sitting in the middle of irrigated fields and paddies.

As we approached Phan Thiet, I spotted the first of many places for which I had received photo requests, Takou (Buddha) Mountain. After taking pictures in three different mediums (still, video, and digital), we drove through Phan Thiet, heading toward Phan Rang. The landscape changed very quickly becoming much more arid with fewer green fields and irrigated rice paddies. Although there is some rice cultivation in Binh Thuan and Ninh Thuan provinces, grape vineyards for the cultivation of table grapes, fishing and salt harvesting are the primary agricultural pursuits here.

Just south of Phan Rang, we stopped at a beautiful, small beach called Ca Na. Buses of Vietnamese on their way up the coast had also stopped here to admire the scenery, take pictures, and buy bunches of large purple grapes, peanuts, and pork and rice cakes wrapped in banana leaves from the many vendors along the beach.

North of Phan Rang, we encountered a turnpike! The local government had set up a toll plaza to raise funds to maintain the road between Ba Ngoi and Cam Ranh. As I had found to be true while driving in other areas of the south on previous trips, the villages along the road paralleling Cam Ranh peninsula were built-up, bustling, and looked fairly prosperous. The area looked nothing like it did in 1969, when instead of houses and shops there was a swath of deserted, desolate scrub reaching back from the road. Signs bore familiar names, Ba Ngoi, Cam Ranh, My Ca, Su Chinh, Dong Ba Thin. I recognized the road that had led to the My Ca bridge and checkpoint over which all traffic to and from Cam Ranh peninsula had to pass. Now the road was blocked by a gate, and a Vietnamese military installation occupied the area between the road and the bay.

Across the bay, I caught a glimpse of Cam Ranh peninsula. I was shocked by the fact that it was covered with trees, up onto the mountains that had split the peninsula down the middle and right down to the shore of the bay. I could not remember any trees on Cam Ranh, only sand and scrub. I wonder is this the fruits of a reforestation project? Even more, I wonder if trees were there before the Americans turned it into a giant supply base, and if so, where did they go? What wiped them out? Dioxin, perhaps?

We passed the site of the headquarters of the 18th Engineer Brigade in Dong Ba Thin. It is now a sprawling Vietnamese Army and Navy base with lots of new construction going on. The actual site of the 18th Engineers Headquarters, where one of my libraries was located, seemed to be a parade ground where Vietnamese sailors were marching and drilling.

Most of the land from Dong Ba Thin to Nha Trang was very built up, but some areas were still rural with rice paddies backing up against the side of the mountains, just as they did in 1969. Missing, though, were the charcoal kilns which had lined the side of the road in 1969. The guide said that they had been removed by the government in order to control pollution.

As we drove into the suburbs of Nha Trang, it was very difficult to recognize anything. Nha Trang is much bigger and there seem to be many more roundabouts (traffic circles). A beautification project was in progress, planting flowers and bushes down a newly constructed concrete median dividing the north and south-bound sides of Highway 1. I caught a glimpse of the large white Buddha sitting majestically on the hill. Practically everyone who spent any time in Nha Trang remembers the Buddha, and I had several requests for pictures of it. We passed the Nha Trang Cathedral and the train station and turned right at the Grand Hotel onto Tran Phu, the street known as Duy Tan in the sixties, that parallels the shoreline and the beautiful white sand beach overlooking the bright blue water of Nha Trang Bay.

We passed the street that had led to the 8th Field Hospital, and what had been the entrance to the Air Base and the Aerial Port, and to Camp McDermott past the CORDS and 8th PSYOPS compounds. Nothing looked the same, really. The city had expanded into much of the area. The Aerial Port is now the Nha Trang Municipal Airport. What had been Camp McDermott was mostly a huge vacant lot. This had been the case with other former U.S. military installations I had encountered on previous trips, so I wasn't surprised to see that it was no different here. While the Vietnamese military have taken over many of these installations, they seem to have no need for so much land, so a small portion is utilized and the rest is left to lie fallow. I probably would have had a very difficult time recognizing the specific areas at all, were I not able to get my bearings from the beach and the street.

My hotel (actually resort is the more appropriate term) was right across the street from the area where Camp McDermott had been located. I had come to this same beach in 1969–1970, and the sparkling white sand and beautiful warm azure sea was just as beautiful as I had remembered it. Many Vietnamese families and individuals enjoyed the beach along with the tourists who were mostly Japanese and European. I didn't encounter any other Americans. Just after sunrise, children engaged in a rousing game of soccer on the sand before heading off to school.

There are few cars and trucks in Nha Trang. Almost everyone travels by motorbike, bicycle or cyclo, although the new motorbike taxis seem to be taking business away from the more traditional cyclos. There is only one high-rise in Nha Trang, the ill-conceived Nha Trang Lodge across the street from the Grand Hotel. The guide said that the city government realized immediately after it was built that it was a mistake and have not allowed any other high rises to be built along the beach.

I spent one day in Nha Trang sightseeing, although it was difficult to tear myself away from the beach. I had only seen the Buddha from the air before, so it was exciting to climb the steps and see it up close. I learned that the Buddha had been built in 1963 to commemorate the sacrifices of the Buddhist monks who had immolated themselves as a protest against the Diem regime. The faces of these men were carved onto the base of the lotus blossom on which the Buddha sits. Halfway up the hill there was a memorial to the one Buddhist nun who immolated herself.

The other major sightseeing attraction in Nha Trang is the Po Nagar Cham Towers. Having visited the Cham Museum in Da Nang in 1994, I was very interested in seeing these ruins. The towers were built between the 7th and the 12th centuries at a location used for Hindu worship as early as the 2nd century AD. There are four towers remaining of the original seven or eight. A restoration project appeared to be in the beginning stages. I knew nothing of these archaeological ruins in 1969 and was glad for the opportunity to see and learn about them now.

The sightseeing trip ended with a ride to one of the rocky promontories that jut out into Nha Trang Bay. There we encountered vendors—men selling soft drinks and bottled water and a woman selling post cards and paperback copies of *Sorrow of War*, *The Lover*, and *The Quiet American*. All of the men were veterans of the South Vietnamese Army. When they learned that I had been in Nha Trang, Dong Ba Thin, and Cam Ranh in 1969–1970, one of them volunteered that he had worked at

Dong Ba Thin in 1972. They all spoke French, and I was able to talk with them in French, just as I had talked with many Vietnamese 30 years ago.

Few of the younger Vietnamese speak French now. Everyone wants to speak English. It seemed to me that almost everyone I met was thirty or younger, and English is the lingua franca. The Japanese tourists and the Vietnamese communicated with each other by speaking English!

I spent one afternoon walking the length of the beach from my hotel to the Grand Hotel and back. Even though it was much the same, at the same time it was very different. I felt, much more strongly than I had in Saigon, that I was leaving Vietnam USA and Vietnam the War behind and entering a tranquil, peaceful place to relax and watch the sun, sea, and surf. Vietnam was becoming Viet Nam, a place for a lovely vacation rather than a place to relive thirty-year-old memories.

The ride back to Saigon was broken up by an overnight stay in Phan Thiet. The hotel was located across the street from a huge 18 hole golf course, but both the hotel and the golf course appeared to be under-utilized. The Vietnamese must prefer Nha Trang, I think, and so do I.

I was glad to have the opportunity to return to the places where I spent my life-changing year in 1969–1970. I was sorry not to be able to go onto Cam Ranh Peninsula, still the site of Russian and Vietnamese military installations and off limits to tourists, but visiting Nha Trang and driving along Highway 1 made the trip more than worthwhile. I was sorry too, not to have included Dalat in my itinerary. I guess I'll just have to go back!

by Ann L. Kelsey
Copyright 1999, Ann L. Kelsey. All Rights Reserved, Used with permission.

To read all Ann Kelsey's 1992 journal, *A Trip Back to Vietnam,* log on to http://grunt.appliedphysics.swri.edu/tripsbk.htm, part of the Vietnam Veterans Home Page. Also at this site, read her journal, *Back To The Past,* about her experiences on her return trip in 1994.

Ann Kelsey served as a civilian librarian with Army Special Services in Vietnam, 1969–1970. Working out of Cam Ranh Bay, she administered libraries in Nha Trang, Dong Ba Thin, and the 6th Convalescent Center.

She returned to Vietnam for the first time since the war in 1992 and made another trip in October 1994 as a member of a humanitarian group, Project: Hearts and Minds, delivering medical supplies to clinics and hospitals. She co-authored an article on civilian women who served in Vietnam for the November 1993 issue of the *VVA Veteran* and wrote a brief history of Special Services in Vietnam for the dedication program of the Vietnam Women's Memorial.

She is currently the Associate Director of the County College of Morris Learning Resource Center in Randolph, New Jersey.

Civilian Women in Vietnam: Army Special Services

The Army Special Services Program in Vietnam began on July 1, 1966. At that time responsibility for providing a diversified and comprehensive recreation program in support of the morale and welfare of United States and Free World Military Forces was transferred from the United States Navy to the United States Army Vietnam (USARV) with operational responsibility being assumed by the 1st Logistical Command.

The Special Services Program was composed of several branches, but the civilians, both women and men, who volunteered to serve one year tours in Vietnam were concentrated in the Arts and Crafts, Entertainment, Library, and Service Club sections. These civilians, many of whom extended for additional one-year tours, staffed and operated craft shops, libraries, and service clubs, and coordinated an array of entertainment programs. These facilities and programs provided off duty recreation and relaxation to service men and women from I Corps at the DMZ to IV Corps in the Delta.

In March 1970, at the time that Special Services was reorganized and centralized as the USARV Special Services Agency (Provisional), approximately 99 civilians managed and supervised the 31 craft and photography laboratories, 6 entertainment offices, 23 service clubs, and 39 libraries in Vietnam. Between 1966 and 1972 an estimated 300–600 civilians, about 75% of them women, served in Vietnam as employees of the Special Services.

In pursuit of their mission, the women who served as Special Services librarians and recreation specialists worked long hours in monsoon mud and dusty heat. Because there were far fewer personnel than there were installations requiring their services, they traveled extensively by any available means: jeeps, 2 1/2 ton trucks, helicopters, fixed wing aircraft, and on foot. They endured rocket attacks, mortar barrages, and commando raids mounted against the installations at which they were located, sometimes spending nights in sandbagged rat-infested bunkers, occasionally composing songs to keep up their spirits.

What did these women do? They managed permanent libraries, similar to small public libraries in the United States, located on larger bases, such as Cam Ranh Bay, Long Binh, Bearcat, Chu Lai, Nha Trang, and Dong Ba Thin. They supervised 250 field library units, and arranged the field distribution of 190,000 magazine subscriptions and 350,000 paperbacks. They offered assistance and instruction in metal enameling, model building, lapidary, photography, painting, and leather working. They directed a variety of recreational programs and activities, from Ping-Pong tournaments to song fests, running them from service clubs in such places as Tay Ninh, Cu Chi, Dong Tam, An Khe, Phu Bai, and Quang Tri. They coordinated USO tours of entertainers and celebrities, and produced, directed, and acted in little theatre productions at larger base camps. They developed Command Military Touring Shows, composed of in country military personnel, who entertained their fellow soldiers in areas that commercial shows could not go for security reasons.

The women who volunteered to serve with Special Services in Vietnam did so for a variety of reasons. They went for adventure, in search of exciting and rewarding opportunities, and because it presented a challenge, both professional and personal. They went out of patriotism. But mostly they went because they cared about their fellow men and women.

They wanted to serve their country and help to boost the morale of soldiers far from home. Their effectiveness in accomplishing these objectives under extremely difficult working and living conditions was underscored in 1971 when the USARV Special Services Agency was recommended for a Meritorious Unit Commendation.

Women in Special Services assumed a lot of responsibility, learned a lot, did things they had never done before. Their sense of humor, enthusiasm, creativity, and excitement saw them through. They felt they were a real part of Vietnam, as much a part as any soldier. They gave much, but in return they received a strong sense of satisfaction and accomplishment, something to look back on for the rest of their lives. The women of Special Services, when all is said and done, were just that—special people who provided a very special service.

Sources: General Historical Records, Relating to the Entertainment Branch, 1970–1972 Folder, Entertainment Branch History Files, RG 472 Records of the United States Army Vietnam, Special Services Agency (Provisional), Entertainment Branch, Box 1, National Archives, Suitland Reference Center. Department of the Army Overseas Recruitment Center film, *Special Services: Where the Action Is*, 1970.

by Ann L. Kelsey
Copyright 1993, Ann L. Kelsey, DAC, USARV Special Services, Library Branch, 1969–1970. All rights reserved. Used with permission.

CHAPTER 26

The Vietnam Veterans' Memorial

As virtuous men pass mildly away,
And whisper to their souls to go,
Whilst some of their sad friends do say,
The breath goes now, and some say no.
                    John Donne, 1572–1631

The Wall

Kneeling down facing "The Wall,"
tears rolling down their cheeks.

Bring them flowers, bring them love,
bring them back we can only wish so.

Remember our fallen comrades now
on the granite wall.

Touch "The Wall" and listen to their final
expressions…Medic, I'm hurt, I'm losing my blood,
I got hit, please help me.

We've traveled many miles, and years.
Part of their lives were left unfulfilled,
fathers never to be.

No more warm nights for them ever.
Only frigid ones on "The Wall."

So many hands touching "The Wall,"
so many feelings displayed for them all.

"The Wall" feels so cold to our touch.
Granite wall so dark and cold,
and yet holding so many warm hearts.

All colors, creeds and genders united we stand.
Nearly 60,000 names of fallen soldiers rest.

Fallen names still waiting at "The Wall."
The dark and rectangular bricks on the
floor are once again covered with tears.

by Frank Zamora

Frank Zamora was a specialist, E-4, with the 1st Infantry Division, 1st Aviation Battalion (Headquarters), Phu Loi, Vietnam, January 26, 1967, to January 25, 1968.

Frank Zamora's Vietnam Web site with more of his poetry is on the Internet at www.geocities.com/fyzamora1. Frank Zamora works for a Sea Food Importing Company in Washington State where he lives with his wife. They have two children. See Zamora's poem in chapter 13; his quote, chapter 28; and his poem *Thanksgiving Day,* chapter 27.

The Vietnam Veterans' Memorial

The Vietnam Veterans' Memorial, "The Wall," was dedicated in 1982, in the constitution gardens in Washington, D.C.

In 1993, Americans rejoiced at the dedication of the Vietnam Women's Memorial. Finally, the thousands of military and civilian women who served and volunteered during the Vietnam War have a tangible memorial to call their own.

"This monument will ensure that all of America will never forget that all of you were there, that you served, and that even in the depths of horror and cruelty, there will always beat the heart of human love...and therefore, our hope for humanity."—General Colin Powell.

"A legacy of healing and hope," is the motto of The Vietnam Women's Memorial Project, VWMP, incorporated in 1984 as a non-profit organization located in Washington, D.C.

The VWMP's mission is "to promote the healing of Vietnam women veterans through the placement of the Vietnam Women's Memorial on the grounds of the Vietnam Veterans' Memorial in Washington, D.C.," according to Diane Carlson Evans, RN, Vietnam veteran, 1968–1969. Evans served as a nurse with the Army Nurses Corps from 1966 to 1972. Evans is the founder and chair of the Vietnam Women's Memorial Project, Inc. The Vietnam Women's Memorial Project's mission also is "to identify the military and civilian women who served during the Vietnam War; to educate the public about their role; and to facilitate research on the physiological, psychological, and sociological issues correlated to their service." For more information and pictures on the Vietnam Women's Memorial Project, Inc., see www.vietnamwomensmemorial.org on the Internet.

Diane Evans.

The Vietnam Women's Memorial Project also provides Sister Search, a program for military and civilian women who served during the Vietnam War to find contacts, peace, and healing.

Glenna Goodacre sculpted the bronze statue that portrays the American women who served in Vietnam. For more about Goodacre and her sculptures, see www.glennagoodacre.com on the Internet.

My Brother

You were there for me
When I faced the Wall
For that first time

You gave me back
A part of me
Taken from me
By others
In that place
So many years past

You didn't scorn me
Nor expect me to be
Bright and vivacious

You allowed me tears
Held prisoner inside me
Trapped by years
Of pain and denial
Of fear and confusion
You acknowledged
That I was a veteran

My brother
You were a God-send
Allowing me to grieve
And giving me laughter
In the midst
Of all those emotions
That were strangers to me
For too many years

Your Words
Your arms comforted me
You, a combat veteran
Gave me the courage
To celebrate my life
My service

To hold my head
High with pride
To join
My brothers and sisters
In a place
Of healing and honour

My brother
I thank you
For your gift to me
You helped me journey home
To allow my spirit
To fly free and soar

by Penni Evans

Read about Penni Evans and her poetry, *Sisters,* chapter 1; *Ambushed,* chapter 15; *Souvenirs,* chapter 18; and *Folded Flag,* chapter 27.

Images of Freedom

The starkness of a silhouette
upon a field of black,
The image of one who fought for us
but did not make it back.
P.O.W./M.I.A.
we all know the names,
Prisoner of War/Missing in Action
is their claim to fame.
We must never forget these lost souls
nor the price they paid so dear,
Hold them close in your heart forever—
year after year.
When you see the Stars and Stripes
blowing in the wind,
Say your thanks and your prayers
for each one of them.
We may not have known them—
someone's father, brother, son,
But with each life given
someone's family is missing one.
Stand at the great black wall,
read the names and count the cost,
Our precious freedom gained
for the many lives lost.
Freedom we take for granted
with no thought of our own,

For the P.O.W./M.I.A.
who may never come home.

by Diana Waite

Read about Diana Waite and her poem *The Angels of Vietnam*, chapter 1.

Honoring our Heroes

"A soldier isn't dead until he is forgotten."
We'll observe their absence eternally,
and I shall pay respects with
my everlasting silence.

by Frank Zamora

CHAPTER 27

In Memory

*When one man dies,
one chapter is not torn out of the book,
but translated into a better language.*
John Donne, 1572–1631

Folded Flag

The triangle shape denotes
The loss of one of our own
The stars on the blue background
Do not twinkle as those in the sky

The colours of our flag
Are represented by the life blood
Of our fallen comrades
Their honour is not diminished

The pain of their death
Remains in our souls
We stand together
As taps is played

The salute of rifles
Fired in honour
Punctuates our loss
As the folded flag is handed to the family

by Penni Evans

Read about Penni Evans and her poetry, *Sisters,* chapter 1; *Ambushed,* chapter 15; *Souvenirs,* chapter 18; and *My Brother,* chapter 26.

Roll Call

The following are the American, Australian, and New Zealand civilian and military women who lost their lives while serving in Vietnam.

United States Army

2nd Lt. Carol Ann Elizabeth Drazba—born December 11, 1943, from Dunmore, Pennsylvania, assigned to the 3rd Field Hospital near Saigon. Drazba, age 22, was one of the first two women to die in Vietnam. She died February 18, 1966, in a helicopter crash. She was headed for a weekend of R&R (rest and recreation). Drazba's name is on the Vietnam Memorial Wall in Washington, D.C. 2nd Lt. Elizabeth Ann Jones was also killed in the accident.

2nd Lt. Elizabeth Ann Jones—born September 12, 1943, from Allendale, South Carolina, assigned to the 3rd Field Hospital near Saigon. Jones, age 22, was one of the first two women to die in Vietnam. She died February 18, 1966, in a helicopter crash. She was headed for a weekend of R&R. The helicopter pilot, Lt. Col. Charles M. Honour Jr., was her fiancé, whom she had met in country. Jones' name is on the

Vietnam Memorial Wall in Washington, D.C. 2nd Lt. Carol Ann Elizabeth Drazba was also killed in the accident.

Capt. Eleanor Grace Alexander—born September 18, 1940, from Westwood, New Jersey, assigned to the 85th Evacuation Hospital, Qui Nhon. Alexander, age 27, died November 30, 1967, when her plane crashed returning to Qui Nhon from a hospital in Pleiku where she had been sent to help. Alexander was posthumously awarded the Bronze Star. The city of Riverside, New Jersey, named a park in honor of Alexander. Her name is on the Vietnam Memorial Wall in Washington, D.C. 1st Lt. Hedwig Diane Orlowski was also killed in the accident.

1st Lt. Hedwig Diane Orlowski—born April 13, 1944, from Detroit, Michigan, assigned to the 67th Evacuation Hospital, Qui Nhon. Orlowski, age 23, died November 30, 1967, when her plane crashed returning to Qui Nhon from a hospital in Pleiku where she had been sent to help. Orlowski was posthumously awarded the Bronze Star. Orlowski's name is on the Vietnam Memorial Wall in Washington, D.C. Capt. Eleanor Grace Alexander was also killed in the accident.

2nd Lt. Pamela Dorothy Donovan—born March 25, 1942. Donovan was born in Ireland, and grew up in Allston, Massachusetts. She was assigned to the 85th Evacuation Hospital, Qui Nhon. Donovan, age 26, became seriously ill after three months in country and died July 8, 1968. A road leading to the St. Gabriel's Monastery in Brighton, Massachusetts, was named in her honor in 1969. Her name is on the Vietnam Memorial Wall in Washington, D.C.

Lt. Col. Annie Ruth Graham—born November 7, 1916, from Efland, North Carolina, Chief Nurse at 91st Evacuation Hospital, 43rd Medical Group, 44th Medical Brigade, Tuy Hoa. Graham, age 52, suffered a sudden internal hemorrhage while on duty. She died three days later on August 14,

1968. Graham, a career Army nurse since graduating from nursing school in 1942, was a veteran of World War II and Korea. Graham's name is on the Vietnam Memorial Wall in Washington, D.C.

1st Lt. Sharon Ann Lane—Army Nurse Corps, born July 7, 1943, from Canton, Ohio, assigned to the 312th Evacuation Hospital, Chu Lai, RVN, was 25 at the time of her death.

1st Lt. Sharon Ann Lane was the sole American military nurse in the Vietnam War to die under enemy attack. Sharon had been in country less than two months, and her nursing responsibilities consisted of caring for Vietnamese civilian men, women and children, South Vietnamese soldiers, NVA, and VC POWs at the 312th Evacuation Hospital in Chu Lai, RVN, in April 1969.

Sharon spent her free off duty day caring for American soldiers in the surgical ICU. She especially loved the Vietnamese children patients, and declined transfer from the Vietnamese ward. She became an inspiration to her colleagues by her compassion, kindness, and caring in treating all her patients with dignity, humanity, and respect despite the uniform they wore.

On June 8, 1969, a 122mm rocket directly struck Ward 4, the Vietnamese Ward, killing Sharon and a twelve-year-old girl, and severely injuring twenty-seven Vietnamese patients. It was 0530 in the morning, shortly before her shift was to have been completed.

Sharon was posthumously awarded the Purple Heart, the Bronze Star with a "V" for Gallantry, the National Defense Service Medal, the Vietnam Service Medal, the National Order of Vietnam Medal, and the (South) Vietnamese Gallantry Cross with Palm.

Numerous awards and honors have been given to Sharon. In 1970, Fitzsimons Army Hospital in Denver, Lane's assignment prior to her volunteering for Vietnam, dedicated the recovery room in her honor. A bronze statue of Lane was erected in 1973 at Aultman Hospital in Canton, Ohio, where she attended nursing school, and is the site of the annual Day of Remembrance Ceremony sponsored by the local Vietnam Veterans Chapter, the Sharon Ann Lane memorial Chapter 199 of Canton, Ohio, to commemorate her memory. The statue also bears the names of 110 local service members killed in Vietnam. Lane's name, along with her brother and sister veterans, is etched on the black granite of the Vietnam Memorial Wall in Washington, D.C.

Sharon is among the eight female and two male American military nurses to have perished in the Vietnam War. A biography, *Hostile Fire, the Life of 1st Lt. Sharon Ann Lane in Vietnam* by Phillip Bigler, is available from our group, The Friends of Sharon Ann Lane.

The Friends of Sharon Ann Lane have established the Sharon Ann Lane Foundation with a vision of building a Medical Memorial Clinic in honor of Sharon Ann Lane in Vietnam. Six veterans traveled to Chu Lai to explore the construction of such a clinic in the Chu Lai District in March, 2001. The Foundation has initiated in Hue city a liaison with the Medical School in the hopes of creating a Pediatric Fellowship in conjunction with an American medical school. Committed physicians, medical students, and physician assistant students may spend a portion of their medical studies in Vietnam as members of a Medical Educational Exchange Program which will eventually permit reciprocal exchange of Vietnamese physicians and students in the United States.

It is our desire to assist in healthcare services and in the delivery of much needed medical care to the children and people of Vietnam. We believe this will be a continuation of the legacy of Sharon's nursing practice demonstrated more than thirty years ago by this American military nurse who served in Vietnam and lost her life caring for her Vietnamese patients. Her dedication to these patients remains an act of kindness of the human spirit in the midst of the horrors of war and is a beacon of hope to have come from the pain, trauma, and suffering of the Vietnam War.

For more information or to make a tax deductible donation contact the Sharon Ann Lane Foundation:

The Friends of Sharon Ann Lane, Box 90, Media, Pa 19063
Kathleen Fennell, PA-C, R.N., 12th Evac Hospital, Cu Chi, RVN, 1968–1969, mach06@earthlink.net
Patricia Powell, USMC, cody47@juno.com

United States Air Force

Capt. Mary Therese Klinker—born October 3, 1947, from Lafayette, Indiana, flight nurse, 10th Aeromedical Evacuation Squadron, Travis Air Force Base, temporarily assigned to Clark Air Base in the Philippines. Klinker, age 27, died April 4, 1975, in the Operation Babylift (chapter 22) crash, a C-5 Galaxy evacuating Vietnamese orphans outside Saigon. She was posthumously awarded the Airman's Medal and the Meritorious Service Medal. Klinker's name is on the Vietnam Memorial Wall in Washington, D.C. Klinker was the last nurse, and the only member of the Air Force Nurse Corps, to be killed in Vietnam.

Royal Australian Army Nurse Corps

Lt. Barbara Black served at Vung Tau. She died due to illness in 1971.

American Red Cross

Hannah E. Crews died in a jeep accident, Bien Hoa, October 2, 1969.

Virginia E. Kirsch, 21 years old, from Brookfield, Ohio, was murdered by a U.S. soldier in Cu Chi, August 16, 1970.

Lucinda J. Richter died of Guillain-Barre Syndrome, Cam Ranh Bay, February 9, 1971.

Army Special Services

Rosalyn Muskat died in a jeep accident, Long Binh, October 26, 1968.

Dorothy Phillips died in a plane crash, Qui Nhon, 1967.

Catholic Relief Services

Gloria Redlin, shot to death in Pleiku, 1969.

Central Intelligence Agency

Barbara Robbins, died March 30, 1965, when a car bomb exploded outside the American Embassy, Saigon.

Betty Gebhardt, died in Saigon, 1971.

United States
Agency for International Development

Marilyn L. Allan, murdered by a U.S. soldier in Nha Trang, August 16, 1967.

Dr. Breen Ratterman, American Medical Association, died October 2, 1969, from injuries due to falling from her apartment balcony in Saigon.

U.S. Department of the Navy
Officer in Charge of Construction

Regina "Reggie" Williams, died of a heart attack in Saigon, 1964.

Journalists

Georgette "Dickey" Chapelle, died in 1965. Chapelle was killed by a mine while on patrol with Marines outside Chu Lai.

Philippa Schuyler died May 9, 1967, when the helicopter she was on crashed into the ocean near Da Nang.

Marguerite Hall Higgins, born in 1920, foreign correspondent in Korea and Vietnam. Higgins died January 3, 1966, from a disease she contracted in Vietnam. She is buried in Section 2 of Arlington National Cemetery.

Missionaries

Carolyn Griswald
Ruth Thompson
Ruth Wilting
All three women were killed in a raid on Leprosarium in Ban Me Thuot during Tet 1968.

POW/MIA

Evelyn Anderson, born 1950, from Quincy, Michigan, missionary for Christian Missions of Many Lands. She was captured by the North Vietnamese October 27, 1972. She was burned to death approximately five days later along with Beatrice Kosin in Kengkok, Laos. Her remains were returned to the United States.

Beatrice Kosin, from Ft. Washakle, Wyoming, missionary for Christian Missions of Many Lands. She was captured by the North

Vietnamese October 27, 1972. She was burned to death approximately five days later along with Evelyn Anderson in Kengkok, Laos. Her remains were returned to the United States.

Betty Ann Olsen, born October, 22, 1934, from New York, New York, a missionary nurse with the Christian Missionary Alliance. She was captured February 1, 1968, during a raid on Leprosarium in Ban Me Thuot during Tet 1968. Olsen was killed in captivity, and fellow POW Michael Benge buried her somewhere along Ho Chi Minh Trail.

Dr. Eleanor Ardel Vietti, born November 5, 1927, from Houston, Texas, surgeon with the Christian and Missionary Alliance. Vietti was taken prisoner May 30, 1962, at Leprosarium in Ban Me Thuot. Vietti is still listed as POW.

Operation Babylift

April 4, 1975, a C-5 Galaxy evacuating Vietnamese orphans from the country, known as Operation Babylift (chapter 22), crashed outside Saigon. The following women died in the crash. Except for Laurie Stark, a teacher, and Sharon Wesley, all of the women were employed by United States government agencies in Saigon. Wesley had worked for both the American Red Cross and Army Special Services. She chose to stay on in Vietnam after the pullout of U.S. military forces in 1973.

Barbara Adams, Clara Bayot, Nova Bell, Arleta Bertwell, Helen Blackburn, Ann Bottorff, Celeste Brown, Vivienne Clark, Juanita Creel, Mary Ann Crouch, Dorothy Curtiss, Twila Donelson, Helen Drye, Theresa Drye (a child), Mary Lyn Eichen, Elizabeth Fugino, Ruthanne Gasper, Beverly Herbert, Penelope Hindman, Vera Hollibaugh, Dorothy Howard, Barbara Kauvulia, Barbara Maier, Rebecca Martin, Sara Martini, Martha Middlebrook, Katherine Moore, Marta Moschkin,

Marion Polgrean, June Poulton, Joan Pray, Sayonna Randall, Anne Reynolds, Marjorie Snow, Laurie Stark, Barbara Stout, Doris Jean Watkins, and Sharon Wesley.

Australia, Civilian, Entertainer

Cathy Wayne (Warnes) was shot by a soldier who was shooting at his commander.

New Zealand Foreign Affairs Ministry

Lesley Estelle Cowper, civilian member of the New Zealand Surgical Team based at Qui Nhon in 1966.

Lesley Estelle Cowper was born in Auckland, New Zealand, in 1932. She obtained her teaching diploma from the Ardmore Teachers Training College before deciding upon a career in nursing. She earned her SRN (State Registered Nursing) Diploma in 1954.

In 1955, she went to London to take up a private nursing appointment. While there, she joined the British Army and became a lieutenant in the British Army Nursing Service. She served for two years in London and another two years with BOAR (British Army on the Rhine), based in Germany. She then went to Australia and worked as a Sister in a Melbourne Hospital for 18 months. She returned to New Zealand where she worked as a Ward Sister at Middlemore Hospital in Auckland. She enlisted into the Royal New Zealand Army Nursing Corps in 1964 as a lieutenant. A year later she was promoted to captain. She served as a Nursing Officer with 1 (NZ) Casualty Clearing Station, based at Sylvia Park, Mount Wellington, Auckland. In November 1965, she requested a year's leave of absence so she could join the New Zealand Surgical Team (Civilian) based at Qui Nhon Hospital, Vietnam. Qui Nhon Hospital was supported by the New Zealand

Department of Health as part of New Zealand's Foreign Aid Programme.

Sister Cowper was described by all as a tireless worker, but early in 1966 she developed an illness which did not improve with treatment by the team's doctors. They decided that she should be transferred to the Holy Grail Hospital in Saigon. However, her condition worsened and May 2, 1966, Sister Lesley Cowper died from renal metabolic disorder.

Her body was returned to New Zealand, and she was buried at Waikumete Cemetery in Auckland with full military honours. The then Prime Minister of New Zealand, Keith Holyoake, said in a letter to her mother, "Lesley showed courage, dedication and humanity, and her conduct throughout was in the highest traditions of nursing. Her death was most untimely, but I hope that you may be able to draw some consolation from the fact that she was playing her full part in relieving the sufferings of the wounded and sick in a war stricken country when she died."

Sister Lesley Estelle Cowper was (posthumously) awarded The South Vietnamese Legion of Merit (1st Class). She was 34 years old.

Thanks to Mike Subritzky for providing the information on Sister Lesley Estelle Cowper.

Thanksgiving Day

Thanks to those who can no longer enjoy,
Husbands, wives, mothers, sisters, and the rest.
Alive they were before the war,
Now only their memories remain.
Kilometers just north of Saigon,
Silence abruptly arrived to their young lives.
Giving all they had to give,
In a moment's notice they ceased to exist.
Victory, honor and respect now remains,
In solitude so many of us will tomorrow be.
No more hugs and kisses,
Gone forever our Sisters and Brothers rest.

Did they have to go so soon?
Answers we will never have.
Yesterday is now our past, and for them an eternal unknown.

by Frank Zamora

See Frank Zamora's poem, chapter 13; quote, chapter 28; and poems *The Wall* and *Honoring Our Heroes,* chapter 26.

CHAPTER 28

Welcome Home

*Heroes will always be heroes
no matter females or males.
We were all brave human beings.*

Frank Zamora

Gathered In
(For DGS)

Friends who listen with ears that hear,
with hands that touch,
with arms that hold,
with hearts that break along with ours,
with smiles that say we're welcome home.

Angels with innocent, mended hearts,
the powerful patience of quiet minds,
the simple nod, the sparkling eye—
the dogs of war are gathered in,

the dogs of war are once more—Men.
The dogs of war are—Home.

by James M. Hopkins

Gathered In was specifically written for Deanna (Shlee Hopkins, chapter 23) not long after we met but before we were married. Unlike so many women who could not accept their "changed" men after Vietnam, she accepted me with love and understanding, honored my service (even if I couldn't), and sympathized with the on-going problems which it caused me.

So many vets were "strays" when they returned home. Family and friends who knew the men as good (and predictable) sons, now found them altered and de-civilized in unpredictable, usually unpleasant ways. Their fun-loving puppies had become the dogs of war, and they were often rejected and abandoned.

Deanna gathered in and recivilized (to some extent) this abandoned war-dog through love, understanding and acceptance. I am forever in her debt.
James M. Hopkins.

Read James M. Hopkin's poem, *I See You Walking,* chapter 3. See more of Hopkin's poetry at http://vets.appliedphysics. swri.edu/blades.htm or http://www.vietvet.org/blades.htm (a mirror site),The Sound of Whirling Blades—Poems and Reflections at The Vietnam Veterans Home Page.

Also visit http://gecko.gc.maricopa.edu/~dgshleeh/battle.htm, From The Battlefield...any battlefield...anywhere.

"*Battlefield* was created to allow the same poetic outlet to vets of all wars that the VVHP (Vietnam Veteran Home Page, http://vets.applied-physics.swri.edu/) allows only for Vietnam Vets."
James M. Hopkins.

Aftermath

The noises—the sound—
falling rain on sandy ground—
the trees, canopies
the dark and the damp—
brothers, sisters, Base Camp...
the smells, the fears, the letters and tears
the Now and the Why,
the why can't I cry?
No answers—just left forlorn
feeling lost, feeling scorn,
or no feeling, no feeling at all
except the feeling of feeling small.
Chopper sound, circling 'round
Take me home,
go away—
but don't leave me alone...
nightmares,
daymares,
screams in my head—
wondering, pondering
why I'm not dead...
Can't stand loud noises—
hate firecrackers
hate backfires, loud sounds
sounds too much
like mortar rounds.

I sit in the corner,
facing the door—
the enemy doesn't look the same

anymore…
Go to the movies,
have to get out
Can't stand the dark
can't see, can't see—
who sits behind me.

Check the perimeters
check all the locks,
check all my options
synchronize clocks—

who says it's over
who says it ends…
(never over for Dad,
ever so sad—)

Maybe someday for me,
someday for my friends
The War will be over
and we can forget—
but not yet…
not yet.

by Christina Sharik
For all casualties of war, living or dead

Soldier's Farewell

I've saddled up, and dropped me hooch,
I'm going to take the gap,
my Tour of Duty's over mates,
and I won't be coming back.

I'm done with diggin' shell scrapes
and laying out barbed wire,
I'm sick of setting Claymore Mines,
and coming under fire.
So, no more Fire Support Base,
and no more foot patrols,
and no more eating ration packs,
and sleepin' in muddy holes.

I've fired my last machine gun,
and ambushed my last track,
I'm sick of all the Army brass,
and I sure ain't coming back.

I'll hand my bayonet to the clerk,
he ain't seen one before,
and clean my rifle one more time,
and return it to the store.
So, no more spit and polish,
and make sure I get paid,
and sign me from the Regiment,
today's my last parade.

by Mike Subritzky

Reprinted with permission from Mike Subritzky's book *The Happy Warrior—An Anthology of Australian and New Zealand Military Poetry*. This poem is often read at soldier's funerals. See Mike Subritzky's poetry, *Sister,* chapter 8; *Midnight Movie,* chapter 15; and *bird of a single flight,* chapter 29.

What Is A Vietnam Veteran?

A couple years ago, just before Veterans' Day, a college student named Adam wrote to an Internet e-mail discussion list. He was working on a school assignment in which he was supposed to obtain original narratives from "people old enough to have actually been there in person." I asked how I could help, and he asked me to respond to the question, "What is a Vietnam veteran?" This is what I wrote.

Vietnam veterans are men and women. We are dead or alive, whole or maimed, sane or haunted. We grew from our experiences or we were destroyed by them or we struggle to find some place in between. We lived through hell or we had a pleasant, if scary, adventure. We were Army, Navy, Marines, Air Force, Red Cross, and civilians of all sorts. Some of us enlisted to fight for God and Country, and some were drafted. Some were gung-ho, and some went kicking and screaming.

Like veterans of all wars, we lived a tad bit—or a great bit—closer to death than most people like to think about. If Vietnam vets differ from others, perhaps it is primarily in the fact that many of us never saw the enemy or recognized him or her. We heard gunfire and mortar fire but rarely looked into enemy eyes. Those who did, like folks who encounter close combat anywhere and anytime, are often haunted for life by those eyes, those sounds, those electric fears that ran between ourselves, our enemies, and the likelihood of death for one of us. Or we get hard, calloused, tough. All in a day's work. Life's a bitch then you die. But most of us remember and get twitchy, worried, sad.

We are crazies dressed in cammo, wide-eyed, wary, homeless, and drunk. We are Brooks Brothers suit wearers, doing deals downtown. We are housewives, grandmothers, and church deacons. We are college professors engaged in the rational pursuit of the truth about the history or politics or culture of the Vietnam experience. And we are sleepless. Often sleepless.

We pushed paper; we pushed shovels. We drove jeeps, operated bulldozers, built bridges; we toted machine guns through dense brush, deep paddy, and thorn scrub. We lived on buffalo milk, fish heads and rice. Or C-rations. Or steaks and Budweiser. We did our time in high mountains drenched by endless monsoon rains or on the dry plains or on muddy rivers or at the most beautiful beaches in the world.

We wore berets, bandanas, flop hats, and steel pots. Flak jackets, canvas, rash and rot. We ate cloroquine and got malaria anyway. We got shots constantly but have diseases nobody can diagnose.

We spent our nights on cots or shivering in foxholes filled with waist-high water or lying still on cold wet ground, our eyes imagining Charlie behind every bamboo blade. Or we slept in hotel beds in Saigon or barracks in Thailand or in cramped ships' berths at sea.

We feared we would die or we feared we would kill. We simply feared, and often we still do. We hate the war or believe it was the best thing that ever happened to us. We blame Uncle Sam or Uncle Ho and their minions and secretaries and apologists for every wart or cough or tic of an eye. We wonder if Agent Orange got us.

Mostly, we wish we had not been so alone. Some of us went with units; but many, probably most of us, were civilians one day, jerked up out of "the world," shaved, barked at, insulted, humiliated, de-egoized and taught to kill, to fix radios, to drive trucks. We went, put in our time, and were equally ungraciously plucked out of the morass and placed back in the real world. But now we smoked dope or drank heavily. Our wives or husbands seemed distant and strange. Our friends wanted to know if we shot anybody.

And life went on, had been going on, as if we hadn't been there, as if Vietnam was a topic of political conversation or college protest or news copy, not a matter of life and death for tens of thousands.

Vietnam vets are people just like you. We served our country, proudly or reluctantly or ambivalently. What makes us different—what makes us Vietnam vets—is something we understand, but we are afraid nobody else will. But we appreciate your asking.

Vietnam veterans are white, black, beige and shades of gray. Our ancestors came from Africa, from Europe, and Asia. Or they crossed the Bering Sea Land Bridge in the last Ice Age and formed the nations of American Indians, built pyramids in Mexico, or farmed acres of corn on the banks of Chesapeake Bay. We had names like Rodriguez and Stein and Smith and Kowalski. We were Americans, Australians, Canadians, and Koreans; most Vietnam veterans are Vietnamese.

We were farmers, students, mechanics, steelworkers, nurses, and priests when the call came that changed us all forever. We had dreams and plans, and they all had to change...or wait. We were daughters and sons, lovers and poets, beatniks and philosophers, convicts and lawyers. We were rich and poor but mostly poor. We were educated or not, mostly not. We grew up in slums, in shacks, in duplexes, and bungalows and houseboats and hooches and ranchers. We were cowards and heroes. Sometimes we were cowards one moment and heroes the next.

Many of us have never seen Vietnam. We waited at home for those we loved. And for some of us, our worst fears were realized. For others, our loved ones came back but never would be the same.

We came home and marched in protest marches, sucked in tear gas, and shrieked our anger and horror for all to hear. Or we sat alone in small rooms, in VA hospital wards, in places where only the crazy ever go. We are Republicans, Democrats, Socialists, and Confucians and Buddhists and Atheists—though as usually is the case, even the atheists among us sometimes prayed to get out of there alive.

We are hungry, and we are sated, full of life or clinging to death. We are injured, and we are healers, despairing and hopeful, loved or lost. We got too old too quickly, but some of us have never grown up. We want, desperately, to go back, to heal wounds, revisit the sites of our horror. Or we want never to see that place again, to bury it, its memories, its meaning. We want to forget, and we wish we could remember.

Despite our differences, we have so much in common. There are few of us who don't know how to cry, though we often do it alone when nobody will ask, "what's wrong?" We're afraid we might have to answer.

Adam, if you want to know what a Vietnam veteran is, get in your car next weekend or cage a friend with a car to drive you. Go to Washington. Go to the Wall. It's going to be Veterans Day weekend. There will be hundreds there—no, thousands. Watch them. Listen to them. I'll be there. Come touch the Wall with us. Rejoice a bit. Cry a bit. No, cry a lot. I will. I'm a Vietnam Veteran; and, after 30 years, I think I am just beginning to understand what that means.

by Daniel Mouer
U. S. Army 511th Engineer Company (PB)
70th Engineer Battalion (Combat)
An Khe, RVN, 1966–1967
Copyright 1996 L. Daniel Mouer, All Rights Reserved. Reprinted with permission.

Daniel Mouer is happily married with one son, two granddaughters, and a hound dog named Mr. T. He is a professor of anthropology and archaeology at Virginia Commonwealth University, specializing in American culture history. To read more about Mouer, visit Dan Mouer's Wild World Web at http://www.people.vcu.edu/~dmouer/homepage.htm.

If Only

If only Mother Earth
could speak
of the atrocities she's seen;
of all her clear streams running red
and fallen men upon her green—
If only she could tell about
the damage that's been done
by politicians ordering
one man to fight a mother's son;
If only Mother Earth could cry
She would be crying still
at the child-like foolishness of Man
and his stubbornness of Will.

by Christina Sharik

Read about Christina Sharik, chapter 1, and see her poetry, *The Woman Veteran/Women Who Served*, chapter 1; *The Night Before*, chapter 2; *The Suitcase And The Duffle Bag*, chapter 2; *I Am Sadness*, chapter 3; and *The Cab Driver*, chapter 29.

CHAPTER 29

God Bless America

God Bless America
Irving Berlin, 1888–1989

On September 11, 2001, terrorists killed over 3,000 people in an unprovoked attack on America. The terrorists hijacked and crashed four commercial airplanes: American Airlines flight 11 flew into the North Tower of the World Trade Center at 8:45 a.m. Eastern Standard Time; a few minutes later, United Airlines flight 175 crashed into the South Tower of the WTC. Both of the 110-story towers collapsed. The terror continued as American Airlines flight 77 crashed into the Pentagon in Washington, D.C. A fourth hijacked airplane, United Airlines 93, redirected for Washington, D.C., crashed into the Pennsylvania countryside.

Americans united in their mixed emotions of shock, fear, anger, and grief.

Many were vividly reminded of wars in which they had personally been involved. World War II veterans compared this attack to Japan's bombing on Pearl Harbor, December 7, 1941. The attacks also triggered memories in thousands of Vietnam veterans as they recalled the horrors they had experienced firsthand in that country.

The attacks shook Americans to their core. Our friends from other countries were disturbed and grieved as well. In his address to the nation on September 20, 2001, President George W. Bush announced America's plan to fight terrorism: "We will not tire; we will not falter; and we will not fail."

The following poems are in tribute to all of us, those who survived and those who didn't, one Tuesday in September, in America.

bird of a single flight

we met only once,
it was that morning
but i will never forget you,
your life is part of mine now
and i will always remember.

you wore a white blouse,
so very bright in the morning
sunlight,
whilst i was unshaven
and in my dressing gown.

you had become the kotuku,
that beautiful bird
of a single flight
whilst i was earth bound
and became your epitaph.

it was early,
and i had woken
from that same old
dream of africa

>   the machine guns,
>   the blood, and the angry black faces.
>
>   i remember the way your hair,
>   billowed in the wind,
>   and as i watched you fall
>   i began to bless myself
>   in the old way
>   'In nomine Patri, et Filio'...
>   and pray that when your journey
>   ended,
>   God would hold your soul
>   forever,
>   in the palm of his hand.

by Mike Subritzky
In Memory of all who died that day on September 11, 2001.

Kotuku is a New Zealand native heron, which is pure white and very rare. Ancient Maori believed that if a Kotuku was ever sighted, it heralded the death of a Great Chief. It is regarded as the magical "Bird of a Single Flight."

A Stronger America

I have seen three tiers of public response to the acts of terror. First there was shock and disbelief. Second came a remarkable unity, a resolution of spirit, bonding a nation to police, firefighters and other rescuers working with deeply ingrained emotion, brotherhood, and the love that makes our country great. I felt us all brought together in ways we had not felt in a long time. Scenes of bravery and patriotism, and sheer, unadulterated love for our fellow man thrilled me to the core. Third came a paranoid fear and trepidation arising from the original shock and disbelief, threatening to wreak even further havoc upon a distressed nation. Life will never be the same as it was before September 11, that infamous day when terror reigned, but from the ashes of devastating horror will grow a greater strength that can make America stronger.

by Gary Jacobson

The Cab Driver

I have to take the cab these days
just to work, one way—
my husband picks me up
at the end of the work day.

This morning was so different
I was glued to the TV
with ash and fire and screams
that will always stay with me.

I had to call the cab
when it was time to leave
and when he came to get me,
I could tell he couldn't believe

all that had just happened
so swift and suddenly
and then I saw him shaking
as he softly talked to me.

At first, I was just nervous
and then realized his age,
He said that he was angry
and was really in a rage.

And then it dawned on me
he might have been a vet
so I mentioned who I was
He said he'd seen me on the net.

When we got to work, he
walked around,
He opened up my door—
he thanked me for my writing
I said I wish I could do more.

I paid him and I turned away
and then turned back again,
I shook his hand
and Welcome Home, I said.

At first he seemed surprised,
and then he bowed his head,
at my gesture and my words,
I asked are you ok, and
this is what I heard:

I'm fine, he said, I'll truck along
We're the finest country yet,

But thank you for that welcome home;
I'm a shaken old Vietnam vet.

by Christina Sharik, written September 11, 2001

My Fellow Americans

My fellow Americans—I am disturbed! There was a tragic crime committed against us, and we as Americans will indeed see those that perpetrated that tragedy rewarded with their just dues. The terrorist act in New York and Washington, D.C. will not stand. But brothers and sisters, we are aiding the terrorists! We're helping them perpetuate their horrible reign with collateral damage far greater than those desert fanatics ever dreamed.

We are doing this by being paranoid! We are letting fear be our guide. Certainly there is a lot to be afraid of, and I am not trying to minimize it, but we are Americans! We must walk tall with bravery and courage. We must be careful more than ever before, but we must be steadfast, to not let the terrorists change completely our way of life.

Sure there will be increased security restrictions, but we must continue to use the airlines, and to travel as we did before, or the airlines are going to go bankrupt, and the terrorists will have won another round! We must be bullish on America, and buy as before, instead of bailing out of the stock market, for our economy will flounder into recession and chaos to the point of collapsing, and the terrorists will have won round three. We must not be afraid to congregate in sports stadiums and theaters, unless we want our tormentors to have won, evermore hiding in the shadows like them.

We must know our enemies are not Muslims but a radical faction. Most American-Muslims love America as much as we—sometimes they revere it more, because they chose to leave their homeland behind and come to this home of the brave, to make a new life among the free. My brothers and sisters, we must walk in justice and pride like Americans!

by Gary Jacobson.

God Bless America

God Bless America.
Land that I love
Stand beside her, and guide her
Through the night with a light from above.
From the mountains, to the prairies ,
To the oceans, white with foam
God bless America
My home sweet home.

God Bless America,
Land that I love
Stand beside her,
And guide her,
Through the night
With the light from above,
From the mountains,
To the prairies,
To the ocean,
White with foam,
God bless America,
My home sweet home.
God bless America,
My home sweet home.

by Irving Berlin

Irving Berlin, 1888–1989, wrote *God Bless America* in 1918. He never used the song until 1938. He made some changes, and Kate Smith sang it on November, 11, 1938, Armistice Day, in a radio broadcast.

ABOUT THE AUTHOR

Jan Hornung served her country as a UH-1 helicopter pilot in the 1980s. After leaving the U.S. Army, she continued to serve her country as a writer/editor for a military newspaper in Germany. She holds a bachelor's degree from Texas A&M University and a master's in aeronautical science from Embry-Riddle Aeronautical University.

"I have always held the Vietnam veterans in the greatest esteem. Had I been born a few years earlier, I know I would have volunteered to go," she says.

Many of the Vietnam veteran helicopter pilots were still serving in the Army when Jan served. "These were some of the finest and most daring men that I had the privilege to fly with," she says.

Having been a woman in the military and friend to many Vietnam veterans, she pays tribute with this book to the unsung heroines of Vietnam—the women.

"No one can tell their stories better than the women themselves and the men who knew them. I knew that as an author I could provide the means to let them tell their own stories, to let them continue their journey of healing."

She has earned several writing awards, and in addition to *Angels in Vietnam: Women Who Served*, she has published three other books: *This Is The Truth, As Far As I Know: I Could Be Wrong* (www.geocities.com/janine2121), *If A Frog Had Wings* (no longer in print), and *KISS the Sky: Helicopter Tales* (www.geocities.com/helicoptertales).

She currently resides with her active duty Army husband and two Siberian Huskies.

Feel free to send your comments, thoughts, or questions via e-mail to Jan Hornung at Book212121@aol.com.

To contact writers, poets, and artists featured in the book, do so via their Web sites listed in the book or through Jan Hornung at Book212121@aol.com.

APPENDIX

Web Sites of Contributors

- A Circle of Friends, Deanna and Mike Hopkins
  http://gecko.gc.maricopa.edu/~dgshleeh
- A Shaman's Site, Diana Sebek
  http://hometown.aol.com/chitownshamyneuz/
  Chicago_Shamanindex.html
- A Tribute To My Daddy and All Veterans Lest We Forget, Maria Sutherland
  http://msbeliever.tripod.com/WWII.html
- A Trip Back To Vietnam, Ann Kelsey
  http://vets.appliedphysics.swri.edu/kelstrpt.htm
- A Year To Kill, Jim McColloch
  http://vietnam67.home.att.net
- American Red Cross Vietnam Donut Dollies
  http://www.donutdolly.com
- Angels in Vietnam: Women Who Served
  http://www.geocities.com/vietnamfront
- Army Mom's Safe Haven, Christina Sharik
  http://www.the-revetment.com/armymom
- The Australian Involvement in Vietnam, The Mildura Vietnam Veterans' Web site
  http://users.mildura.net.au/users/marshall

- Bushranger's Revetment, Anthony W. Pahl
  http://www.the-revetment.net
- Corpsman Up, Paul Baviello
  http://www.corpsman.com/corpsbook.html
- Dan Mouer's Wild World Web
  http://www.people.vcu.edu/~dmouer/homepage.htm.
- David H. Hackworth
  http://www.hackworth.com
- Deanna's Stories, Deanna Hopkins
  http://gecko.gc.maricopa.edu/~dgshleeh/dsstorie.htm
- Dien Cai Dau Express, Joe Casal
  http://hometown.aol.com/number1gijoe/DDExpress.html;
  http://members.aol.com/vet66a/page/index.htm
  http://www.geocities.com/vet66a
- Donut Dollies: Frequently Asked Questions
  http://www.geocities.com/catellen/faq.html
- The Flak Jacket Collection, New Zealand War Poetry
  http://www.geocities.com/mike_subritzky
- Frank Zamora
  http://www.geocities.com/fyzamora1
- From The Battlefield
  http://gecko.gc.maricopa.edu/~dgshleeh/battle.htm
- General Issue Blues, Sonny Gratzer
  http://www.sonnygratzer.com
- Glenna Goodacre
  http://www.glennagoodacre.com
- Information and Search Aids Index
  http://grunt.appliedphysics.swri.edu/infoindx.htm

- The International War Veterans' Poetry Archives
  http://www.iwvpa.net
- It's Just A Nam Thing, Dane Brown
  http://www.itsjustanamthing.com
- Janis Nark
  http://www.nark.com
- Jimmy Mac Music Company, Jim McColloch
  http://jimmy.mac.home.att.net
- Lightworks, *A Time To Honor,* Diana Sebek
  http://www.lightworks.com/MonthlyAspectarian/1996/December/1296-09.html
- Metro Volunteers
  www.metrovolunteers.org
- Military Living, Ann Caddell Crawford
  http://www.militaryliving.com
- My Vigil at the Vietnam Wall
  http://grunt.space.swri.edu/dgsvigil.htm
- Navy Corpsman
  http://www.corpsman.com
- Pararescue, Gone But Not Forgotten
  http://members.aol.com/Berly100
- Project Concern International
  http://www.projectconcern.org/contact.html
- The Punji Pit
  http://maori2000.com/moller
- Sharon (Vander Ven) Cummings, American Red Cross, SRAO
  http://www.illyria.com/rccummings.html
- The Sound of Whirling Blades, Poems and Reflections, James M. Hopkins

http://vets.appliedphysics.swri.edu/blades.htm
http://www.vietvet.org/blades.htm (a mirror site)
- The Veterans Resource Network Association
  http://www.vrna.org
- The Vietnam Experience, Bill McDonald
  http://www.vietnamexp.com
- Vietnam Nurses Haven
  http://vietnamnurses.com
- Vietnam Nurses Haven "closed" discussion/support list
  http://groups.yahoo.com/group/VietNamNursesHaven
- Vietnam Picture Tour, Gary Jacobson
  http://pzzzz.tripod.com/namtour.html
- Vietnam Veterans Home Page
  http://vets.appliedphysics.swri.edu/
  http://www.vietvet.org (mirror site)
  http://vietvet.infopsyc.com (mirror site)
- Vietnam Women's Memorial Project, Inc.
  http://www.vietnamwomensmemorial.org
- Vigil
  http://vets.appliedphysics.swri.edu/dgs.htm
- The Virtual Wall, Jim Schueckler
  http://www.virtualwall.org
- Walk With Me, Karen Offutt
  http://walkwithme.netfirms.com
- What A Long, Strange Trip, 18th Surg, Quang Tri, Mary "Chris" Banigan
  http://www.illyria.com/chris/vnchris7.html
- World War II Red Cross Clubmobile
  http://www.clubmobile.org

Medals

Medal of Honor

The Congressional Medal of Honor is the highest honor bestowed upon an individual for valor. It is presented to the recipient by the President of the United States in the name of Congress. Two hundred and forty-three Vietnam veterans received the Medal of Honor for their military service in Vietnam, less than 70 of those recipients are alive today.

Silver Star

The Silver Star is the third highest military award given for distinguished gallantry in action against an enemy of the United States or while serving with friendly forces against an opposing enemy force. The Citation Award was established in 1918 and redesignated in 1932 as the Silver Star.

Legion of Merit

The Legion of Merit is for exceptionally meritorious conduct in the performance of outstanding service.

Distinguished Flying Cross

The Distinguished Flying Cross, established in 1926 and retroactive for actions after 1918, is awarded for heroism or extraordinary achievement while participating in an aerial flight, evidenced by voluntary action above and beyond the call of duty. Charles A. Lindberg was the first recipient of the Distinguished Flying Cross. Commander Richard Byrd and Amelia Earhart also received the award.

Soldier's Medal

The Soldier's Medal is for heroism by those serving with the Army in any capacity that involves the voluntary risk of life under conditions other than those of conflict with an opposing armed force. It was established in 1926.

Airman's Medal

The Airman's Medal is for heroism in a non-combat situation. Established in 1960, the Airman's Medal is equivalent to the Army Soldier's Medal.

Bronze Star

The Bronze Star Medal is awarded for heroic or meritorious achievement of service, not involving aerial flight in connection with operations against an opposing armed force. It may be awarded either for combat heroism, valor, or for meritorious service. The Bronze Star was authorized on February 4, 1944, and is retroactive to December 7, 1941.

Purple Heart

The Purple Heart is awarded for wounds or death as result of an act of any opposing armed force, as a result of an international terrorist attack or as a result of military operations while serving as part of a peacekeeping force. It is the oldest military award, known as George Washington's "Badge of Military Merit" from 1782. It was redesignated the Purple Heart in 1932. It may also be presented posthumously to the next of kin of personnel killed in action or who die of wounds sustained in action.

Meritorious Service Medal

The Meritorious Service Medal is awarded for outstanding non-combat meritorious achievement or service to the United States. It was established in 1969.

Air Medal

The Air Medal is awarded for meritorious achievement while participating in aerial flight.

Army Commendation Medal

The Army Commendation Medal is for heroism, meritorious achievement or service in which the soldier distinguished him/herself. It was authorized in 1945.

Combat Infantryman Badge

The Combat Infantryman Badge was established in 1943. It is awarded to soldiers in the MOS of infantry. The soldier must have been engaged in active ground combat to receive this badge.

Army Meritorious Unit Commendation

The Army Meritorious Unit Commendation is awarded to an Army unit for at least six months of outstanding service during a period of combat on or after January 1, 1944.

National Defense Service Medal

The National Defense Service Medal is for active federal service in the armed forces, including the Coast Guard, regardless of the station of duty (for Vietnam), from January 1, 1961, to August 14, 1974. It was authorized April 22, 1953. (This medal also includes time periods for the Korean and Persian Gulf Wars.)

Vietnam Service Medal

The Vietnam Service Medal is for service in Southeast Asia from July 4, 1965, to March 28, 1973. It was authorized in 1965.

Vietnam Gallantry Cross with Palm Unit Citation

The (Republic of) Vietnam Gallantry Cross with Palm Unit Citation was awarded by the Republic of Vietnam to units for valorous combat achievement.

Glossary

Boonies—Boondocks, a rural area, or remote area of dense brush.
Bouncing Betty—An explosive.

C-rats, rations—Combat Rations, canned meals for military in the field.
Charlie—Slang term for Viet Cong; from phonetic alphabet for VC (Victor Charlie).
Chopper—Helicopter.
Claymore—Antipersonnel mine.
Cobra—Attack Helicopter.
Cyclo—A two-person cab powered and steered by a third person on a bicycle.

Defence—British spelling of defense.
Deuce and a half—A 2 ½ ton military truck; also deucy.
Dog Tag—Identification tags for military personnel.
Duffle or Duffel Bag—a large bag used by military for moving personal gear.
Dust Off—Also dustoff or dust-off; medical evacuation helicopters.

Evac—Evacuation.

Frag—Grenade.
Freedom Bird—Any airplane that took the Americans home from Vietnam.

Gook—A derogatory nickname for people of Asian decent.
Grunt—Nickname for an Army infantryman.
Gung ho—To be dedicated and enthusiastic.
Gunship—An armed helicopter.

Helo—Helicopter.
Hooch—also hootch; Living quarters, such as a hut, tent, house.
Huey—UH-1 utility helicopter.

In country—In Vietnam.

Kilometers—km, equals 0.62 of a mile.
Kiwi—New Zealander nickname.

Longhouses—A long communal dwelling, typically built of poles and bark and having a central corridor with family compartments on either side.

Mama-san—Older Vietnamese woman.
Medevac—Medical Evacuation.
Montagnard—People inhabiting the mountains and highlands of southern Vietnam.

Nam—Vietnam or Viet Nam.

Petrol—Gasoline.
Psych—Psychiatric.
Pyjama—British spelling of pajama.

Recognise—British spelling of recognize.

Steel pots—Helmets worn by soldiers.

Stryker—Medical equipment company.
Succour—British spelling of succor.

Tet—Tet is the Vietnamese Lunar New Year holiday period. On Tet's Eve, January 30, 1968, the NVA/VC began a surprise offensive attack against the South. Historians consider this the turning point in the war for the NVA.

The Wall—The Vietnam Veterans' Memorial.
World—When used in Vietnam, the "world" referred to the United States.

INDEX

A Brief History of Red Cross Clubmobiles in W.W.II, 130
A Christmas Visit Remembered, 151, 153
A Circle of Friends, 228, 309
A Daughter's Love, 27-28
A Dogfaced Soldier, 24
A Measure of Success, 55
A Moment, 225
A Soldier's Prayer, 161, 182
A Stronger America, 87, 238, 301
A Tribute To My Daddy, 162-163, 309
A Trip Back To Vietnam, 266, 309
A Woman Looks Back At War, 173, 177
A Year To Kill, 157-158, 309
Aftermath, 3, 16, 22, 43, 291
Alestra, Vinny, xxiii, xxix, 42
Ambushed, 10, 160, 184, 275, 278, 293
American Red Cross, 6, 10, 51, 100-101, 103, 105, 116, 124-125, 128-131, 145, 151, 157, 186, 192, 206-207, 210, 225, 282, 285, 309, 311
An Affair To Remember, 87, 236
And The War Goes On, 197, 200
Angel of Mercy, 73-74, 78, 80, 83
The Angels of Vietnam, 10, 276
An Khe, 156, 268, 297

ANZAC, xxi, xxv, 89, 94, 98-99, 161, 243, 247-248
Are You A Vet?, 178
Army Mom's Safe Haven, 3, 309
Army Nurse Corps, 5, 47, 49, 53, 63, 65-66, 70-72, 138, 280, 282
The Art of Medicine, 83-85
Australia and New Zealand in Vietnam, 90
Ba Ngoi, 262-263
Banigan, Mary, xxi, xxx, 68-70, 312
Ban Me Thuot, 284-285
Barrie, James M., 100
Baviello, Paul, xxiii, xxix, 37, 38, 310
Beautiful Vietnam, 65-66
Becky Died, 26-27, 207
Berlin, Irving, 299, 305
Better Than Medicine, 4
Biedermann, Narelle, Dr., xxii, xxix, 95-97
Bien Hoa, 25, 186, 196, 282
Binh Thuan, 262
Binh Thuy, 63
bird of a single flight, 90, 171, 293, 300-301
Bits and Pieces, 55
Blended Like A Fine-Tuned Instrument, 31
Body Bags, 91-92, 95
Boosting Morale, 157

Brown, Dane, xxiii, xxix, 31, 311
Browning, Robert, 255
Broyles Jr., William, 52
Bushranger's Revetment, 23, 310
The Cab Driver, 3, 22, 43, 298, 302
Camp Pendleton, 11
Cam Ranh Bay, 66, 105, 177, 258, 267-268, 282
The Car, 98-99
The Caring Was From The Heart, 32
Carol-Has It Been A Hundred Years, 16, 30
Carrying on the Tradition, 103
Casal, Joe F., xxiii, xxix, 46, 310
Central Intelligence Agency, 6, 283
Christmas in Vietnam, 1966, 149
Chu Lai, 68-69, 104-105, 108, 113, 120, 152, 186, 268, 280-281, 284
Civilian Women in Vietnam: Army Special Services, 267
Colonel Maggie, 12, 15, 17, 30
The Colors of Christmas, 53-54
Cowper, Lesley Estelle, 286, 287
Crawford, Ann Caddell, xxii, xxix, 249, 254, 255, 256, 311
Cu Chi, 10, 40-41, 127, 196, 268, 282
Cummings, Sharon Vander Ven, xxii, xxix, 101, 128, 129, 311
Daines, Mary Hyland, xxii, xxix, 41
Da Lat, 141-142, 144, 147
The Dam Burst, 168-169
Dam Pao, 141, 146, 148-149

Da Nang, 28, 43, 53, 55, 57, 59, 104-105, 108, 115, 119, 121, 151, 196, 241-243, 265, 284
Dan Mouer's Wild World Web, 297, 310
The Day It Snowed In Vietnam, 140
Deanna's Love Story, 226
Deanna's Stories, 228, 310
Dear Little Boy of Mine, 63, 165
Dempsey, James P., xxiii, xxix, 34, 156
Di An, 112, 154
Dog Tags, xv, 1
Doing Their Best, 32
Dong Ba Thin, 258, 263, 265-268
Dong Tam, 268
Donne, John, 270, 277
Donut Dollies: Frequently Asked Questions, 128, 310
Donut Dolly Blue, 101
Do You Know, 193
Duet With Death, 38
Earhart, Amelia, 196, 313
Elgin, Sandra K., xxii, xxix, 28
Evans, Diane, xxii, xxix, 272
Evans, Penni, 9-10, 161, 184, 274, 275, 278
Farewell, 52
Fay, Elma Ernst, xxii, xxix, 131
Fennell, Kathleen, xxix, 282
Field, Kate, 5
Finding Judy, 83
Fitzsimons Army Medical Center, 212
The Flak Jacket Collection, 89-90, 310
Flashbacks, 161, 172, 184

Folded Flag, 10, 161, 184, 275, 277-278
Fort Bragg, 15
Fort Lewis, 25, 175
Fort Polk, 36
Fort Riley, 206
Fort Sam Houston, 55, 174, 206, 211
Fortenberry, Patty Bright, 115, 118, 120
Fortenberry, Steve, xxi, xxix, 115, 122, 123, 225
For Your Information, 217
Franklin, Benjamin, 18
Frank Zamora's Vietnam Web site, 271
From The Battlefield, 290, 310
Gary's Angel, 73, 238
Gathered In, 289-290
General Issue Blues, 103, 310
God, A Soldier, and A Red Cross Worker, 203
God Bless America, 299, 305-306
God, I'd Really Like To Know, 27, 206-207
Goodacre, Glenna, 273, 310
Gratzer, Sonny, xxiii, xxix, 103, 310
Grenfell, Wilfred, xxxiii, 217
Gulf of Tonkin, 219, 222
Gung Ho, 11-12, 318
Hackworth, David, xvii, xviii, xxiii, xxix, 310
Haiphong, 262
Hanoi, 219, 262
Harty, Larry, xxiii, xxix, 36
Hay, Melody, xv, xxi, xxix, 1
Hay, Sarah, xv, xxi, xxix, 45

Hewatt, Pat, xxii, xxix, 186, 190, 192
Hinckley, Gordon B., 4
Ho Chi Minh, 220-221, 223, 259-260, 285
Hollywood, Doc, xxiii, xxix, 195
Honoring our Heroes, 276, 288
Hope, Bob, 117, 118, 153
Hopkins, Deanna Gail Shlee, xxii, xxix, 34, 225, 227, 228, 290
Hopkins, James M., xxii, xxix, xxxiv, 33, 34, 226, 227, 228, 290, 311
Huffman, Sharon Long, xxii, xxx, 25
Hutcherson, Johnny, 194
I Am Off To War, My Gentle Carol, 16, 28
I Am Sadness, 3, 22, 42, 298
I Can Still See Her Face, 34, 156
I Felt I'd Died, 79, 81
I Only See Blue Pajamas, 210
I See You Walking, 32-33, 290
I Stand and Salute, 37
I Wish I Knew Her Name, 36-37
If Only, 3, 22, 43, 186, 298
Images of Freedom, 12, 275
The Injured, 50-51, 101
In My Heart Forever, 35, 156
The International War Veterans' Poetry Archives, 3, 23, 87, 93, 311
It's Just A Nam Thing, 31, 311
Jacobson, Gary, xxiii, xxx, 73, 78, 81-83, 86, 87, 238, 302, 305, 312
Jimmy Mac Music Company, 158, 311
Johnson, Lyndon B., 15, 210, 219, 220, 222
Judy's Story, 47

Julie, 165
Keller, Helen, 60, 124
Kelsey, Ann, xxii, xxx, 266-267, 269, 309
Kennedy, John F., 183, 219, 222
Kenny, Pat, xxiii, xxx, 44
Kigin, Judy Blackman, xxii, xxx, 85
Klein, Marsha, xxii, xxx, 67
Lai Khe, 104-105, 107-110, 112-113, 115-117, 122, 225
Landauer, Nancy, Rev., xxii, xxx, 205, 206, 209-211
Lane, Sharon, 280-282
The Last Step, 93
Lend Me, 45-46
Lewis, Rick, xxiii, xxx, 27, 207
Lilja, Nancy Quirk, xxii, xxx, 62-64, 165
Long, Arthur E., xxiii, xxx, 25-26
Long Binh, 10, 37, 127, 151, 153, 185-186, 188, 196, 206, 261, 268, 283
Long Thanh, 36, 261
Love and War, 233
Love's Good Vibrations, 87, 228
Mandela, Nelson, 203
McBride, Bill, 226
McColloch, Jim, xxiii, xxx, 156, 158-159
McDonald, Bill, xxiii, xxx, 15-17, 29-30, 312
Mekong Delta, 32, 100, 159
Memories Penetrating the Shroud of Death: PTSD, 64, 163
Midnight Movie, 90, 169, 293
Miley-Terry, Pam, xxii, xxx, 97-99

Military Assistance Command, Vietnam, 141-142, 196, 201, 246-247
Military Living, 254-255, 311
Moller, John, xxiii, xxx, 92-93
The Morning After, 40-41
Mouer, Daniel, xxiii, xxx, 297, 310
My Brother, 10, 161, 184, 197, 273-274, 278
My Ca, 263
My Fellow Americans, 87, 238, 304
My Name Is Karen, 196
My Thirty Year Anniversary Trip, 257
My Vigil at the Vietnam Wall, 226, 228, 311
My Visits With Jack, 138, 239, 242
Nan, 169
Nark, Janis, xxii, xxx, 6, 173, 177-178, 180-181, 311
Nelson, Phyllis, xxii, xxx, 212, 215-216
The New Zealand Involvement in Vietnam, 97
Nha Trang, 66-67, 73, 79, 258, 260, 262-268, 283
The Night Before, 3, 18, 43, 234, 298
Nightmare of a Soldier, 194
Ninh Thuan, 262
Nixon, Richard M., 221-222
Nolen-Walston, Alice, xv, xxx
Norris, Jackie Lively, xxii, xxx, 105
Nui Dat, 23, 92, 96, 98
Offutt, Karen, xxii, xxx, 196, 200, 201, 202, 312
Operation Babylift, 218, 282, 285
Pahl, Anthony W., xxiii, xxx, 22-23, 310

Parade of Fear, 207
Pararescue, Gone But Not Forgotten, 28, 311
Parker, Julie, xxi, xxx, 159, 225
Parris Island, South Carolina, 11
Parts is Parts, 190
Patterson, Andrew Barton, 88
Penn, William, 132
Phan Rang, 262
Phan Thiet, 81, 140, 147-148, 261-262, 266
Phouc Tuy (also Phuoc), 92, 96
Phu Bai, 31, 268
Phu Loi, 13, 15-16, 30, 116, 271
Phuoc Loc, 36
Phuoc Tuy (also Phouc), 92, 96
Phuoc Vinh, 25
Pilot in Triage, 53
Pleiku, 40, 187, 279, 283
Poe, Edgar Allen, 160
Powell, General Colin, 272
Powell, Patricia, xxx, 282
Project Concern International, 148-149, 311
Proud To Be A Donut Dolly, 105
Psyched, 184
PTSD, 46, 63-64, 163, 168-169, 171-172, 192
The Punji Pit, 92-93, 311
Quan Loi, 108
Quang Tri, 9-10, 68-70, 135, 138, 239, 242, 244, 247, 268, 312
Qui Nhon, 34, 49, 161, 279, 283, 286
RAANC, Royal Australian Army Nursing Corps in Vietnam, 94
Raye, Martha, 12, 15, 17, 153

Reagan, Ronald, 220
Roll Call, 278
Roosevelt, Eleanor, 1
Saigon, 12, 32, 72, 107, 114, 150, 152-153, 183, 196, 217, 219, 223, 249-250, 254-256, 258-261, 266, 278, 282-283, 285, 287, 295
Sandburg, Carl, 212
Schneider, Chris, xxii, xxx, 24, 53-59
Schneider, Karli, xxii, xxx, 24
Schueckler, Jim, xxiii, xxx, 148, 312
Schuller, Robert H., Dr., 249
Seasons of Siege, 187, 192
Sebek, Diana, xxii, xxx, 138-139, 247, 309, 311
Shakespeare, William, 31
Sharik, Christina Smith, xxii, xxx, 3, 20, 22, 43, 292, 298, 304, 309
Sharon Ann Lane Foundation, 281
Sister, 88
Sisters, 7-9
Sister Search, 83, 85, 272-273
Smith, David Lloyd, xxiii, xxx, 37
Smith, Kate, 306
Soc Trang, 14
Soldier's Farewell, 90, 171, 293
Soldier's Medal, 201, 313-314
The Sound of Whirling Blades, 34, 290, 311
Souvenirs, 10, 161, 183-184, 275, 278
Spellman, Francis Joseph Cardinal, 153, 155
Standard, Mary M., xxii, xxxi, 40, 41

Subritzky, Mike, xxi, xxxi, 78, 89, 90, 92, 99, 161, 171, 287, 293, 301, 310
Su Chinh, 263
The Suitcase and The Duffle Bag, 3, 20, 43, 298
Sutherland, Maria, xxii, xxxi, 162, 163, 182, 309
Tan Son Nhat, 259
Tay Ninh, 268
Tet Offensive, 41, 66, 95, 104, 112, 223, 234, 252
Thanksgiving Day, 271, 288
Thank You, Ma'am, 35
They Are Angels, 41-42
They Brought Smiles, 100
Thomas-Bowles, Kimmie, xxii, 28
To Say Goodbye, 96, 132, 134
To The Nurses, 43
Turpin, James, Dr., 148
Tuy Hoa, 279
USO, 6, 125, 268
Veteran of the Vietnam War, 22-23
Veteran's Day, 60, 62, 165, 176
Veterans Resource Network Association, 178, 180-181, 312
The Vietnam Experience, 16, 294, 312
Vietnamization, 223
Vietnam Light, 249, 251-252, 254
Vietnam Nurses Haven, 50, 312
Vietnam Picture Tour, 86-87, 312
Vietnam Veterans Home Page, 3, 34, 226, 228, 266, 290, 312

The Vietnam Veterans' Memorial, 148, 176, 178, 270, 272, 319
Vietnam Women's Memorial, 83, 85, 148, 176, 267, 272-273, 312
The Virtual Wall, 148, 312
Vung Tau, 23, 90, 97-98, 116, 261, 282
Waite, Diana, xxii, xxxi, 11-12, 276
Walk With Me, 200, 312
The Wall, 8, 60, 62, 126, 152, 176, 179, 253, 270-273, 288, 297, 319
The War Comes Home, 212
War No More, 86
Warrior and The Nurse, 74, 85
Watching for Dustoff, 45
Weilbacher, Lindsey Stringfellow, xxii, xxxi, 151, 152, 155
We Smiled Anyway, 124, 127
Westmoreland, William, General, 223
What is a Vietnam Veteran?, 294
What They Said, 219
When Did It Begin?, 123
Where Is Vietnam?, 219
Who Was Ho Chi Minh?, 221
Why?, 181-182
Why Vietnam?, 222
Williams, Judith Baker, xv, xxii, xxxi, 49-50
Wolfe, Eileen P., xxii, 161
Wolfe, Thomas, 257
The Woman Veteran/Women Who Served, 2, 22, 43, 298
Women in War, 5
Women's Army Corps, 196, 201

World War II Red Cross Clubmobile, 131, 312
Xuan Loc, 261
You, 23-24
You're In The Army Now, 65
Zamora, Frank, xxii, xxxi, 140, 271, 276, 288, 289, 310

0-595-24090-9

Printed in the United States
75935LV00004B/49-57